Life of
SRI RAMANUJA

By
Swami Ramakrishnananda

Translated from Bengali
by Swami Budhananda

Sri Ramakrishna Math
Mylapore, Chennai-600 004

Published by :
Adhyaksha
Sri Ramakrishna Math
Mylapore, Chennai - 4

XI-2M 3C-6-2011
ISBN 978-81-7823-421-2

Printed in India at
Sri Ramakrishna Math Printing Press
Mylapore, Chennai - 4

PREFACE

On March 11,1885, when Girishchandra and Narendranath (later Swami Vivekananda) were engaged in Sri Rama-krishna's presence in a heated discussion as to whether God assumes a human body or He is 'beyond word and thought' and also 'If God is infinity, how He could have parts', the Master said to M. (the author of the *Gospel of Sri Ramakrishna*):

'I do not enjoy these discussions. Why should I argue at all? I clearly see that God is everything; He himself has become all. I see that whatever is, is God. He is everything; again, He is beyond everything. I have come to a state in which my mind and intellect merge in the indivisible.... I cannot utter a word unless I come at least two steps from the plane of Samadhi. Sankara's nondualistic explanation is true, and so is the qualified nondualistic interpretation of Ramanuja.'

Many years later while describing the 'reaction movements' of resurgent Hinduism that followed the decadence of Buddhism in India, Swami Vivekananda wrote in a paper entitled *The Historical Evolution of India.*

'.... The movement of Sankara forced its way through its high intellectuality, but it could be of little service to the masses, because of its adherence to strict caste laws, very small scope for ordinary emotion, and making Sanskrit the only vehicle of communication. Ramanuja, on the other hand, with a most practical philosophy, a great appeal to the emotions, an entire denial of birthrights before spiritual attainments and appeals through the popular tongue, completely succeeded in bringing the masses back to the Vedic religion.'

When, with this background of knowledge and experience, Swami Ramakrishnananda, a direct disciple of Sri Ramakrishna, came in March 1897 to live in the South and saw and felt the tremendous living influence of Sri Ramanuja on the spiritual and philosophical heritage of India, he almost felt an anguish—the impression of which can be seen in his own forceful introduction to the book—that in the Bengal of his time people unfortunately knew so little about this great Acharya. Notwithstanding great hardships imposed on him by his very trying circumstances, he kept on studying Ramanuja's life from all available sources, and from February 1899 began to write this life serially from the fourth issue of the *Udbodhan,* the newly started Bengali Journal of the Ramakrishna Order. And the writing continued for nearly eight years, providing delight and inspiration to earnest readers. Subsequently these articles were published in a book entitled *Sri Ramanuja-charita.*

The book which he so painstakingly wrote for the enlightenment of the people of Bengal had been all the time serving a great purpose, being perhaps the best available life of Sri Ramanuja in Bengali. What was given from the South specially to the people of Bengal, is today through this translation presented to all the English knowing people of the world.

To be sure, this book will not give the reader any information on Sri Ramanuja's life which is not already available in some book or other. But it will surely communicate the transforming power—and who can say we do not require it so urgently today in this distracted world of ours—of the great life of a mighty and magnanimous world-teacher written by an illustrious apostle of another great world-teacher.

Whether one belongs to the ranks of orthodox followers or to those of the heterodox, in the pages of this book one will surely feel the faith as well as the fervour of the writer who was, in the words of Swami Vivekananda, 'more orthodox than the most orthodox man of the South and at the same time unique and unsurpassed in his worship of God and meditation on Him.'

At a time when a detailed English biography of Sri Ramanuja is not easily available, this book, we hope and trust, will meet a felt need of the reading public, and help serve the cause of Bhakti movement in the world.

Holy Mother's Birth Tithi   THE PUBLISHER
January 1, 1959

TRANSLATOR'S NOTE

Life of Sri Ramanuja is a translation of *Sri Ramanuja-charita* written in Bengali by Swami Ramakrishnananda. In Bengali literature the work is considered to be a classic.

This English translation in its turn was serially published in the *Vedanta Kesari*—an English monthly Organ of the Ramakrishna Order—from May 1949 to April 1954. At the request of friends and after careful editing, the serial is now appearing as a book.

Rare and blessed indeed is the occasion when a saint, an illumined soul, undertakes the task of writing a biography of an Acharya, a world-teacher; for no writer, however erudite and accomplished, can bring to his work that revealing insight which a saint does by virtue of his illumination. On this view, Swami Ramakrishnananda's *Sri Ramanuja-charita* may be considered a singular work.

The translator of such a work, written in an ornate classical style, faces a dilemma: should he make the translation faithful to the letter, or should he make it free and readable? With the help of good friends, a compromise has been worked out which we hope will commend itself to the English reader.

Coming from the North as he did, Swami Rama-krishnananda could not have direct access to some of the source-books of Sri Ramanuja's life which are in Tamil. It would appear that, except in case of Sanskrit source-books like Anantacharya's *Prapannamritam,* he had to depend largely on the help of scholar-friends. It was therefore thought proper to get the entire manuscript scrutinized, if necessary edited, by one who was well-grounded in the original lore and thoroughly conversant with the written and unwritten traditions of Sri Vaishnavism. Such a scrutiny of the manuscript has been done by Swami Paramatmananda,

Editor, *Sri Ramakrishna Vijayam,* the Tamil Organ of the Ramakrishna Order. As the editor of the book, he has found the necessity of giving some foot-notes presenting some other current versions of certain incidents and making some minor changes in one or two places in the body of the book. The translator is thankful to him for his ready labour of love, and to Swami Adidevananda for writing the monograph on 'Visishtadvaita, the philosophy of Sri Ramanuja', which is included in the Appendix.

The book abounds in Sanskrit quotations, all of which are found in the Bengali original. In the translation, we have put all the Sanskrit quotations as foot-notes, giving their renderings in the body of the book. Only in one chapter where the entire *Stotraratna* of Sri Yamunacharya is rendered, we have for the sake of convenience put the Sanskrit slokas in the Appendix. In fixing up many of the references of the Sanskrit citations and in checking up the nuances of their meanings in their renderings, we thankfully acknowledge the help we have received from Sri V.S. Venkataraghavachari, M.A., B.O.L., Lecturer, Department of Sanskrit, Vivekananda College, Madras. In tracing some references we have also received help from some other scholars. To them and to other friends who have joyfully participated in the labour of producing this book by way of typing the manuscript, reading proofs and preparing the Index, we tender our thanks collectively. The references of some of the quotations could not be traced. If any one could provide us with the same, we shall be glad to use them in the subsequent editions.

Certain allusions occasionally come up in the book which, though more or less familiar to Indian readers, will not be easily traceable by non-Indian readers. Such allusions we have given in the Appendix which we hope will be found useful by all who are not in close touch with ancient Indian literature. Such Indian words which have special associations of their own and do not have adequate and satisfactory synonyms in the English language, have been used in the translation as they are in the original and explained in the Glossary.

Apart from the usual Glossary and Index, we are also adding a list of the Tamil equivalents of the Sanskritized names used in the book for the benefit of those readers who may find them more familiar. Owing to some technical difficulties, we could not use diacritical marks for non English words in the body of the book, but we are showing them in the Glossary and the Index.

FOREWORD

THE life-story of Sri Ramanuja, the great saint and teacher, was almost unknown to the common people of Bengal a few years ago. Once in a while during the course of discussion on the *Brahma-sutras,* some students of scriptures would come to know his name and of the *Sribhashya* written by him. And they would be content with the general notion 'that the doctrine of Visishtadvaita, preached by Sri Ramanuja, is a rival one to Advaita as propounded by the great Sri Sankara.' In recent times it was Acharya Swami Vivekananda alone who in his speeches made clear references to Sri Ramanuja and the quintessence of his doctrine and thus drew to them the attention of the common people. And it was Swami Ramakrishnananda, the writer of this book, that for the first time wrote serially in the *Udbodhan* for the enligh-tenment of the common people of Bengal a detailed account of the wonderful life, teachings and activities of the Acharya. Staying as he was for a long time in Madras, the birth-place of the Acharya, he was in a position to consult the necessary source-books for the purpose.

This fairly big book was published serially in the *Udbodhan* for eight long years beginning from the month of Phalgun of 1305 (Bengali Era) to the month of Kartik of 1313. And the readers of the *Udbodhan* are not unaware of the charm of the *Sri Ramanuja-charita.* We had the idea of presenting to the readers this book which was the fruit of the selfless labour of Swami Ramakrishnananda in the life-time of its author. But the publication of the book was delayed owing to adverse circumstances, especially the passing away of the author on August 21, 1911 (4th Bhadra, 1318), leaving incomplete the work of correcting the manuscripts.

Swami Ramakrishnananda, the highly accomplished President of Sri Ramakrishna Math, Madras, attained Maha-samadhi at 1-10 p.m. on August 21, 1911. Himself whole-heartedly dedicated to Sri Ramakrishna, the Swami was one of the pioneer preachers of the Ramakrishna Mission.

Born in 1863, he lived only for forty-nine years with us here on earth. But he has left a deep impression behind. On the one hand, his supreme devotion to the Guru, fixity of purpose, absorption in service, blazing renunciation and devotion to God made the winsome Swami an ideal to the devotees; on the other hand, his learning, discernment, humility, knowledge of scriptures, sympathy and generosity made him a haven of hope and peace for the people scorched by the miseries of the world.

While yet a student, first at the Olbert College and then at the Metropolitan College, a fervent yearning for spiritual attainment was noticed in Swami Ramakrishna-nanda. By witnessing his attachment to ritualistic worship in boyhood, his subsequent study of such books as the *Bible,* the *Chaitanya Charitamrita,* etc., and his enthusiastic attendance at religious lectures and the prayer-chapel of Keshab Chandra, the great Brahmo preacher, one could understand how keen that yearning was in his heart! This yearning reached its final consummation in October 1883, when, yet a student, he came to the feet of Sri Ramakrishna, where he found eternal peace.

Though this contact had brought about a complete transformation in his life, he continued to live at home, frequently visiting Sri Guru. Then he renounced his home and came to stay at the residence of the Sri Guru in the Cossipore garden house. And, at last, after the passing away of Sri Guru in 1886, he lived for about twelve years in the Baranagore Math with the sole preoccupation of serving and worshipping his Sripaduka (holy sandals).

After his great work in the West, the most revered Acharya Swami Vivekananda returned for the first time to the Math in the beginning of 1897 and with the help of his brother-disciples, established various welfare projects for the good of the people. In obedience to the command of Swami Vivekananda, Swami Ramakrishnananda went to Madras in March 1897 with a view to establishing there a centre of the Ramakrishna Math and the Ramakrishna Mission. And for about fourteen years, from 1897 to 1911, he lived there and, following the footsteps of Swami Vivekananda, taught the people of South India the transcendent message of Sri Guru which reconciles all sects.

As a result of the divine life lived and self-immolating labours done by Swami Ramakrishnananda, a veritable hero among those who had found shelter at the feet of Sri Guru, many noble deeds came to be performed in Madras and in South India generally. Great was the grief of the people of Madras and South India at his passing away. Even today his memory is cherished by them with reverence and gratitude.

EDITOR, 'THE UDBODHAN'
(Swami Saradananda)

Contents

PART I
THE SPIRITUAL BACKGROUND

PART II
LIFE OF SRI RAMANUJA

Introduction

Few in Bengal know about Bhagavan Sri Ramanuja. This is so because here there are very few who follow the doctrines of that Mahatma and belong to what is known as Sri-sampradaya. But their influence is paramount in South India. It is time that people of this part of the country knew what religious doctrine he preached and on the basis of what philosophical conclusions (Siddhanta); whether this doctrine was in vogue prior to his time; why his followers are known as Sri-sampradayis; and whether there is any agreement between his and Bhagavan Sri Sankaracharya's doctrine of non-duality. It is sheer shortsightedness to remain ignorant of the life and teachings of that great soul, who is worshipped by his followers as the manifestation of Sri Lakshmana, the prince among devotees; whose loving heart is the refuge of one and all, right from Brahma to a blade of grass; and whose incisive and well-reasoned arguments stand arrayed to meet the impregnable Advaitic doctrines of Bhagavan Sri Sankaracharya of immeasurable intellectual powers. He is still a great influence among the followers of his school whom his teachings have enabled to withstand the materialism and atheism of the present century and to reflect, even in spite of all the changes that have come over their mode of life, a little of that overflowing love of his Rishi-heart in their pure vegetarian habits,[1] which is a token of their acceptance of the principle that it is a heinous sin to slaughter fellow living beings for the upkeep of this corrupt body of ours.

---

1. खच्छन्दवनजातेन शाकेनापि प्रपूर्यते ।
   अस्य दग्धोदरस्यार्थे कः कुर्यात्पातकं महत् ॥

Why on earth should one commit such a heinous sin for this wretched stomach,, which can be filled with vegetables and greens growing lush in the forests? *Hitopadesa:* 'Mitralabha', 68.

1

The lives of the great ones are always consecrated to the good of the many. They descend on earth for no selfish ends of their own. They are ever preoccupied with the thought how to remove the afflictions of the lowly, the indigent and the helpless. This is why searching and thorough study of their lives is immensely beneficial. By knowing and following the path discovered by these great ones by their deep and constant meditation on the good of all living beings, one can live one's life here on earth in supreme happiness and, what is more, can find one's way to heavenly bliss or liberation here-after. Is it not the paramount duty of all intelligent people to drink, from the life-stories of the great ones, the elixir which brings good in this world and the next?

Supremely glorious and large-hearted, Sri Ramanuja is among the foremost of such Mahatmas. The path shown by him is established on Sattva. Not being unsteady and fleeting like those resting on Rajas and Tamas, it yields everlasting results. All who aspire to share in ever-abiding supreme bliss should follow in the footsteps of the magnanimous ones like Bhagavan Sri Ramanuja. 'There is no other way but this.' The rich and the poor, the erudite and the unlettered, the high and the low,—all can tread the path shown by this Mahatma with great ease and much benefit.

One word more. It is more profitable to study the lives of the great ones than to repeat parrot-wise hard and abstruse homilies. When the maxims—which, being abstract, are difficult to grasp—find concrete expression in the lives of the great ones, they can be easily comprehended and followed by average people. By even unthinkingly following in their footsteps, men advance in the path of virtue, gradually overcome animal impulses, and become fit to find refuge in the Divine. From one's very boyhood, one continually hears it said that to tell the truth is one's duty. But after witnessing the systematic violation of truth wherever one may turn one's eyes, one gets almost convinced that the maxims about truthfulness can at best adorn the pages of books of ethics and that in practice speaking of unalloyed truth is an utter impossibility. Such an idea would have established itself in the human mind, like the immovable and unshakable Mount Sumeru, had there not been born in this world those noble ones who are veritable images of truth itself.

God, the all-powerful Father of all, out of infinite compassion for His children, comes into this world, assuming the forms of holy men, to resuscitate religion and help men forward in the path which leads to good here and hereafter. Is it not then the duty of every one to study the lives of such holy personages?

SRI RAMANUJA

1

Influence of the Line of Teachers

THE GLORY AND THE METHOD OF CHANTING
THE NAMES OF DEVOTEES

The Vaishnavas of Sri-sampradaya, when they sing the glory of their previous Gurus, Sri Ramanuja and others, feel themselves as pure as sinless divine beings through the influence of the holy ones. However thick might be the pall of gloom in the heart of the Vaishnava, however perturbed might it be with sufferings and misfortunes in this rough ocean of Samsara, all afflictions fly away as soon as he remembers those holy names. What is this due to? Sri Ramakrishna has given the answer to the question. As by a single stroke of a match-stick the inside of a room where darkness has dwelt a thousand years can be instantaneously illumined and that thick darkness dispelled, even so by once remembering the name of any one who is as pure and effulgent as fire, all the deep-rooted mental agonies are put to flight. If such is the power of the mere names of those great ones, how great must be the influence of their real personalities?

But darkness cannot be possibly dispelled by striking the match-stick at the wrong end, even though one might continue the futile process for a hundred years; this would only be labour lost. Similarly, for uttering the names of the noble ones too, there are principles, without the knowledge of which mere repetition of names not only brings no merit but may even land one in atheism. What is that principle? Sri Gaurangadeva, the incarnation of devotion, laid it down as follows:

He, who deems himself lowlier than even a blade of grass, is patient like a tree, craves not honour for himself but is

7

always eager to offer it to others—he alone is fit to chant the name of Hari.[1]

'Bhagavata, Bhakta, and Bhagavan—these three are one.' Therefore, the discipline which is essential for uttering the name of God is also necessary for uttering the names of those noble ones—the devotees of God. Why is it that there is no difference between the Bhakta and the Bhagavan? Because the heart of the genuine devotee is the eternal abode of God. The devotee is a slave of God and the doer of His behests. All the physical and mental activities of the slave are, in fact, the activities of the Lord Himself. The slave does not do or think of anything for himself. His deeds and thoughts are not his own but his Lord's. The activities of my hands and feet, which are mere servants of my wishes, are counted to be my activities rather than those of my hands or feet. Even so, the deeds and thoughts of the slave should be counted to be those of the Lord rather than his own. Where then is the difference between the Bhakta and the Bhagavan?

Again, the Bhagavatas too are engaged in singing the glories of the Lord. And one can probe into the divine mysteries through the study of the Bhagavata. This is why Bhagavan Vyasa introduced in his *Brahma-sutras* the aphorism[2] which means that Brahman is revealed and realised through the Sastras alone. The Bhagavata, being permeated with the Divine, is verily another name for the Bhagavan. Singing the glory of the name of the Bhaktas is only for the steady, the humble, the pure and the tranquil-minded. It is not for those egotistic ones who deem themselves successful and omniscient merely because they have found some cheap means to sense-enjoyment through their intelligence—which is tossed about by numberless questions on all odd topics—and

1.   तृणादपि सुनीचेन तरोरिव सहिष्णुना ।
     अमानिना मानदेन कीर्तनीयः सदा हरिः ॥
                              Sri Krishna Chaitanya's Sikshashtakam, 3.

2.   शास्त्रयोनित्वात् ।   *Brahma-sutras* 1.1.3.

imagine themselves leaders and teachers of humanity just because they have read 'modern' science and philosophy which promise the mundane happiness. Nor is it for those whose entire quest has been, through infatuation for discursive knowledge, reduced merely to hunting for earthly pleasures; who, light-hearted as they are, think themselves to be the very ideal of all seriousness and gravity, and are unclean with sullenness, puffed up with pride and insolence. For him who thinks, 'Who is there equal to me?'[1] or 'Who is there greater than I?'—it is impossible to be lowlier than a blade of grass, to be as patient as a tree. Such a man is avaricious for honour for himself; his throat is parched with a burning thirst for fame. How can such a man accord honour to others, see the virtues of others?

When a man has freed himself from the clutches of temptation, when he is no longer attracted by earthly pleasures, when he is carried far away from the tumults of social life and is driven deep into the secret cave of his own heart in search of the waters of peace and the bliss which is beyond speech and mind, when he has taken a plunge in the transmuting river of divine love flowing out of the fountain of the devotees' hearts, then and then alone he becomes fit to take the Name and touch Immortality. Then alone, being aware of his own insignificance, he can think himself to be lowlier than a blade of grass, realise that the universe is permeated with the Divine, and be ready to worship even the tiniest insect. Only then he deserves the title of real Vaishnava. Is it for such a Vaishnava to be perturbed by the rebuffs of the world? Knowing everything to be the sport of the Lord, he goes about at ease even as a lunatic or a lad, playing, laughing and dancing over the breakers of the ocean of Samsara. Such beings represent the Godhead in different forms. One can earn as much merit by singing their names as by singing the names of God. Such Vaishnavas do not belong to any caste; they are neither Brahmana nor Kshatriya, neither Vaisya nor Sudra. There is another

---

1.   कोऽन्योऽस्ति सदृशो मया ।   *Gita*, XVI, 15.

eternal, transcendental caste which can be grasped through the purified mind and intellect alone. They belong to this noble fold. To chant their names, one has to observe the rule laid down by Sri Gaurangadeva. One with a heart full of devotion and faith can, with great ease and much benefit, chant their names. Though the Vaishnavas belonging to any particular caste may not all be real Vaishnavas in the sense mentioned above, yet they have their devotion, faith and natural confidence in Vaishnavism as such. This is why, when they chant the name of their previous Gurus, the light of that influence drives out from their hearts all the darkness of impurity.

So, let us also become fit to plunge in the nectar-ocean of Sri Ramanuja's life by purifying ourselves by chanting with heartfelt devotion the glories of the names of the previous Gurus. In the Tamil language, the supreme devotees of Lord Vishnu are called 'Alvars'. 'Alvar' literally means 'one who sinks or dives deep.' The Alvars dive deep into the ocean of the countless auspicious attributes of God, and being overwhelmed by an insatiate longing for incessant communion with Him, remain immersed in the devout contemplation of His divine glories. They are the eternal and everfree devotees of the Lord who once at His behest came down in human form to demonstrate, both by precept and example, the nature of true devotion to the benighted and erring mortals below. Sri-vaishnava tradition has fixed their number once for all as twelve, since their peerless devotion is deemed unapproachable to ordinary bound souls, however exalted be their illumination and purity.

2

Poigai, Bhuta, Pey and Tirumazhisai Alvars

The sum total of that Jnana, through the help of which this beginningless and endless process of creation is going on in a well-ordered and unobstructed manner, is called the Vedas, which are necessarily without beginning and end. Therefore, He, from whom the universe originates, in whom it rests and finds its dissolution in a successive order, who is always fulfilling the desires of all created beings, who is the truth of all truths,—that Supreme Purusha alone is truly the Vedavit or the Knower of the Vedas. That is why Sri Krishna says to Arjuna:

> I am the Author of the Vedanta and the Knower of the Vedas as well.[1]

All beings are born of Him alone. He addresses Arjuna again to say:

> In whatever way men worship me, in the same way do I fulfil their desires; it is My path, O Son of Pritha, that men tread in all ways.[2]

Consequently all religions that are in vogue on earth are none but the paths laid by God. Obviously then the devotees of Sri-sampradaya commit no error when they claim that the doctrine of Visishtadvaita primarily came out of the lotus-mouth of Padmanabha, and that the entire Vedas preach that doctrine alone. It would, however, be wrong and narrow-minded to hold that none but the doctrine of Visishta-dvaita is the true one. The pure-natured devotees, whatever might be the doctrine of their adoption, can never

---

1. वेदान्तकृत् वेदविदेव चाहम् ।   *Gita*, XV, 15.
2. ये यथा मां प्रपद्यन्ते तांस्तथैव भजाम्यहम् ।
 मम वर्त्मानुवर्तन्ते मनुष्याः पार्थ सर्वशः *ibid*. IV, 11.

11

be narrow-minded. They can never be frogs in the well.
Their natural humility enables them to discern the
underlying principles of Reality. Knowing as they do how
to pay respect to one and all, they are capable of seeing the
beauty embedded within everyone. No wonder, therefore,
that in different religions they see only their own chosen
deities, in diverse apparels. Can such noble ones speak ill
of any religion?

In pursuance of their example, as an invocatory rite, let us
meditate on the blessed feet of Sriman Narayana and of the
celebrated Acharyas:

I worship Sriman Narayana, who is ever determined to establish the genuine truth of Vedanta on earth and who shines
in the midst of liberated souls and worthy preceptors.[1]

POIGAI ALVAR

I take refuge in Saroyogi, who was born of a golden lotus in
the month of Aswina (October-November) under the influence
of the asterism Sravana (twenty-second stellar mansion) in
the Dvapara Yuga[2] in the city of Kanchipura, who is the
incarnation of Panchajanya (the conch of Vishnu).[3]

In Kanchipuram there exists even today a temple under
the waters of the lake Deva-sarovara. Within that temple
the image of this Mahapurusha, known as Poigai Alvar, is
enshrined in a recumbent posture with eyes closed in
meditation. The conch which Vishnu, after slaying the demon
Panchajana, got made out of his bones, goes by the name
Panchajanya. This conch is very dear to Vishnu, because at
its very sight the feeling wells up in Him that He is the
chastiser of the demons and people of unclean minds, and

1. श्रीमद्वेदान्तसिद्धान्तस्थापनानित्यदीक्षितम् ।
   श्रीमन्नारायणं वन्दे भान्तं सूरिगुरुत्तमैः ॥
          Brahmatantraswatantra Swami's *Divyasuristotram*, 1.
2. See Appendix A.
3. तुलायां श्रावणे जातं कांच्यां काञ्चनवारिजात् ।
   द्वापरे पाञ्चजन्यांशं सरोयोगिनमाश्रये ॥   *Divyasuristotram*, 2.

that He is the greatest friend of those whose minds are noble, clean and directed to the good of others. That very cage of bones, whose occupant (the demon) at one time employed many a missile to bring about His annihilation, is now, by its tremendous sound, drying up the heart-blood of His enemies. In the Kurukshetra, it was the thundering sound of this Panchajanya that rent through the heart of the Kurus, the earth and the heavens. In like manner, the Panchajanya fills the enemies of Vishnu with fear and robs them of their prowess. Such are its attributes. And where these attributes are present, one discerns the Panchajanya there. It is because the great Poigai sped like an arrow against the hearts of atheists and wicked people and by his sweet and moving speech threw them into convulsions that he is regarded as an incarnation of Panchajanya.

To annihilate evil-doers, Bhagavan Vishnu holds the discus in one hand and the club in another. And to increase the joy of his devotees and the dismay of those who bear malice towards cows, the Vedas and holy men, He holds the lotus and the conch in the other two hands. These, being the unfoldment of the Vishnu-power, are verily the manifestations of Vishnu Himself. Wherever the manifestation of the Vishnu-power is noticed, there we acknowledge a partial advent of Vishnu. To do so is by no means irrational. They who unthinkingly ridicule this concept can only be told to reflect deeply over the subject. Now let us worship the feet of the previous Acharyas again.

BHUTA ALVAR

I adore the saint Bhuta who was born in the month of Aswina (October-November) under the influence of the asterism Sravishtha (twenty-third stellar mansion) from within the blooming lotus as the manifestation of the (Kaumodaki) club at Mallapuri (Mahabalipuram) situated on the seashore.[1]

---

1.   तुलाश्रविष्टासंभूतं भूतं कल्लोलमालिनः ।
     तीरे फुल्लोत्पलान्मल्लापुर्यामीडे गदांशकम् ॥   *Divyasuristotram, 3.*

The earlier name of the place, Tirukadalmalli, a few miles southward from Madras, was Mallapuri, where Mahatma Bhuta Alvar was born. Because he used to make the atheists kiss the ground, people worship him as a manifestation of the mace of Vishnu.

PEY ALVAR

Him I adore, that celebrated Mahatma, who was born out of a water-lily blossoming within a well in Mayurapura, in the month of Aswina (October-November) under the influence of the asterism Satabhisha (twenty-fourth stellar mansion) as a manifestation of Nandaka (the sword of Vishnu).[1]

The southern part of the Madras City is known as Mylapore or Mayurapura. Even today one can find a well there from within which Pey Alvar was born. He is worshipped as the incarnation of the sword of Vishnu, for he used to cut asunder the fetters of delusion that bind the infatuated. The word 'Pey' means a ghost. As he always used to be absorbed in God-consciousness, wandering along indifferent to all the concerns of the world, he looked like a ghost.

These three Alvars were born in the Dvapara Yuga, i.e., before 4302 B.C.[2]

TIRUMAZHISAI ALVAR

I worship Bhaktisara, who was born as the son of Bhargava in Mahisarapura (Tirumazhisai) in the month of Pausha (January-February) under the influence of the asterism

------

1. तुलाशतभिषग्जातं मयूरपुरकैरवात् ।
   महान्तं महदाख्यातं वन्दे श्रीनन्दकांशकम् ॥   *ibid. 4.*

2. These and other dates of Alvars as given here and elsewhere, pushing the same back to the B.C's., are the traditional dates given in the verses of Sri Manavala Mamuni. Modern historians, however, place all the Alvars between the 5th and the 2nd of the 8th century A.D. See Appendix A.—*Editor.*

Makha (tenth stellar mansion) as a manifestation of the discus (Sudarsana, of Vishnu).[1]

The name of this great one is Tirumazhisai Alvar. He is renowned to have been born as the manifestation of the 'discus', because his ever-sharp discrimination would remove delusion root and branch. He was born in the last year of the Dvapara Yuga, i.e., in the year 4202 B.C., at the village Tirumazhisai, two miles west of Poonamallee. In olden times this village was known as Mahisara. The only occupation of this great one was to pluck flowers and Tulasi leaves and offer fascinating garlands made out of them to Sri Govinda. Though he was no ruler of any kingdom, he was, is, and will remain more honoured than any sovereign emperor. The flavour of his devotion was so captivating.

---

1. मखायां मकरे मासे चक्रांशं भार्गवोद्धवम् ।
     महीसारपुराधीशं भक्तिसारमहं भजे ॥   *Divyasuristotram, 5.*

3

Sathari, Madhura Kavi and Raja Kulasehara Alvara

SATHARI ALVAR

I worship Sathari, the incarnation of the commander-in-chief (Vishvaksena) of the army of Sri Vishnu, who was born in the beginning of Kali Yuga as a son of Kari at Kurukapuri in the land of Pandya in the month of Vaisakha (May-June) under the influence of the asterism Visakha (sixteenth stellar mansion).[1]

Kurukapuri (Kurukur or Alvar Tirunagari) is situated on the banks of the river Tamraparni—the southern most river of India. Kurukur is situated near the town of Tinnevelly. The eastern portion of the southern part of the Deccan beginning from Trichinopoly right down to Cape Comorin used to be called Pandyadesa. The western expanse of the land beginning from the Cape and Trivandrum, inclusive of the Western Ghats up to Cannanore went by the name Malabar (Malayaladesa) or Kerala. North of this was the Kannada Province. West of the Kannada country is the Konkanadesa. The south-eastern part of Konkana was known by the name Karnataka (Mysore Province). The eastern province from Trichinopoly to Nellore bore the name Cholarajya of which Kanchipura (Conjeevaram) was the capital. The expanse of the land on the north of the Godavari, from Nellore to Rajahmundri, was called Andhradesa. From Rajahmundry to Ganjam toward the east was known as Kalinga. To the north and to the east of Kalinga lay the Odradesa or Orissa. The current language of the Pandya

---

1.   वैशाखे तु विशाखायां कुरुकापुरिकारिजम् ।
     पाण्ड्यदेशे कलेरादौ शठारिं सैन्यपं भजे ॥   *Divyasuristotram, 6.*

16

and Chola provinces is Tamil; of Kerala, Malayalam; of Karnataka, Kannada; and of Andhra and Kalinga, Telugu. These four are known as the Dravidian languages which one has to learn to know of the devotees of South India.

Vishvaksena is the alter-ego of Narayana. He is the commander-in-chief of the Vaishnavi-sena (the army of Vishnu). Of moon-like shining complexion, he has four arms, and is the destroyer of all difficulties. The Vaishnavas worship Vishvaksena in the place of Sri Ganapati and Sri Kartikeya. Being the dispeller of difficulties Vishvaksena is the Commander-in-chief of Lord Narayana.

Desirous of a son, Mahatma Kari, along with his wife, once went to the temple of Narayana where they offered worship and observed fasts. Pleased with them, Bhagavan Vishnu revealed to them through an oracle that He Himself was going to take birth as their son. Accordingly, Satha-ripu—Satharipu, Sathari and Sathakopa are synonymous—was born. He was of such a sweet and loving nature that whoever happened to exchange a word with him would love him as a blood brother. He was so dear to God that He once referred to him as 'Our Alvar', and his name came to be 'Nammalvar', the word 'nam' meaning' our'. Another name of his was 'Parankusa', the iron goad; this he got by controlling the wild elephants of other systems of philosophy. Mahatma Kari, his father, was a rich landlord. Nammalvar was born in 3102 B.C., the first year of Kali Yuga.

MADHURAKAVI ALVAR

I take refuge in him, who was born in the month of Chaitra (April-May) under the influence of the asterism Chitra (fourteenth stellar mansion) as a manifestation of Garuda, the king of birds, and who had great devotion to Parankusa Satharipu.[1]

Nammalvar had a very aged devotee who was known as Madhura Kavi Alvar, because he was a singer of sweet

---

1.   चैत्रे चित्रासमुद्भूतं पाण्ड्यदेशे खगांशकम् ।
     श्रीपरांकुशसद्भक्तं मधुरं कविमाश्रये ॥   *Divyasuristotram*, 7.

songs. He was born in the transition between the Yugas. Tamil scholars have pointed out 3224 B.C., to be his year of birth.

His birth-place was near that of Satharipu.

KULASEKHARA ALVAR

I take refuge in King Kulasekhara (the ruler of Kerala), who was born in Cholapattana (Tiruvanjikkolam) of Kerala, in the month of Magha (February-March) under the asterism Punarvasu (seventh stellar mansion) as the manifestation of the Kaustubha (the gem of Lord Vishnu).[1]

He was the composer of the Mukundamala. Rare indeed is a devotee like him. He was born on a Thursday, which was the twelfth day of a bright lunar fortnight in 3102 B.C. Vaishnavas worship him as the manifestation of the Kausthubha gem of Narayana because he was a radiant Rajarshi.

1. कुम्भे पुनर्वसुभवं केरले चोलपट्टने ।
   कौस्तुभांशं धराधीशं कुलशेखरमाश्रये ॥ *ibid. 8.*

4

Periyalvar, Andal and Tondaradippodi Alvar

PERIYALVAR

I take refuge in Vishnuchitta (whose mind would ever remain permeated with Vishnu-consciousness) who was born at Dhanvinahpura (Srivilliputtur) under the influence of the asterism Svati (fifteenth stellar mansion) in the month of Jyeshtha (June-July) as the manifestation of Vishnu's chariot, who was reputed as the father-in-law of Vishnu (his daughter being married by Narayana Himself) and who belonged to the Brahmana community called *Purassikha* (who wore tufts on their foreheads).[1]

The name of the daughter of this Mahapurusha was Andal. From her very childhood, Andal would keep herself occupied in the worship of Narayana and would say that she was going to marry none other than Narayana Himself. On her growing up, the father felt concerned for her marriage. But the daughter was determined not to marry any one but Vishnu Himself! The father, not knowing what to do, began to meditate on Narayana. Tradition says that on that very night Vishnu appeared before him in a dream and said: 'Do not hesitate to offer Me your daughter, for she is Lakshmi Herself.' The very same night the priest (Archaka) of the Vishnu temple was thus commanded in a dream: 'Tomorrow morning you will go to Andal's father's house with all the necessary paraphernalia for a matrimonial ceremony and, getting Andal apparelled in beautiful garments, escort her here to My temple in a palanquin.' The priest acted accordingly. Immense was the father's joy when he heard

---

1. ज्येष्ठे स्वातीभवं विष्णुरथांशं धन्विन: पुरे।

प्रपद्ये श्रशूरं विष्णोर्विष्णुचित्तं पुर:शिखम्॥ *Divyasuristotram, 9.*

this good news. Andal went in a palanquin to be married to Sri Purushottama. Countless people followed her. As Andal entered the inner shrine, Narayana received her with outstretched arms and embraced her. In that embrace, Andal dissolved and became one with that blessed image. None did see her any more. At the anxiety of her father, Sri Purushottama smiled and said, 'From today you have become My father-in-law. Please go back home. Your daughter will always remain in Me.' Overwhelmed with joy and thrilled to the core of his being, Andal's father prostrated himself again and again before Vishnu, the sustainer of all, the Supreme Purusha, and went back home. From that day onward he became famous as the 'Periya Alvar', which literally means 'The Great Alvar '. He was born in 3056 B.C..

ANDAL OR GODA

I worship Sri Ranganatha's consort (Andal) who was born in a Tulasi grove in the month of Ashadha (July-August) under the influence of the asterism Purvaphalguni (eleventh stellar mansion) in Pandyadesa; who is the manifestation of Bhudevi (supporter of the Universe) and who is the superb artificer of language.[1]

Sri Lakshmi appears in three manifestations. Sridevi is Her first manifestation, as She sports in the heart of Vishnu. Bhudevi, Her second manifestation, is the delight of Vishnu's vision. Niladevi, the third one, deems Herself blessed in singing the sweetness and glory of Narayana and remaining ever-overwhelmed and intoxicated drinking the elixir of His love. It was Bhudevi who incarnated in the form of Andal.

Periyalvar had one day gone to his own Tulasi-grove to gather leaves for the worship of Sri Vishnu. As tradition has it, while busy plucking the leaves, all on a sudden he was simultaneously surprised and moved by an upsurge of

---

1. आषाडे पूर्वफल्गुण्यां तुलसीकाननोद्भवाम् ।
पाण्ड्ये विश्वंभरां गोदां वन्दे श्रीरङ्गनायकीम् ॥ *Divyasuristotram, 10.*

profound affection at the sight of an exquisitely beautiful baby lying on the ground, smiling and briskly plying her limbs. Having no children, he considered himself lucky to receive the gift of such a lovely daughter. A natural flow of love towards Narayana characterised this girl from her very childhood. She did not like playing with other children. One would often find her sitting before the temple, and talking endlessly to herself. Sometimes she would be laughing and, at other times, in a fit of pique towards the Deity, shedding blinding tears and then, being assuaged, dancing and clapping her hands for joy. Again, when there was none to spy, she would steal into the temple, throw around her own neck the garland meant for Narayana and then put it back in its place. One day, noticing that she had put around her neck the wreath of Tulasi leaves which was meant for Vishnu, her father scolded her. No garland could be offered to Vishnu that day. At night, the Lord appearing in a dream said to her father, 'Why, pray, did you not offer Me the Tulasi-wreath today? I derive greater joy out of things that have been touched by My devotee. Think not Andal to be a mere mortal.' To his surprise, the next day Periyalvar found that the Tulasi-wreath worn on the previous day by Andal had not faded; on the contrary, it was looking brighter and more beautiful than a freshly made garland. Without any more hesitation he took the garland and set it on the image. Thrilled to witness the uncommon efflorescence of the Lord's beauty that day, his heart was filled with great joy. As tears of love flowed down his cheeks, he became immersed in ineffable peace.

Even after she had come of age, Andal was that same simple child, that same loving heart, wholly given over to the Lord. Devotion to Vishnu formed itself, as it were, into an image in the person of Andal. The one hundred and seventy-three incomparable verses, composed by her in Tamil, with exquisitely mellifluous words drown the readers in the nectarine ocean of love and will for all time be counted the most precious treasures by the devotees of God. It was as if her love-laden heart melted and flowed as the sweetness of these verses.

'Goda', in Sanskrit may mean the giver of sweet hymns; one who was given by the earth; or the giver of garlands. In all these senses the name is appropriate to Andal. Because this sweet-speaking one was married to Sri Ranganatha she came to be known also by another name, Ranganayaki. She descended on earth in 3005 B.C.

TONDARADIPPODI ALVAR

I take refuge in that greatest of devotees known by the name 'Dust-of-the-Devotees' Feet', who was born under the influence of the asterism Jyeshtha (eighteenth stellar mansion) in the month of Agrahayana (December-January) as a manifestation of Sri Vishnu's Vanamala (the garland made of forest flowers) at Mandangudipura (near Tiruchirapalli) in the kingdom of Cholas.[1]

The great joy of this Alvar was the weaving of garlands for offering to Sri Vishnu. Hence the devotees have concluded that he was an incarnation of the blessed forest-flower-garland of Vishnu. Serving Narayana was his only work and with this the Lord was well pleased. He was born in 2814 B.C.

It is said that[2] one day Sriman Narayana was praising this great devotee before Sri Lakshmidevi in glowing words

1. कोदण्डे ज्येष्ठानक्षत्रे मण्डङ्गुडिपुरोद्भवम् ।
चोलोर्व्यां वनमालांशं भक्तांघ्रिरेणुमाश्रये ॥   *Divyasuristotram, 11.*

2. The following is another popular version of the story:

It was Devadevi, a courtesan, who one day happened to observe, on her way, Vipranarayana (the previous name of Tondaradippodi), an embodiment of pure Sattva, toiling in his garden with great devotion, entirely oblivious of the external world. Though struck by his unique devotion and complete indifference to worldly concerns, she, in her mischievous way, thought that he was offering a challenge to her powers of captivating any one by her charms and wiles. She appeared in the simple guileless dress of a devotee and expressed to him her intense desire to participate in the glorious service he rendered to the Lord day after day. Vipranarayana agreed and she, true to her word,

that in the three worlds there was no power which could impede the unbroken flow of love from this devotee's heart. The Mother of the Universe smiled at this and said, 'There is nothing impossible for the glance of a woman.' And to prove Her own words. She secretly directed one of Her attendants to remain ever within sight of this great devotee, and that, in her most ravishing dress. One day when, after plucking flowers from his own garden, Tondaradippodi was busy making a garland out of them, there appeared before him a bright-eyed maiden of exquisite charm with a celestial garland in her hand, who addressed him hesitantly: 'Swamin, will you take pity on me and accept this garland woven by this servant of yours and put it round the blessed neck of Sri Govinda-deva? A stranger here, I wish to stay for some time. But I have none to call my own in this place. Being a noble soul, you are a kinsman to one and all. Emboldened by this thought, I am here at your feet.' At the sight of that beautiful garland, the devotee naturally felt a longing to bedeck his Chosen Deity with it. And his heart too had perhaps melted a little at the sweet address of the maiden. So he accepted the garland with great eagerness. Henceforth, the maiden would every day present a garland for the Deity and water the plants in the garden like a servant. The modest and sweet behaviour of the young woman gradually

---

continued to help him in various activities for months. One evening as there was a continuous and heavy downpour of rain, she could not go home and was obliged to spend the night in Vipranarayana's hut. She got the long-expected opportunity and made Vipranarayana yield to temptation. He was so much in the grip of lust that he spent the nights afterwards in her house only and squandered all his wealth in his pursuit of sense pleasure. But on the day he became penniless, he was mercilessly turned out of her house, and he had to spend the night in dire distress. Unable to bear his sorrow, the merciful Lord Ranganatha in human form, calling himself a servant of Vipranarayana, took the golden bowl of His temple and offered it to Devadevi in her house in his master's name. This made her admit Vipranarayana into her house to his great glee. But next morning, the Lord's bowl was found to be missing, and after a vigorous search it was discovered in the possession of Devadevi. She was summoned to the palace to depose before

lured the mind of the great devotee away from the path leading towards the blessed feet of the Lord. Brooding constantly over her, he progressively became bewitched by her. At last, instead of being mad for God, he longed for union with the woman. And she too employed all her wiles to infatuate him all the more. When finally he opened his mind before her, she demanded gold coins of him. The penniless Brahmana was at a loss and began to weep. That day he failed to go to the temple. Knowing the cause of the absence of His devotee, Narayana Himself went in disguise to the Brahmana and offering him His own golden bowl, said, 'Why are you weeping? Take this and have your desires fulfilled.' When in great glee the Brahmana hastened into the maiden's room, lo! in her stead, there he saw his own Chosen Deity,—Narayana and His consort Sri Lakshmi. At this sight, the feelings of shame and self-contempt brought him near to death. And at last with profuse tears of love rolling down his cheeks, he muttered: 'O Ocean of mercy! You have saved me today from falling into eternal hell. Boundless is Your kindness.' Since that day, he lost himself in the love of God. Real wisdom had dawned on him. Never more could the glance of any maiden tempt him.

the king. She admitted that it was given to her by a servant of Vipranarayana. When Vipranarayana was next questioned, he pleaded complete ignorance of the whole affair, whereupon the king put him in prison. Again the agony of his devotee moved the Lord to appear before the king in his dream and reveal the part that He played out of compassion for His devotee. The king liberated Vipranarayana who, stung with remorse for his wretched part, expiated his sin by purificatory deeds. Soon he became his previous self again and, out of the fullness of his devotion and humility, came to be reckoned as 'the dust of the feet of the devotees'.—Ed.

5
Poigai, Bhuta and Pey Alvars Meet Together

An interesting story is told about Poigai Alvar, Bhuta Alvar and Peyalvar. One day, the sky was overcast by thick clouds and it began to hail, while thunder roared. Violent gusts of wind added to the foulness of the weather and the fury of Nature. The rain and storm went on for two days incessantly. Not a single pedestrian was seen on the way. Even indigent and homeless people had taken shelter in mountain caves or hollows of trees to save themselves from the sweeping squalls and the cruel beatings of big hailstones.

At this time, on a vast lonesome plain, bare of even trees and creepers, a seeming madman clad in rags and shivering in the cold, became a plaything of the fiendish wind. All the malice of the storm beat on the poor man as if to tear his tatters by force away from him. But the man's hands held his clothes securely round his shivering frame. The wind, failing in its purpose, began to utter angry groans. As if to help the gale, the clouds sent down a big hail-stone, aiming it at the crown of the poor pedestrian. As soon as the man let go his grip over his cloth to save his head with both the hands, the gusty wind snatched away the wrapper. Insolent nature expressed exultation by lashing winds, fierce lightning and crashing thunder. Nature was behaving with this patient wayfarer as if his was not a body of flesh and blood, as if he was an inert thing without any sense of pleasure and pain. As nature giggled forth when his wrapper was blown away by the wind, the wayfarer too squared the humour by laughing outright. Not sorry in the least, he expressed the great delight of his own pure heart by singing a song in the following strain:

O Hari, fickle by nature, You rush hither and thither.
To make others dance, You dance Yourself.

Some You fascinate by so sweetly smiling;
Others, like Gopis, You captivate with Your flute.
Though You have gorged the universe into Your belly,
You steal butter in order to allay Your hunger.
Unaware of Your trick, the fond milk-maidens in
                their pique quarrel with Your mother.
Now You startle the simple cow-boy by disfiguring
                Your face with a frown.
Instantly You lock him in close embrace and kiss
                his face again and again.
Now You are awful, now captivating to the heart;
Sometimes You are volatile, sometimes You are
                absolutely inert.
Once You don regal apparel, then appear in tattered robes.
Who can ever describe You adequately?
By robbing me of my clothes You giggle aloft.
Cunning One, I have seen through Your craft.
Play on, my Lord, have jokes to Your fill.
Your eternal servant is delighted at Your delight.

Not in the least grieved at this dire adversity, the wayfarer wended his way dancing in joy. Though starving for two days and tortured as a plaything at the hands of the hail-storm, this great devotee began to dance in thrilling joy. Such was his unprecedented reaction to the troubles he had to undergo! But now as he seemed to feel a little exhausted, he proceeded towards a very small cottage noticed in the front. The doors being closed fast—and there did not seem to be anyone inside—it was impossible to enter inside the cottage. Attached to the cottage, however, there was a thatched terrace, where one could lie with great difficulty, curling up oneself like a dog. Exhausted as he was, the wayfarer lay down there. When he was almost succumbing to the soft touch of sleep—the assuager of all afflictions—there appeared on the scene another wayfarer in the same plight and asked the former one: 'Good Sir, is there any resting place here for one driven by cold, rain, hurricane, and hunger? 'Do come, you are welcome,' said the former, sitting up instantly; 'there must be enough sitting space for two where there is lying space for one.' The latter went in promptly to find himself seated by the former's side for the much-needed life-saving rest. When the goddess of sleep was lulling them both in her soft lap with a view to steal away their afflictions, presently there appeared with quick steps a third shivering wayfarer in rags, extremely exhausted, driven as he was like the former two by the terrible gusts of wind, and enquired, 'Good Sirs, any space for a third man there?' 'Come, do come in,' said the former two standing up eagerly. 'Where two can sit, three can remain standing at ease.' Gladly the third one drew in, and being sheltered by their side, got relieved to a great extent of his weariness.

As soon as the third wayfarer had found shelter, all on a sudden the storm and rain ceased simultaneously. It seemed, as if only to endanger these three, the rain and storm had joined in conspiracy and brought about this foul day. The sky now became absolutely clear. The juvenile sun shot forth its celestial rays on all quarters. Meanwhile the first wayfarer visualised that on the lap of smiling Nature, was shining the Crest-Jewel of the Lord, holding in His four hands the conch, the discuss, the club and the lotus, smiling sweetly and bewitching the mind. At this vision, he hymned the Lord in the following words:[1]

> Dear Friend, pray, why this new dress again?
> Erstwhile You were all furious intentness!
> Delighted am I exceedingly to see Your fascinating figure.
> Oh, how shall I propitiate You?
> What wealth either is there on this earth?
> The lamp of this earth holds a vast sheet of oil

---

1. Another version of the episode is as follows:

The three devotees were spending their time in delightful conversations on God, His Divine forms, attributes, etc. Suddenly in the darkness they felt on their persons the pressure of the body of an unknown stranger in their midst. Suspecting that a fourth man had entered into their midst without notice, and intending to find out who he was, Poigai with his song lit the lamp of the sun in the receptacle of the earth containing the oil of the sea; while Bhuta with his song lit the lamp of wisdom in the receptacle of love holding the oil of intense affection in which is soaked the wick of the mind melting in bliss; as the result of the illumination generated by both the lights, Peyalvar saw that the fourth person was the Supreme Vishnu Himself with a tremendous form, and he sang in praise of Him. Then the other two Alvars also enjoyed the beatific vision.—*Ed.*

On which the juvenile sun appears as the flame.
With this lamp I make You light-offering to my
                                        heart's content.
Dear Friend, do please accept this worship of mine
And thus bind Your servant with the chord of Your love.

In his upsurge of joy, the second wayfarer too worshipped the world-bewitcher in the following strain:

Ah me! so sweet Your beauty, that
All my afflictions are at an end.
Melting my heart in the lamp of love and therein
Kindling the flame of wisdom, I perform
Your ecstatic worship. Do accept, dear Friend,
This offering of mine and thus enmesh me with the
                                        net of Your love.

Intoxicated by the supreme shining beauty of the Lord, the third wayfarer forgot all about worship. Drunk with love, he began to sing while dancing:

I have seen, I have seen, dear Friend,
I have seen You today.
Enmeshed in Your lustre, the sun weeps to be free.
The moon and stars hide their faces in Your exquisite
                                        beauty.
And I, Your eternal slave, am today totally beholden to
                                        Your feet.

While thus dancing, this God-lover lost his consciousness. Meanwhile, Hari, the enchanter of the hearts of Yogis, too hid Himself in the lap of smiling Nature.

The birds now began to sing His glory in their morning anthem. The three wayfarers had by now discovered each other's identity, and there ensued a love-squabble among them on the issue of worshipping one another's feet. Each one of them had started from his Ashrama, desiring to see the other two. Then fallen into a strange cycle of events and driven by various providential events, they had at last suddenly gathered at one place and had the vision of God. After thus realizing the supreme ends of their life and attaining ineffable peace, they again took different paths towards their respective destinations. The names of the three wayfarers were Poigai Alvar, Bhuta Alvar and Pey Alvar. ❈

6

Tiruppanalvar

I take refuge in Munivahana known as Sripana, who was born
in Nichulapura in the month of Kartika (November-December) under the influence of the asterism Rohini (fourth stellar
mansion), who is the manifestation of (Vishnu's) Srivatsa
and who is foremost among singers (of the Lord's glory).[1]

We have thus sung the glories of the names of the
former Acharyas, most of whom, the Vaishnavas hold, were
born either just before or at the beginning of the Kali Yuga.
After springing forth from the lotus-mouth of Sriman
Narayana and illuminating continually the hearts of the
Gurus, the Vishtadvaita-vada (the doctrine of Qualified Non-
dualism) has progressed up to the middle of Kali Yuga.
Through what we call historical time, which is counted from
the time of the birth of the Son of Mary, the Visishtadvaita-
vada has been flowing uninterruptedly, illuminating the
hearts of the devotees, sometimes in a discernible way and
sometimes otherwise. The course of the stream that sprang
from the will power of God cannot be held up anywhere.

Tiruppanalvar was born of a low-caste family. He used
to pass his days even as a lunatic, always singing the glories
of God to the accompaniment of Vina. So deep was his
absorption while singing the name of the Lord that he would
lose all outward consciousness. Once while singing the
glories of the Lord in single-minded devotion, sitting on the
bathing ghat in the Kaveri in front of the gigantic temple
of Sri Ranganatha, he was so much overwhelmed with
ecstasy that he lost all outward consciousness. At that time
an attendant of Sri Ranganatha-swami, Lokasaranga Muni

---

1. कार्तिके रोहिणीजातं श्रीपाणं निचुलापुरे।
   श्रीवत्सांशं गायकेन्द्रं मुनिवाहनमाश्रये॥ *Divyasuristotram, 12.*

29

by name, was about to return to the temple with the water
for the holy ablutions of the Deity. Finding a man, presum-
ably of a low-caste, across the way, fallen asleep as it were,
when he was playing on his Vina, he called him aloud three
or four times. But there was no response. At last he warned
the man by throwing a stone at him from a distance. Called
back to consciousness by the stone and realising that he had
blocked the way of an attendant of Sri Ranganatha, he
called a thousand curses on himself and, repeatedly begging
pardon of the worshipper for his offence, ran away from
the spot trembling all over in fear.

On the other hand, when Lokasaranga Muni approached the temple-gate, he found the doors closed from within.
One by one, he called all the priests by their name. None
was inside and so there was no response. Meanwhile all the
priests of Sri Ranganatha had assembled there outside the
temple. They were all bewildered and terrified to see the
temple door closed at this unusual hour. All the priests were
standing outside the temple; then who could have closed the
doors? They did not know. The bathing time of the Lord was
passing by. All kept standing there in fear and wonder.
Muni thought that he might have committed some serious
offence because of which Sri Ranganatha Himself must have
closed the doors and prevented him from entering the temple.
With folded palms, he began to pray to the Lord seeking
pardon for the offence. Tears of remorse began to roll down
his cheeks. 'My Lord,' supplicated Muni, 'deign to tell Thy
servant what offence he has committed. He will try his best
to expiate that.' Praying thus for a long time, he heard some
one speaking from within the temple, 'Muni, today you have
struck Me with a stone and I shall not allow you to come
near Me any more.' 'When did I strike You, my Lord, with
a stone?' Muni enquired. The answer came from within:
'The Mahapurusha who was chanting My name with the
vina in his hand on the bathing ghats of the Kaveri is verily
My other self. If you circumambulate the temple carrying
him on your shoulders, the doors of the temple will be

opened, otherwise not.' As soon as he heard this oracle, Muni ran like a madman towards the bathing ghat of the Kaveri. On finding Tiruppanalvar there, he rushed to him with folded palms in sincere contrition. Frightened at this sight, Tiruppanalvar fled to a distance and with folded hands submitted imploringly, 'My Lord, I am a despicable low-born. I have certainly committed an offence. Do therefore punish me, please, by pelting stones from a distance. Do not defile your pure body by touching this Chandala.' But Muni rushed toward him and seizing him forcibly took him upon his shoulders and, carrying him thus, circumambulated the entire seven-walled temple of Sri Ranganatha. Since then Tiruppanalvar came to have the name 'Munivahana'.

7

Tirumangai Alvar and His Founding the Temple of Sri Ranganatha

I take refuge in Kaliyam (Tirumangai) who was born in the month of Kartika (November-December) under the influence of the asterism Krittika (third stellar mansion) as a manifestation of Sri Vishnu's Saranga bow and who was the crest-jewel among the poets accomplished in four kinds of poems and the writer of six Prabandhas.[1]

O Tirumangai Alvar, born in the eigth century A.D., was a devotee par excellence. Even from his youth, going on pilgrimages and visiting the shrines of gods and goddesses were very dear to his heart. He was a natural genius, a great poet. During his pilgrimages, attracted by the loftiness of his personality, four accomplished persons with miraculous powers accepted his discipleship and began to travel far and wide along with him. The name of the first disciple was 'Tola Vazhakkan' or 'the-polemic par excellence'. He came to have this name because none could defeat him in controversy. The name of the second disciple was 'Taluduvan', which means 'The opener of doors'. He could open any lock by a mere puff-of his breath without the help of any key. The name of the third one was 'Nizhalai Mithippan' meaning the 'shadow-catcher'. He whose shadow he touched with his feet would lose his power of movement. The name of the fourth disciple was 'Neermel Nadappan' or 'walker on water'. He could stroll about on water just as he could on land.

After visiting many a place of pilgrimage, along with his four disciples, Tirumangai arrived at the temple of

---

1. कार्तिके कृत्तिकाजातं चतुष्कविशिखामणिम् ।
   षट्प्रबन्धकृतं शार्ङ्गमूर्तिं कलियमाश्रये ॥ *Divyasuristotram, 13.*

Sri Ranganatha situated on an islet in the Kaveri. At that time the temple—a very small one and a haunt of bats etc.— was in an almost dilapidated condition and surrounded by thickets and forests. Once by the day end the priest would come there, offer some flowers and a little water to the Diety and then flee away thence for fear of hyenas and jackals. On seeing this plight of Sri Ranganatha, Tirumangai felt a strong desire to build a suitable temple for the Lord. And soon this desire became an absorbing passion with him. Himself penniless, he knew not whence to get the necessary funds for the purpose. After consulting his four disciples, he resolved to procure money by begging from the rich in different parts of the country. The campaign began; whenever he heard the name of a rich man, he would rush to him, explain his purpose and beg money for the same. But none of these rich men gave him even a small coin and, what was worse, they revealed their godlessness by calling him a thief.

The great devotee that he was, Tirumangai did not mind his treatment. But the thought that the Lord of the universe stood uncared-for in the forest, so to say, without service and worship and surrounded by hyenas and jackals, pierced his heart and caused him much suffering. As a soft earthen pot gets hardened by fire, likewise his naturally tender heart, passing through the fire of wrath, became as relentless as a thunderbolt. He at last burst out before his four disciples, saying, 'My boys, haven't you seen enough of these rich men's devotion to God? They will ever remain atheists and heretics! What then is our duty? Which is better,—to lick the feet of these fiends, while keeping Sri Ranganatha in this plight, or to humble those rogues by building a temple of surpassing magnificence for the Lord of the universe, who is the cause of creation, sustenance and dissolution, and the refuge of all? 'The disciples answered, 'The service to the Lord is our duty, not subservience to these rogues.' 'Then get prepared,' said the guru. 'From today see to it that all the wealth of these avaricious men is spent in constructing the temple. These rich men, who are cruel by nature have been robbing the poor who work hard and are still without sufficient food. Come then, let us rob the rich and spend their wealth for building the temple and feeding the poor.' The disciples were only too ready to carry out the bidding of the master.

Tola Vazhakkan said, 'Revered Sir, it is not given to any one to defeat me in a wrangle. When I engage and enmesh a rich man and his attendants in argument and make them forget everything else, then you can, with your men, easily carry off his wealth.'

'Revered Sir,' said Taludhuvan, 'with a mere puff of my breath, I can open any door however securely it might have been closed. The doors of the rich men's treasuries are always open to me.'

Nizhalai Mithippan added, 'My Lord, any one whose shadow I touch with my feet loses his power of movement. So, from today the wealth of rich wayfarers is yours.'

'Revered Master,' submitted Neermel Nadappan 'the royal castles with moats around are always open to me, for I can easily walk over water. Therefore, from today, yours are all the treasures of kings.'

Helped by the miraculous powers of his disciples, Tirumangai soon became the leader of a big gang of robbers. And boundless wealth began to be stored up in some secret place of the island.

Spending huge sums, Tirumangai brought the best architects from different parts of the land and laid the foundation stone of the temple at an auspicious moment.

The *sanctum sanctorum,* encircled by the first ring of walls and crowned with a high steeple, was completed in two years. After thousands of architects, working day and night for two years, had finished the construction of the inner apartments, work on the first circle of the outer apartments began. Four years' labour, day and night, brought its construction to completion. In this way, a band of more than a hundred thousand architects took six years for the construction of the second, eight years for the third, ten years for the fourth, twelve years for the fifth, and eighteen

years for the sixth ring of apartments. It took sixty years
in all to complete the construction of the temple. By now
Tirumangai had entered his eightieth year. And his four
dear disciples were younger by one or two years only.

When the construction of the inner apartments was
over, the kings of their own accord began to send him money,
convinced that Tirumangai was a genuine devotee. Moreover, he was the ring leader of a gang of more than a
thousand robbers. Such was his prowess that it struck terror
even in the hearts of kings. Lest Tirumangai should one day
come to plunder them of all they possessed, they helped him
with men and money. He used to keep the architects satisfied with regular payments. With his farflung fame and
powerful retinue, he was in fact the paramount ruler of the
time, other rulers being either his subsidiaries or allies.
Still, his habits and behaviour were extremely simple. Once
at day-end he took the food cooked by his own hands out
of the doles he got by begging. Few men had achieved such
mastery over their senses as Tirumangai had done. So intense was his love of God that there was no knowing when
tears would gush out of his eyes. None in that part of the
land suffered the pinch of poverty during the time of his
ministry. Only the rich used to go about terror-stricken.

Now, the construction of the magnificent seven-walled
temple was completed. Tirumangai rewarded the architects
in generous measure. Not a coin was left in his purse.
Meanwhile, some other people—a thousand in number-who
were his accomplices in robbery came to demand money of
him. He thought for long, but did not know how to meet their
demand. In a flash he took aside Neermel Nadappan and
whispered something into his ears. Neermel soon got a huge
boat brought into the northern stream of the Kaveri. It had
been used for carrying blocks of stones for the temple.
Nadappan entered into the boat and remained there for two
hours and then reported himself to his Guru. Thinking that
Tirumangai had returned insolvent, the robbers had, in the
meantime, conspired to kill him outright. Just then Neermel

Nadappan stepped in and addressed them as follows: 'Dear brothers, hidden somewhere on the northern bank of the Kaveri lies a huge treasure belonging to our master; let us all go there and share the wealth among ourselves. The boat is ready. I shall take you there and show you the spot where the treasure lies hidden. You will apportion it as you please. Whatever you give us, we shall be pleased to take. We have been plundering the land for sixty years. Now, there is hardly anything left with the people. Come, let us pass the rest of our days happily, after sharing the treasures left in our hands.' Pleased with these tidings, they all meekly followed Nadappan, abandoning their resolve to do away with the leader.

All boarded the boat. It was the rainy season. The deep waters of the Kaveri, which now stretched across a mile, were flowing at torrential speed, eddying and whirling with a terrific roaring sound. It was evening time. The sky being overcast with dark clouds made it look like midnight. The ship was now plying in the middle of the river. Along with his three other disciples, Tirumangai was standing on the southern bank gazing at the ship, which could be now discerned only very indistinctly. Suddenly there shot forth a horrible cry of distress from the bosom of the Kaveri. And then all was quiet. The boat could be seen no more. In the roaring, rough bosom of the Kaveri nothing else was noticed. After a short while, one man walking with steady strides over the water came near Tirumangai and bowed down at the feet of this devotee and former ringleader of robbers. The man was none other than the fourth disciple, Neermel Nadappan. Tirumangai heaved a sigh and said, 'Rise up, my child. Sri Ranganatha has assuredly taken His children to His lap. Do not feel concerned for that. Leaving this earth behind, all of them have gone to Vaikuntha. Tell me, is not that better than continuing to live the life of robbers? Come, let us also pass the remaining days of our life in the service of Sri Ranganatha. That, for which we adopted the way of robbery, is now accomplished. We have no other duty now but the service of the Lord.'

In the fulness of time Tirumangai and his four dear disciples attained the sanctuary of Vishnu's feet.

The northern branch of the Kaveri, the place of the death of the thousand robbers, is still known by the name 'Kollidam' (Coleroon), i.e., 'the place of murder'.

It is also said that, once while going to plunder the palace of a king, Tirumangai entered a temple therein. The image of Sriman Narayana stood installed in the temple.[1] Finding the ornaments of the Deity, all studded with costly diamonds and jewels, Tirumangai removed all of them but one. He could take all the ornaments, but one diamond ring sat so close around the flower-like finger that all his attempts with his hand to remove it failed. Then he sought the aid of his teeth to take that out. When the teeth touched the finger of the Lord, divine wisdom flashed within him. Mad with the love of God, he sang a thousand slokas in His praise. Even today these hymns are reputed as 'Tirumozhi' (sacred utterances).

1. Another version of the incident is as follows:

The Lord and His Divine Consort assuming human forms walked on earth along a street within the sight of the Alvar. Both of them were loaded with costly jewels from head to foot. Seeing them the Alvar stopped them and forced them to part with all their jewels, which they did willingly! A ring in the toe of the Lord was so tight that it had to be removed by the Alvar with the aid of his teeth. The Alvar made a bundle of all the jewels and proceeded to walk away with it, but lo! it was too heavy. Alvar suspected foul play on the part of his male captive and in a fit of rage addressed Him, * Have you kept me spell-bound with the aid of Mantras?' Thereupon the captive replied, 'Yes, undoubtedly. But I shall teach you that Mantra of divine power,' and forthwith initiated the Alvar by giving him the sacred Ashtakshara. This initiation and the touch of the Lord instantaneously wrought a spiritual metamorphosis and Tirumangai, the robber, became Tirumangai Alvar.—*Ed.*

8

Nathamuni and Yamunacharya

NATHAMUNI

I adore Acharya Nathamuni, the greatest among the preceptors, who was born at Viranarayanapuram in the month of
Jyeshtha (June-July) under the influence of the asterism
Anuradha (seventeenth stellar mansion) as an incarnation
of Gajavadana (a courtier of Vishvaksena).[1]

About 908 A.D. the stream of Sri-vaishnava spiritual
tradition described in the early Chapters flowed with such
force into the heart of a great devotee, Sri Nathamuni by
name, that it promised to swell into a mighty deluge.

A scion of a good Brahmana family, Nathamuni had a
son, Isvaramuni by name. In his youth, Isvaramuni—a man
of rare beauty and brilliance—married and enjoyed worldly
happiness for some time. But before long, he had to end his
play in the world. His premature death was a heavy blow
to his loving father, Nathamuni, who needed all the strength
of his wisdom to bear the pain.

A beautiful child was born to the newly married wife
of Isvaramuni. It was this child who afterwards became
famous by the name Yamunacharya. Nathamuni, so the
story goes, had visited the places of pilgrimage in Aryavarta
along with his wife, son and daughter-in-law. Because the
child had been conceived on the banks of the Yamuna near
Sri Brindavan, he was named Yamunacharya by Nathamuni
who was the foremost scholar of his time.

After the demise of his son, he renounced the life of the
householder and became a Sannyasin. People conferred on

---

1. ज्येष्ठेऽनुराधासम्भूतं वीरनारायणे पुरे ।
   गजवक्त्रांशमाचार्यमाद्यं नाथमुनिं भजे ॥   *Divyasuristotram, 14.*

him the title 'Muni', because he used to lead as pure a life as the Munis of yore. He was also called 'Yogindra' in view of his attainment of perfection in Yoga. He wrote some books in which he systematised his philosophical views. Of these, *Nyaya Tattva* and *Yoga Rahasya* are and will ever be valued and venerated by all Sri-vaishnavas.

YAMUNACHARYA

I worship that Yamunamuni who was born at Viranarayana-puram in the month of Ashadha (July-August) under the influence of the asterism Uttara-ashadha (twenty-first stellar mansion) and who was reputed to be an incarnation of the throne of Sri Vishnu.[1]

Yamunacharya had lost his father at an early age. And his grandfather Nathamuni became a Sannyasin. Yamunacharya was, therefore, brought up with great difficulty by his old grandmother and his own mother. But through the boundless powers of his intellect, he was soon able to propitiate the goddess of fortune. At the age of twelve he secured half the throne of the kingdom of Pandya!

Because Sri Vishnu alone was seated in his heart, the Vaishnavas worship him as the manifestation of Sri Vishnu's throne. He was born about 953 A.D. in Madura, the capital of the Pandya kingdom. Though an orphan, he proved a prodigy and excelled all his fellow-students in mastering all the branches of study. His preceptor, Srimat Bhashyacharya, used to hold him in very great affection because of his proficiency in all the Sastras. His sweet nature captivated the hearts of all his fellow-students who were only too glad to take lessons from him.

---

1. आषाढे चोत्तराषाढासम्भूतं तत्र वै पुरे ।
सिंहासनांशं विख्यातं श्रीयामुनमुनिं भजे ॥ *Divyasuristotram, 45.*

9

Yamunacharya Wins a Kindom

When at the age of twelve Yamunacharya was studying under Bhashyacharya, a Pundit of the Pandya court was
making all the scholars of South India look pale before him
by the lustre of his learning. In whatever assembly the all-
conquering Pundit appeared, he would create a great uproar
among scholars by defeating all rivals. So his name was
'Vidvajjanakolahala', which means 'One who throws the
learned men into convulsions'. The Pandya king held him
in high regard, as the invaluable ornament of his court. The
invincible Vidvajjanakolahala used to extract, by order of
the king, a yearly tax from the scholars whom he defeated.
Yamunacharya's Guru too had been paying him the tax. But
owing to want of money, two or three years' dues from him
had fallen into arrears. One day a disciple of Kolahala
appeared before the seminary of Bhashyacharya in order to
realise the arrears of tax. On that day Bhashyacharya had
gone out on some business, leaving Yamunacharya in charge
of the school. All the other students too had gone home after
their daily lessons. Yamunacharya was there alone seated
on his mat. As soon as he appeared at the place, the disciple
of Kolahala asked Yamunacharya in a churlish manner,
'Where is your preceptor?' At this, Yamunacharya enquired
in a steady and calm manner, 'May I know, revered Sir,
wherefrom you are coming?' Kolahala's disciple replied in
a ruder manner still: 'Don't you know whence I am? If not,
hearken! I am the most fortunate disciple of that large-
hearted and noble-minded one, the lustre of whose learning
illumines all South India. Well versed in all the Sastras, he
is a terror to all scholars and destroyer of their pride. The
Pandya king is his most obedient servant. By establishing
his sovereignty over all learned scholars, he has reduced

them to the position of his tax-payers. No one failing to pay him tax will be spared by the Pandya king. Methinks, your preceptor has lost his head and so he has kept two to three years' tax in arrears. What does he mean? Does he want to face my invincible preceptor in a scriptural debate again? Is your Guru in the mood of a moth foolishly going to fall into fire?'

Closing his ears with his fingers for fear of hearing any more calumny of his preceptor, Yamunacharya told the disciple of Kolahala: 'Fie upon you! How stupid you are! But what else could the disciple of a stupid one be! As by the fruit one can judge the quality of the tree, so by seeing you I know already the range of your preceptor's learning. Undoubtedly the preceptor who teaches his disciples to be proud, and instead of cleansing their minds makes them all the more dirty, is perfectly hollow within. Is he not an idiot who raises a hurricane to carry off a blade of grass? Why challenge my revered preceptor to defeat Vidvajjana-kolahala in a wrangle? Should a lion go to scare away a fox? Go you and tell your pedantic teacher that one of the most insignificant of the disciples of the venerable Bhashyacharya wants to argue with him. If he is strong and bold enough, let him send me word without delay. I am here quite ready to meet him.'

Kolahala's disciple was too indignant to give any reply. With eyes red and body quivering with rage, he rushed to his preceptor and described the incident exactly as it took place. Kolahala could not help laughing when he learned the age of his rival. All present in the court of the king said that the disciple of Bhashyacharya had only shown the pertness so natural in a boy of his age and that it was proper to admonish him for that. In order to ascertain if the boy did really mean what he said and if he was a normal or an insane creature, the Pandya king sent another man with the words: 'If he really wants to argue, get him here without delay. He should be reprimanded forthwith.'

When the messenger of the king communicated the royal behest to Yamunacharya, he replied: 'By all means I am bound to obey the order of His Majesty the king. But as I am going to argue with a Pundit of Kolahala's eminence, please submit to His Majesty that I expect to be escorted from here with the honour due to a scholar; that is to say, he may either send a conveyance here to take me to the court or send Kolahala here.'

The king and his courtiers were duly apprised of this by the messenger. After much discussion, it was settled that it was but meet to send a conveyance. Accordingly, a very costly palanquin was sent along with a hundred footmen.

On returning home, Bhashyacharya heard that his disciple had trodden on the deadly serpent that was Vidvajjanakolahala, and he almost swooned as he had no more hope of life, since the Pandya king, though generous by nature, treated those who insulted his court Pundit with the utmost cruelty amounting even to capital punishment. But the disciple consoled Bhashyacharya saying, 'There is no reason, revered Sir, for you to be alarmed. You may be certain that, by your grace, I will smash the pride of Kolahala.' As the conversation was going on, the king's men appeared before the seminary with the palanquin. The boy Yamuna-charya duly worshipped the feet of his Guru and mounted the palanquin, assuming the serious air of a great scholar. A great crowd had already assembled on the way.

It was an unprecedented thing for a boy to go to meet the chief Pundit of the royal court in a debate on the Sastras. Men, women and children hastened to have a glance of this wonderful lad. The Brahmana Pundits blessed him from the depth of their hearts: 'Even as Vishnu dethroned and displaced Bali by assuming the form of a dwarf, so may you too return after laying low the insolent pedant! 'A huge crowd followed his palanquin up to the palace gate.

In the meantime, in the royal court a difference of opinion arose between the king and the queen as regards

Yamunacharya. The king said, 'As a cat plays with a mouse, even so will Kolahala defeat and destroy the boy.' 'As a single spark of fire,' replied the queen, 'turns a mountain of cotton into ashes, so will this little boy bring Kolahala's mansion of pride to the ground.' The king cried out indignantly, 'What would you wager to back your faith in this puny boy? 'The queen replied, 'I would become the slave of your bond-slave.' The king exclaimed, 'You fond woman, forsooth a terrible pledge you have taken. I too promise that, if the boy defeats Kolahala, I will give away half my kingdom to him.'

When, the royal couple were thus wrangling, Yamunacharya alighted from the palanquin and courteously bowed before the king, the queen and the courtiers. Then being offered a seat opposite to Vidvajjanakolahala, he occupied it. Seeing his slight build and tender age, Kolahala said jestingly to the queen, *Ala Vandara?* Is this the boy who has come to conquer me? 'She replied, *Ala Vandar*—yes, this is he who has come to conquer you.'

At the outset, Kolahala began to put him simple questions on grammar and on books like the *Amarakosa*. When, however, he found that Yamunacharya answered these questions with ease, he went on to put really stiff ones. Yamunacharya answered them playfully and told Kolahala: 'A boy as I am, you are slighting me. The great sage Ashtavakra defeated Bandi at the court of Janaka—was he then a boy or an old man like you? Do you judge the learning of a person by his size? Then a huge bullock would be a greater scholar than you are.'

Though Kolahala winced at this scurrilous language, he restrained his feelings and said laughingly, 'Capital! You have given an apt answer. Now you may put questions and I shall reply.' The boy said, 'All right, as you yourself wish, I will place before you three propositions. If you are able to refute them, I shall acknowledge defeat at your hands.' 'Come along, no use delaying,' cried out Kolahala. The lad said, 'My first proposition is this—your mother is not a barren woman. Refute it, if you can.'

'Had my mother been barren, then my birth were an impossibility. But it is a great shame to be unable to refute the boy. What am I to do now? 'So thinking and not knowing what to do, Kolahala kept quiet like a dumb man. All the courtiers were astounded at this.

Notwithstanding Kolahala's best efforts to conceal his state of mind, his flushed cheeks and drooping face betrayed his acute mental agony. After a short pause, Yamunacharya stated his second proposition with the following words: 'Sir, can you not refute my first proposition by dint of your all-conquering intelligence? Then here is my second one: the Pandya king is supremely righteous. Please refute this.'

At this, Kolahala began to see darkness all around. He was at his wit's end. With the king seated right in front of them, how could he say the king was unrighteous? Indeed, could he ever be so ungrateful as to call the king unrighteous? The boy would surely bring about his ruin, he mused. His countenance turned pale. He could not conceal his anger. At this moment, Yamunacharya released his third contention: 'O scarer of scholars, here is my third proposition. I say that the great queen seated in front of us is as chaste as Savitri. Please refute this.'

Overwhelmed with anger and shame, Kolahala now burst out, 'You chap, your sole motive is to muzzle my mouth. Can any loyal person ever say that the king is unrighteous or the queen unchaste? True, my mouth has been gagged, but that does not mean that I am defeated. Now, *you* must refute these sinister contentions of yours. If you cannot do that, you should, by order of His Majesty the king, lose your life; for you have through your insinuations cast aspersions on both the king and the queen.' When red-eyed Koahala shouted this, those on his side exclaimed: 'Bravo! Bravo! ', and the supporters of Yamunacharya shouted: 'Kolahala has already been beaten hollow. He promised to refute all the contentions of Yamunacharya and now he is angry! 'In the midst of this racket on all sides, Yamunacharya said with a smile, 'Pray, be quiet, all of you. I shall refute all the contentions one by one. Please listen to me.

'As to the first contention: It is said in our Sastras that the woman who has but only one child is to be considered barren. So, according to our Sastras, your mother who gave birth to only one son—even if he is a man of such great merits as you—is nonetheless considered to be barren.[1]

'Secondly, in the Kali Yuga, Dharma is one-footed, while Adharma is three-footed. In our holy texts we read: A king who protects in every way his subjects gets a sixth part of their religious merits, and a sixth part of their sins when incapable of protecting them properly.[2] And in the Kali Yuga, irreligion predominates. However able a ruler the king might be, owing to the influence of Kali, the subjects are naturally irreligious and the king has to take his sixth share of the sins committed by them. Therefore on the authority of the holy texts, it can be said that the king has got to bear a heavy burden of unrighteousness.

'And now to the third proposition:

'Manu says: In his regal prowess the king is the veritable manifestation of Fire, Air, the Sun, the Moon, Yama (the lord of virtue), Kubera, Varuna and Indra.[3] Therefore, the queen is wedded not merely to the individual, the king. But, along with that, she becomes the spouse of those eight regents of the various quarters as well. How then can it be said that she is chaste?'

The courtiers and the people were amazed and thrilled. In her great joy the queen exclaimed, 'Alavandar, Alavandar!'

---

1.   एकपुत्रो ह्यपुत्र लोकवादात्।

   Manu-Samhita, IX, 61, Medhatithi Bhashya.

2.   सर्वतो धर्मषड्भागो राज्ञो भवति रक्षतः।
   अधर्मादपि षड्भागो भवत्यस्य ह्यरक्षतः॥   *ibid.* VIII, 304.

3.   सोऽग्निर्भवति वायुश्च सोऽर्कः सोमः स धर्मराट्।
   स कुबेरः स वरुणः स महेन्द्रः प्रभावतः॥   *ibid.* VII, 7.

and took him on her lap. The king addressed him respectfully and said: 'O Alavandar, to-day you have conquered
proud Kolahala by your learning and skill. The star fades
in the face of the rising sun. I surrender to you the pedant
who has brought misery to so many scholars and who sought
to bring capital punishment on you a while ago. You may
deal with him as you please. And please relieve me of a
pledge by accepting half of my kingdom as a prize for your
victory.' So saying, the king took him from the lap of the
queen and seated him beside himself on his own throne. The
people raised a tumult of victory.

It is superfluous to say that Alavandar forgave
Kolahala. After getting half the kingdom, he, though a mere
boy, ruled it with competence. Taking him to be a mere boy,
some neighbouring rulers planned an invasion of his
kingdom. On coming to know of this from his spies,
Alavandar marched against them first. Forced to acknowledge defeat, they now thought themselves fortunate to be
counted as his tributaries or allies.

10

Yamunacharya's Renunciation

Alavandar ruled the kingdom for a long time. Deluded by mundane pleasures, he forgot that this life was perishable. Though by nature a believer in God, he found little time to carry on his religious practices. However, under his rule, the subjects lived happily.

Meanwhile, his grandfather who loved him dearly passed away. Before breathing his last, he called Ramamisra or Manakkal Nambi, his chief disciple, and said: 'Please see that the boy, being immersed in the enjoyment of things temporal, does not forget his duty. I leave him to your care.'

When Alavandar reached his thirty-fifth year, the ascetic Nambi, remembering the last behest of his Guru, appeared at the palace gate to seek an interview with the king.

But seeing the gate crowded with the vehicles of tributary kings and troops of soldiers, and finding that even the biggest aristocrats had to wait long before gaining permission to enter the palace, he, the shabbily dressed Sannyasin Nambi, gave up all hope of getting in through the main gate. Even if the sentries allowed him to enter in, it was clear he could not converse with the king, surrounded as he was by other kings and nobles and ever busy with royal duties. He had therefore to think of some other means to have an interview with the king.

Ascetics like the greens named 'tuduvalai', which is said to develop the quality of Sattva. After collecting some of those greens, Nambi approached the chief cook of the royal kitchen at the backdoor of the palace and said, 'Dear brother, may Narayana bless you! May I entreat you to serve every day to our king, who is spiritually disposed, some preparation of these greens which develop the quality of Sattva? By this his life on earth will be lengthened and his intelligence quickened. I shall get you these greens every day.' The cook was a pious man and knew the rare virtue of these familiar greens. So, he accepted them eagerly and promised to serve them every day.

For about a couple of months Mahatma Nambi supplied a quantity of those greens every day and the cook prepared various kinds of dishes and served them to the king. Alavandar used to take these preparations with great relish. Nambi came to know of this. One day he stayed away deliberately. On that day the king missed the 'tuduvalai' dish and asked the cook, 'Did you not cook the greens today? 'The cook replied, 'The Sadhu who used to get these greens did not bring them today.' 'Who is that Sadhu? At what price do you purchase these from him? 'the king enquired. 'Your Majesty, I do not know the name and whereabouts of that Sadhu. He does not accept any payment. Out of love and regard for you, he procures the greens from somewhere and of his own accord. These greens develop Sattvic intellect and make for longevity. But I do not know why he did not come today.' The king grew thoughtful and then told the cook, 'If he happens to come tomorrow, bring him to me with due courtesy and honour.' 'Yes, Your Majesty,' said the cook and went back to the kitchen. The following day, when the noble-hearted Nambi came with the greens, the cook told him most respectfully, 'Revered Sir, His Majesty the king wants to see you.' Without any hesitation, Nambi asked him to show the way. The cook took him to the king, who seated in a lonely apartment was then absorbed in musing over this very holy man. Now suddenly seeing Nambi presented before him by the cook, he was delighted and said, 'Sir, I salute your holy feet. I am your servant. Please be frank with me. Tell me with what end in view you get these delicious greens every day for me, and take no payment for them. How can I be of some service to you? 'Hearing this, Nambi said, 'I wish to tell you something in private.' The king immediately signed to the cook to leave and, after closing the doors of the room, offered a seat to the Sadhu. The Sadhu in his turn asked the king to take his seat and so he did.

Then Nambi said, 'Your Majesty, it is long since your grandfather, the great-souled Nathamuni, went to Vaikuntha. I dare say you have not forgotten him. I am one of his servants. Before he breathed his last, he left with me an immense treasure to be handed over to you at the right time. Please accept the treasure and relieve me.' Alavandar was very glad to hear of the treasure, for, at that time he was planning an expedition against a rebel king and needed money badly. He could well believe that his grandfather had left a treasure for him; for nothing was impossible for that great man. Therefore, he importuned Nambi, 'Sir, you are really a Sadhu of great renunciation; for, without keeping the treasure yourself, you have been looking for the time to hand it over to me. Now kindly tell me where the treasure is.' Nambi answered, 'If you follow me, I shall take you there, where the treasure lies hidden. It is installed within seven walls between two rivers. A great serpent has been guarding it, and at the end of every twelfth year a demon from the south sea 'goes over there to inspect it. [1] It has been kept shrouded by the power of a Mantra. Through this Mantra aided by the power of a leaf, the treasure will be made visible and accessible to you.' Eagerly the king said, 'I am ready to go over there, with the four divisions of my army. Please be our guide.' 'It is not advisable that many people should assemble there. Your Majesty should follow me alone,' interposed Nambi. For this too Alavandar was prepared. 'I shall do whatever you bid me,' he said 'let us then proceed without delay.' Accordingly the king followed Nambi after making all necessary arrangements so that the affairs of the kingdom might go on in a well-ordered way during his absence.

They proceeded northwards from Madura. At noon, when he was resting somewhere, Nambi began to chant

---

1. See Appendix A. 5

the Bhagavadgita. For long the king had been totally oblivious of the spiritual world. The sweet sounds revived his memory. The world seemed illusory. His home was on the other shore of the ocean of Samsara. Blinded by illusion, all this time he had been considering the unreal to be the real. He had been mistaking a tavern for his home. Thoughts of this kind naturally began to surge up in his mind. He began to relish like nectar the sweet chanting of the Gita. After Nambi had finished chanting, the king with folded hands entreated, 'Revered Sir, if you see no objection, kindly make this servant of yours a rightful drinker of the nectar of the blessed Gita. As I listen to you, I feel like giving up all power and wealth and moving about with you in this world like a wayfarer. Indeed, I am a wayfarer here; my home is elsewhere. Take pity on me and make me a rightful enjoyer of the ambrosia of the Gita. From today I am your disciple.'

On hearing this, Nambi's face lit up with a smile. He said, 'O king, I am exceedingly glad to see my hopes fulfilled. It is not for you to become a disciple of mine, but for me to become one of yours. As desired by you, I shall explain the meaning of the *Gita* according to my ability. If there is no pressure of work, why not stay here and study the *Gita* for a few days? 'The king replied, 'Whatever the pressure of work, the study of the *Gita* is the first and the greatest duty; this I have realised while in your company.' Accordingly, Nambi continued to expound the *Gita* every day. Alavandar forgot all about his kingly duties. The fortunate one who has once enjoyed the beauty of the Divine instantly forgets the world. So the Gopis, separated from Sri Krishna, described the sweetness of His beauty as that which makes one forget all other attractions.[1] The blessed *Gita* is only another form of the Godhead. The Lord Himself has said: 'O Partha, the *Gita* is My heart; the *Gita* is My very quintessence.'[2] It is the sweet

---

1. इतररागविस्मारणं नृणाम्।   *Srimad Bhagavatam*, X. *xxxi*. 14.

2. गीता मे हृदयं पार्थ गीता मे सारमुत्तमम्।

butter that sprang from the churning of the ocean of Sri Krishna's heart.

One may ask, if the *Gita* is really so captivating, why then are all not attracted by it? In reply to this we say that, as it is impossible to feel the sweetness of form, taste, smell, touch and sound without the help of eyes, tongue, nose, skin and ear, in the same way, to enjoy the sweetness of the *Gita* a devout heart and a purified intellect are essential. How can a blind man find joy in the sight of the moon? After one has performed good deeds through many a birth, one attains the purity of heart which brings a spiritual disposition. Only such a devotee can taste the sweetness of the nectar that the *Gita* is. As Sri Ramakrishna says: 'A bird may always utter the holy name of 'Radhakrishna.' But it has not the faculty to taste the sweetness of that name. So, when caught by a cat, it forgets that twin name, which is the only refuge of the entire universe, and displays its natural fear, squawking out *Kriyu, Kriyu,* which is so natural with its species.' Likewise, though many can freely recite the *Gita* from the beginning to the end, yet, as they do it like a bird, they do not reap any benefit therefrom. None the less, the chanting of the holy verses, which came out from the mouth of God, cleanses the heart to some extent.

But Alavandar, as we have already seen, had great powers of intellect. Being concerned with kingly duties for a long time, he had come to be dominated by Rajas, the active and passionate nature. But the Sattvika nature of peace and purity that characterised his father and grandfather had never been effaced from him; it was merely hidden under a Rajasik covering. Now thanks to the help and company of the great-souled Nambi, Alavandar got rid of the covering of Rajas. With his heart illumined by Sattva, he could grasp and comprehend the purport of the *Gita* in the right manner. Gradually the thought of kingly duties and delights faded from his mind. When Nambi sang with tears of love, 'Be absorbed in Me, lodge your mind in Me; thus you shall dwell in Me; do not doubt it here and hereafter,'[1] he exclaimed, 'Alas, alas! all these days I have lived a beastly life, with my mind fixed on lust and lucre. Yet I was proud of my intellect. Fie upon my intelligence! Ah! when will that blessed day come when I shall lift my heart away from the mire and fix it solely on God? O my Guru, when will that blessed day dawn for me? 'And he became very disconsolate. Nambi consoled him with the words: 'O king, your pure mind rests ever on the blessed lotus feet of Narayana. Only, like the clouds covering the sun, desire for worldly objects,, for the time being, hid from sight that blessed image of God as effulgent as a million suns, that imperishable life of all beings. That cloud is about to disperse. The happy sun will shine again and dispel the darkness of your heart.' Alavandar was pacified a little.

From his childhood, Yamunacharya had been brought up with great love and care. He did not know what was meant by suffering. After becoming a king, he had been living in luxury, greatly respected by his subjects. Because of his intellect, he was regarded as Guru by everyone. In this way, he had been ruling over others. He had none to rule over him. Now the attitude of servitude (Dasya-bhava) surged up in his mind. 'The Mother could not wheedle him any more with the sucking toy.'

His heart was illumined with the light of pure intelligence. He mused: 'How could he, who is carried hither and thither by desire, a slave of anger and lust, ever be a lord? What a blunder have I been committing so long, considering myself the master? A slave ought to be dressed like a slave. I shall give up this lordly dress and become a servant of the large-hearted Nambi.' And to Nambi, he said: 'Revered Sir, please make me your servant. After getting rid of slavery to lust and lucre, it would be the greatest glory for me to become a servant of a great man like you who has found in Narayana his sole refuge. Do,

---

1. मय्येव मन आधत्स्व मयि बुद्धिं निवेशय ।
निवसिष्यसि मय्येव अत ऊर्ध्वं न संशयः ॥   *Gita, XII, 8.*

therefore, take pity on me. No longer do I desire to secure the wealth left by my grandfather. Please save me from servility to lust and anger by accepting me as your servant.'

Nambi's heart was filled with joy to see the blazing fire of renunciation in the heart of Alavandar. But he said in a grave voice: 'O king, can a large-hearted great man like you be ever a slave of the senses? You are the eternal servant of Hrishikesa. Your grandfather was among the foremost of the servants of God. You are born in that noble lineage. Today I am seeing in you the manifestation of Mahatma Nathamuni. Blessed indeed am I.' When Nambi stopped, Alavandar spoke in a voice choked with tears, 'My master, please do not praise me. I am really determined to renounce the world and follow you for the rest of my life. In this life's deathly ocean, without a helmsman like you, my poor raft will sink, and the alligators of desire will eat me up. So be kind to me.'

Nambi began to read the eighteenth chapter of the *Gita*. Looking at Alavandar, when, in a celestial tone, he slowly sang the supreme verse,

> 'Lay down all duties
> In Me, your refuge.
> Fear no longer,
> For I will save you
> From sin and from bondage,'[1]

the elixir of that divine promise Revived his innermost being. Hope filled his heart. Gratefully he prostrated himself before Nambi again and again.

After finishing the reading, Nambi said, 'Your Majesty, let us move on towards our destination tomorrow.' Distressed at this, Alavandar said, 'Please do not address me as 'Your Majesty'. I am now a servant and a disciple of yours.' 'My good Sir,' replied Nambi, 'let me first fulfil my

---

1. सर्वधर्मान् परित्यज्य मामेकं शरणं व्रज ।

    अहं त्वा सर्वपापेभ्यो मोक्षयिष्यामि मा शुचः ॥   *Gita*, XVIII, *66*.

promise. Until I hand over to you the treasure of your grandfather, I cannot consider myself free from the debt.' Nambi uttered this in such a serious tone that Alavandar dared not say another word.

The next day they resumed their journey. Four days' walk brought them to the banks of the Kaveri. They performed their ablutions in the holy waters of the river and felt refreshed and blessed. Next day they crossed the Kaveri and set their foot on the holy island formed by the Kaveri in the south and the Coleroon in the north. Here stands the magnificent seven-walled temple of Sri Ranganatha. Nambi walked ahead, followed by Alavandar with folded hands. They proceeded towards the blessed temple of Narayana, in whom rests the universe of which He is the seed and the beginning. One by one they crossed the six gates. Approaching the door of the seventh gate, Nambi looked on Sri Ranganatha and addressed Alavandar: 'O Pure-souled one! There in front of us lies on Sesha, the treasure of your grandfather. He, whose feet are being served by Lakshmi; on whose navel-lotus is seated Brahma the creator; in whom lies coiled up the entire cosmos: who is the very quintessence of supreme beatitude and peace,—He is the treasure of your grand-father. Being his grandson, you are the sole rightful heir to this treasure. Take it and free me of my debt.'

No sooner had Nambi uttered these words than Alavandar ran into the *sanctum sanctorum* like a madman and, stretching his own body before Sri Ranganatha, fell into a swoon. Alavandar accepted with joy the treasure left by his grandfather. Sri Ranganatha became his. Realising Him who is the Lord of the universe, Alavandar had no more desire to go back to his petty kingdom. He received initiation into the spiritual life from Nambi and spent his days in the service of Sri Ranganatha. Alavandar received from Nambi the Mantra of eight syllables which reveals the hidden treasure. Lifting the veil of delusion with the help of that Mantra, he felt the reality of Sri Ranganatha and worshipped Him every day with Tulasi leaves. Alavandar deemed himself blessed in being counted among the daily worshippers of the Supreme Person, upon whom the eternal serpent spreads its hoods as an umbrella, to worship whom comes once in twelve years Vibhishana, the king of the Rakshasas, who had found his only refuge in Sri Ramachandra.

In his later life Alavandar wrote four books in Sanskrit, viz., *Stotraratna, Siddhitraya, Agamapramanya* and *Gitarthasangraha*. In these books, the docrine of Visisht-advaita has been elucidated. He had ideas of writing many more books. But his body gradually became disabled and it was left to Sri Ramanuja to fulfil his desires ere long. Sri Ramanuja was, as it were, the full efflorescence of Alavandar.

PART 2

Life of Sri Ramanuja

1

The Cause of the Descent

I worship Bhagavan Sri Ramanuja, the incarnation of Ananta, who took birth in the month of Chaitra (April-May) under the sixth lunar mansion in the Tundiradesa to establish the philosophy of Vishnu.[1]

Before drinking the nectar of Sri Ramanuja's life, the promulgator of Sri-sampradaya,

I worship the blessed lotus feet of Her, who is endowed with the three forms (of Sri Devi, Nila Devi and Bhu Devi), who dwells in a full-blown lotus, who is the beloved consort of the Lord and the friend of the entire universe.[2]

May we through Her grace be able to complete this work without impediment.

Wherever we turn our eyes in this world, we see the paradoxical combination of Bhava[3] and Abhava,[4] of the real and the unreal. By the play of Abhava on Bhava, the mirage of phenomenal existence, in its boundless variety, is being projected. Innumerable are the physical means invented and lines of thought adopted for securing food, drink and raiment by living beings, who, frightened by their Abhava (want), are anxious to be provided with them. Who knows

---

1. चैत्रार्द्रसंभवं विष्णोर्दर्शनस्थापनोत्सुकम् ।
   तुण्डीरमण्डले शेषमूर्तिं रामानुजं भजे ॥   *Divyasuristotram, 16.*

2. आकारत्रयसंपन्नामरविन्दनिवासिनीम् ।
   अशेषजगदीशित्रीं वन्दे वरदवल्लभाम् ॥ *Sri Yamunacharya's Sri-stuti, 5.*

3 & 4 In philosophical language the words 'Bhava' and 'Abhava' mean 'being' and 'non-being' respectively. In its ordinary sense, the word 'abhava' means want or privation. As in developing his thesis the author has used the words in different shades of meanings in varying contexts, we have preferred to keep the original words in the translation.—*Tr.*

in how many directions in space atoms are thrown about in the confusion caused by the conflict between heat and cold? Abhava is the root of the evergrowing tree of Samsara. We cannot hope to attain eternal peace unless we first get rid of Abhava. Therefore all peace-loving beings, a mixture of matter and spirit as they are, seek first to get rid of the Abhava. The conflict between Bhava and Abhava is unending. This is Samsara. Does the ultimate victory in this battle belong to Bhava or Abhava? Bhagavan Sri Krishna says that we can easily get the answer to this question by pondering over the meaning of the word Abhava. 'The Abhava never is; the Bhava never is not.'[1] My friend, your fear of Samsara is, therefore, a mere delusion. For, what springs from the root of Abhava can never be Bhava. When you realise that all your struggles are against what is not, then you will give them up. That very day, you will earn the right to go to the abode of eternal peace. That very day, realising the fulfilment of yourself, you will know supreme joy. That day alone, you will be the real seer of Truth, for 'only the seers know the distinction between Bhava and Abhava.'[2]

To get rid of Abhava is the nature of all living beings. Everywhere in the world of sentient beings we see the presence of Abhava (want) followed by the attempt to satisfy it. The Jiva who is of the nature of Bhava always looks inimicaly at Abhava and is not ready to harbour it for a moment in his heart. He ever remains in the state of 'fulfilment'. He is indestructible, beginning-less, endless and eternal. This is the supreme truth about Jiva.

We have arrived at these conclusions about the Jiva through reasoning. Now let us see how the Jiva thinks about himself. Every Jiva considers himself to be a body. This is why he thinks that he is born with the body and dies with the body. So the Sruti says:

---

1 & 2. नासतो विद्यते भावो नाभावो विद्यते सत: ।
उभयोरपि दृष्टोऽन्तस्त्वनयोस्तत्त्वदर्शिभि: ॥   *Gita, II. 16.*

To the heedless ignorant person, the path of the hereafter is never revealed. He who thinks that this world alone is and there is no other, falls again and again a prey to death.[1]

In truth there is no creature which does not fear death. None likes to die, for, ordinary men take death to mean the reduction of Bhava into Abhava or termination of life. This is why the Jiva who is of the nature of Bhava and so an enemy of Abhava, regards death with terror and aversion. This is also a proof of the Jiva's everlastingness. Had the Jiva been by nature non-eternal or of the nature of Abhava, he would not cherish such fear and hatred for death.

Sri Ramakrishna has explained the baselessness of this fear by a beautiful simile:

Hari's father brought him a tiger-mask which he was glad to receive. He put on the mask and went to frighten his younger sister Sarala. Sarala was at that time frightfully busy concerning the wedding ceremony of her doll. In the meantime, all on a sudden Hari sprang in front of her with a terrific roar. On hearing this loud cry and seeing the horrible face, the poor girl began to scream, 'Mother, mother', and looked for some means of escape. But unfortunately Hari was blocking the door. Helpless and trembling with fear, she began to scream still louder for her mother. Finding his sister too much frightened, Hari at once removed the mask. When Sarala saw that it was only her brother and not a, tiger, she jumped upon him and, when the excitement subsided a little, she embraced her brother and began to smile. Her fear gone, she resumed her play with a carefree mind.

In like manner, God—who is the Redeemer of Jivas from the troubles the flesh is heir to—also sometimes frightens them by putting on a horrible mask. Then you grow extremely anxious, thinking yourself to be in the grip of bad times. This anxiety is born of ignorance, because you cannot see the smiling face of the loving God within.

---

1. न सांपराय: प्रतिभाति बालं प्रमाद्यन्तं वित्तमोहेन मूढम् ।

अयं लोको नास्ति पर इति मानी पुन: पुनर्वशमापद्यते मे ॥

Kathopanishad, II. 6.

At times you are so much troubled by the miseries of life;
yet why are you reluctant to breathe your last? The reason
is this: God, who also wants His fun once in a while, puts
off the 'tiger-mask', reveals His Compassionate form and, by
thus gladdening your mind and heart, keeps you in fetters
for ever. This is Maya. Therefore, Sri Krishnadvaipayana
Vyasa, the compiler of the Vedas, has said: 'Maya is His
sweet smile that bewitches the mind of all humanity.'[1] Are
there any parents whose hearts are not filled with joy by
the celestial smile on the face of an infant? Which young
man remains undistracted by the smile on the lips of a
maiden? If mere mundane beauty has such power, the heavenly beauty of God is many times more powerful. The sages
of olden times would always perceive His sweetness; they
would always aspire and ultimately succeed in visualising
His entrancing, joyful, ever-affectionate and superbly sweet
Reality behind the wrathful and terrifying appearance. Their
incessant prayers would rise to the feet of the Ruler of the
universe in the following strain:

> O Thou Lord of the universe! As the wind blows
> showering sweetness, as the ocean and the rivers are ema-
> nating sweetness, so may the paddy and barley spread sweet-
> ness over us by growing in abundance; may the nights and
> dawns, even the dust particles of the earth be full of sweet-
> ness; may the high and glorious sky like a father shower
> sweetness over us; may the stately trees bedecked with various
> fruits be sweet unto us; may the sun radiate sweetness; may
> all our cows be all sweetness to us by giving us very sweet
> milk.[2]

By his intrinsic nature man is bliss alone. In expectation of bliss, therefore, he takes refuge in God who is

---

1. हासो जनोन्मादकरी च माया ।   *Srimad Bhagavatam, II. i. 31.*

2. मधु वाता ऋतायते । मधुक्षरन्ति सिन्धवः । माध्वीर्नः सन्त्वोषधीः ।
   मधु नक्तमुतोषसि । मधुमत् पार्थिवं रजः । मधु द्यौरस्तु नः पिता ।
   मधुमान्नो वनस्पतिः । मधुमाँ अस्तु सूर्यः । माध्वीर्गावो भवन्तु नः ॥

   Taittiriyaranyaka, X. 39.

supreme bliss. Can you say whence comes joylessness from one who is naturally full of joy? True, darkness cannot be near light. But, as light appears as darkness to the blind, so too from lack of wisdom the joyful one deems himself to be joyless. Ignorance is the mother of many a mistaken notion of the nature of Reality, but they cannot affect its essential strength. The joyful one remains the joyful one always. The rope continues to be rope; though it may look like a serpent, it never becomes a serpent.

But it is also to be admitted that as long as ignorance fills one's mind, so long one will have to struggle incessantly to realise one's true nature—one will not be able to rest a single moment. This restlessness is called life. A man, in whom this pulse of life is strong, will soon realise that eternity which is also joy. But one with a low vitality is overwhelmed with ignorance and will never find his true self. One has to drive away Tamas by the power of Rajas. And at last one has to forsake both Rajas and Tamas to know one's fulfilment in the light of Sattva and thus get beyond Samsara. This is the only way. 'There is no other way than this.'[1] A man labouring under Tamas is a plaything of sufferings incidental to life. Why does misery have such power over him? Because the perfect one is thinking himself to be imperfect through the influence of ignorance. The king who thinks himself a beggar suffers all the woes of poverty. Likewise, will man, who is Existence-Consciousness-Bliss Absolute, suffer when he thinks himself to be subject to birth, death, old age and disease. When Tamas is overcome by Rajas, Sattva arises, and man is his joyful self again. God, with the tiger-mask on, does not frighten him any more. Then the universe appears all sweetness and bliss to him.

Misery is the constant companion of one steeped in Tamas. When a man is in the grip of afflictions, he tirelessly seeks to get rid of them. He then seeks the person through whose grace he can get rid of them. Like a blind man unable

---

1. नान्यः पन्था विद्यतेऽयनाय ।   *Rig-veda*, X.xc. 17.

to find his way unaided, he seeks refuge at the feet of some noble soul. Hunger drives a man in search of food, thirst in search of water, poverty in search of wealth; in like manner, the three kinds of sufferings which are incidental to life make him seek happiness and beatitude in God. One also finds that along with Abhava, entities denoted as Bhava and destructive of Abhava are also scattered all over the world. For example, everywhere and always there is food as well as hunger, water as well as thirst, wealth as well as poverty, happiness as well as misery. This is the law of nature. When the air of a region, made light through heat, goes up creating a vacuum, at once air rushes in there from all sides to fulfil that Abhava (want of air). That is how great hurricanes take place. All have experienced the fact that wherever there is Abhava, the remedy for it also comes in the wake. As in the world of matter, so too in the realm of spirit, the remedy comes only when there is Abhava. It can be understood clearly by a closer consideration of the world of spirit.

In ancient India, the path of Karma and the path of Jnana were both held in honour. Only those fully qualified were entitled to enter either of the paths. Righteousness or performance of one's duties qualified one for the path of Karma; and the perfect control of all the senses attained through complete desirelessness enabled one to tread the path of Jnana. Everyone acknowledged this and accordingly acquired the fitness to enter the path either of Karma or Jnana. Everybody knows that the observance of duties is easier than the abandonment of desires. Is desirelessness ever attainable by man who is born with desire? Desire alone is Samsara. Desire may make his mind unsteady, but what of that? Unsteadiness is the very nature of the mind. Work which springs out of one's very nature does not cause suffering; it is unnatural work that causes pain. So desire is rather productive of joy than affliction. Such are the ideas of the ordinary man.

Heavenly enjoyments are the *summum bonum* of desires. The Smriti says:

That which is free from the touch of the minutest tinge of suffering, which will not become a prey to afflictions again in future, which is the highest fulfilment of desire—that happiness alone is called heaven.[1]

If one desires heaven, one has to perform sacrifices.[2] This is the main purpose of the Karmakanda of the Vedas. Pleasure-loving man does not want anything higher than that.

But, pleasing though this happiness is, it is not so always; for it is contact-born. The object of happiness, being something external, is not always within the complete mastery of any one. Again, there is no limit to man's thirst for happiness; but earthly happiness is limited by a beginning and an end. Can the craving of man be assuaged by such happiness? Uninterrupted happiness alone can satisfy that craving. It will not do for his object of happiness to remain without; it must be realised within. That is to say, none but he who finds bliss within himself can become the master of eternal bliss. Bhagavan Sri Krishna has beautifully explained this in the *Gita*. To be able to attain to the state wherein one finds delight in one's own self, one has to discard all desires which are of things external. Unless one gives up all contacts with the external, one cannot realize perpetual bliss, without which Abhava (want) cannot be got rid of either. Where there is Abhava there will be affliction.

Therefore, the only way to attain supreme bliss is to renounce desire. The ordinary man is unable to understand this. He cannot just comprehend how happiness is possible in the absence of objects of enjoyment. This is why the majority of people have liking for the ritualistic portion of the Vedas (Karma-kanda). Karma enslaves one. Therefore, though the sacrificial rites prescribed by the Vedas are not now so much in vogue as of yore, one does not find any the

1. यन्न दुःखेन संभिन्नं न च ग्रस्तमनन्तरम् ।

अभिलाषोपनीतश्च तत्सुखं स्वःपदास्पदम् ॥

2. स्वर्गकामो यजेत ।   *Taittiriya-samhita*, II. v. 5.

least diminution of Karma in human society. The doctrine of Karma has been flowing uninterruptedly from time immemorial and will flow on. The type of Karma, however, may change.

In ancient times they would kindle a sacred fire on a level piece of ground covered with sand for a sacrifice and would pour clarified butter into it as an offering to the gods and the fathers and thus worship them. Afterwards they built temples of various designs and, installing images of various gods and goddesses within them, conducted worship with fragrant flowers, incense, light and food offerings. As society changes, the mode and trend of Karma vary. The modes of Karma that were prevalent in the Vedic times are rarely found today. The present mode befits the present age. Though the aim of Karma is ever the same, the methods vary with the change of times.

But in the philosophical portion of the Vedas (Jnana-kanda) there has been no change whatsoever, for Jnana is essentially the same for ever. Self-evident laws like those of Euclid will always remain the same. The 108 Upanishads are the same today as they were in ancient times and will remain so in times to come. They all say unanimously, that through renunciation alone the great ones crossed the ocean of birth and death and attained immortality.[1] Renunciation alone can destroy man's delusion and enable him to realize supreme bliss.

From what has been said it can be clearly understood why pilgrims on the path of Jnana are very rare in this world. If a person with overwhelming desire for Karma enters the path of Jnana, he causes great harm to himself and to society.

The basis of Karma is righteousness or observance of one's duties. He who is averse to observing his duties has no right to enter the path of Karma. That a man is able to perform his duties is because he has to some extent

---

1. त्यागेनैके अमृतत्वमानशुः ।   *Kaivalyopanishad*, 2.

gained mastery over his senses. The man led by his senses is always wilful. Sometimes in the past the sacrificial priests and performers of Yajnas fell victims to sense-indulgence. The responsibility of carrying on the Yajnas being in their hands, they invented, in order to surfeit their stomachs and to indulge their senses, various violent sacrifaces marked by use of wine and flesh and propagated them as sanctioned by the Vedas.

We have seen above that wherever there is Abhava (want), there is also provision for its fulfilment. According to this natural law, there arose at the foot of the Himalayas the Sarvarthasiddha Buddha (literally, the Enlightened One who has achieved the fulfilment of all ends), the personification of compassion and magnanimity. Growing disgusted with life marred by death, decrepitude, disease and afflictions, he became a mendicant in his youth. And at long last discovering the path to the abode of unalloyed peace, he led all afflicted mankind—even the lowliest—along that path and made them all rightful aspirants for immortality. All created beings, from Brahma the highest, down to an insignificant insect, equally found room in his expansive heart. Only these two seemed despicable in his eyes: The horrible image of the fabricated Sruti and the diabolic creator of the universe as innovated by the sacrificial priests. Therefore, after banishing both the 'Sruti' and 'God' of his times, he enjoined the performance of good deeds. Good and bad deeds will bear good and bad fruits. O man, therefore, do good deeds and you will live happily. Ignorant people call Buddha an atheist, for he did not recognise a Godhead. It is a thousand times better to be an atheist than to be a theist by acknowledging the sort of 'God' whom he refused to acknowledge.

Was Buddha really an atheist? Deeds are nowhere found without doers. He acknowledged good deeds and thereby recognized the doer of good as well. God alone, who is endowed with all auspicious qualities, is the

Doer of Good. Then, how can we say that Buddha was an atheist?

His all-embracing and magnanimous heart wanted the supreme good of all creatures without any distinction. He could not pick and choose those who were fit to receive his doctrine. The righteous and the unrighteous, the young and the old, men and women, the rich and the poor, scholars and idiots, all were made by him pilgrims on the path of Nirvana. But as dyspeptics cannot digest Pilau, those who were unfit failed to assimilate his invaluable precepts. Thus his sacred and theistic teaching deteriorated into atheism and nihilism. 'When truth, untruth, religion, irreligion,— everything was a mere fib and there was no author for the universe, who then was to be feared?' Labouring under such ideas, the followers of the Blessed One grew wilful and intractable. There was again Abhava (want) of happiness and peace in the world. The earth was tormented by the weight of the demoniac Buddhists. Therefore, in order to relieve the world, the all-good God incarnated Himself as the teacher of mankind, assuming the name Sri Sankara.

Bhagavan Sri Sankaracharya was then a mere lad of sixteen. But, as darkness cannot stay in the face of the rising sun, atheism or perversity could not stay before his bright face lit up with divine genius. Like the stars that fade at dawn, the wayward Buddhists disappeared from the Indian scene. The light of wisdom spread in all the four directions. The kingdom of peace was again established in Bharatavarsha. Sankara, the master of the Sruti, again unfolded the Vedic truth carefully to those who were fit. The banner of Sanatana-dharma was unfurled everywhere from the Himalayas to Cape Comorin. The gods and the manes were again delighted with the Mantras 'svaha 'and 'svadha'. The Rishis—the very embodiments of wisdom—who were slumbering for long, were again roused up by the sacred chanting of the Upanishads. And the joy of Mother India knew no bounds.

After accomplishing his work, the Siva-like Sankara passed away, in his thirty-second year, to his own supreme abode.

With the passage of time, however, many of the so-called followers of Sankara's creed, who had donned the dress of the Sannyasin but were servile to the senses, brought a great calamity on themselves and on society by perverting the Acharya's exposition of the purport of the four Mahavakyas containing the very essence of the four Vedas. The dictum 'I am Brahman'[1] was understood by them to mean that the physical man—who is three and half cubits in height, made up of seven kinds of secretions, and subject to birth, death, old age and disease—is Brahman who is imperishable, beginningless, endless, all-pervading, omniscient, all-containing and the abode of supreme bliss. As water does not moisten a lotus leaf, virtue or vice, proper or improper conduct, truth or untruth—nothing can touch Brahman. So, they thought that, whatever they did, they could not receive any stain. Could there be a doctrine more devilish than this? Those who, unable to comprehend the supremely pure religion expounded by Sankara, laboured under such false notions, established once again the reign of evil ways, avarice, malice and untruth in India. Happiness, peace and truthfulness disappeared. The noble one who incarnated himself to bring about a change was Sri Ramanuja-charya, the propagator of the doctrine of Visishtadvaita. Nothing of the nature of Abhava can stay in the domain of Bhava. Bliss, peace, truth, generosity, righteousness characterize Bhava; and affliction, want of peace, narrowness, malice, unrighteousness, untruth, avarice—these are characteristic of Abhava. It has been proved that whenever Abhava appears, its remedy also follows. In accordance with this law, the advent of Sri Ramanujacharya took place at the right time in the land of Bharata. ❈

---

1. अहं ब्रह्मास्मि ।   *Brihadaranyaka-Upanishad*, I. iv. 10.

2

The Birth of Sri Ramanuja

There is a prosperous village called Sriperumbudur, thirty miles southwest of Madras. In the village there is a beautiful and spacious temple consecrated to Lord Vishnu. Within the *sanctum sanctorum there* stands only the Lord Sri Adikesava Perumal, with a smiling face casting gracious looks equally on all. On the other side of the temple court-yard stands another shrine, within which is seated with folded hands, in the place of the chief servant, the prince among ascetics (Yatiraja), Sri Ramanujacharya, the Commentator. A hero among devotees and a lover of them too, he is to Vedanta what the sun is to the lotus. In the front a spacious tank of limpid water, rippleless like the pure heart of a devotee, reflects within it the entire temple. Besides, the natural beauty of the place is attractive. Shaded by various kinds of trees and creepers, sonorous with the sweet twittering of birds, lit up and fragrant with blossoming flowers, and inhabited by happy, good, healthy people, the place abounds in peace, sweetness and beauty. The sight of it strikes one as if, the Consort of Lakshmi, incessantly engaged in the task of preserving the universe, sometimes gets tired and goes over here to rest with His most beloved servant.

More than a thousand years ago a pious Brahmana, Asuri Kesavacharya by name, lived in this village. Sri Yamunacharya (Alavandar), after renouncing his throne and accepting the discipleship of Nambi, was at that time living at Srirangam as a mendicant. After the passing away of his Guru, Alavandar was accepted as the leader of the entire Vaishnava community of the time. His uncommon renunciation, dispassion, erudition, humility and steadfastness towards his Chosen Ideal were admired by all the

70

Vaishnavas. All pious men considered themselves blessed in eagerly learning and memorising the sweet hymns composed by him. Truly speaking, in his hymns Mahatma Yamunacharya has dedicated himself to the lotus feet of God in such a candid manner and with such tremendous devotion and love that, on reading them, devotion springs up in the heart of even a heretic. Devoted Vaishnavas coming from all quarters deemed themselves extremely fortunate in being his disciples. Among them were one or two who, like him, adopted the life of Sannyasa. By living in his company and being engaged in his service, they gained a sense of perfect fulfilment in their lives.

Periyatirumalai Nambi (also called Sri Sailapurna), of advanced age, was Yamunacharya's chief disciple. Towards the end of his life he renounced the life of a householder and receiving Sannyasa from his Guru, continued to live with him. He had two sisters. The name of the elder one was Bhumi Piratti, Bhudevi or Kantimati; the name of the other was Periya Piratti or Mahadevi (called Sridevi or Dyutimati).

Asuri Kesavacharya of Sriperumbudur married Kantimati. And the younger Mahadevi was wedded to Kamala-nayana Bhatta of the nearby village Aharam. The marriage of the two sisters being over, Sri Sailapurna devoted himself entirely to the meditation on God with a free mind, and at last finding a great Guru like the Mahatma Yamunacharya, came to enjoy supreme bliss by living in his company.

Asuri Kesavacharya was very much attached to the performance of Yajnas and so the Pundits gave him the title 'Sarvakratu', which literally means the performer of all Yajnas. So his full name was Srimad Asuri Sarvakratu Kesava Dikshita. After their marriage, the couple were living happily for many years at Sriperumbudur. But as no child was born to them, Kesavacharya began to feel concerned. At last the hope of getting a son by the grace of God by pleasing Him with the performance of Yajnas arose in his mind. For there is the scriptural statement:

'The performance of the Yajna is the highest duty; it is pleasing to God. It grants all desires. So Yajna is the greatest refuge.'[1]

He decided to go to Sri Parthasarathi, the dweller of Vrindaranya on the shores of the sea, with a view to supplicate the Lord and perform sacrifices to that end. Accordingly, he, accompanied by his wife, appeared in Vrindaranya on the banks of Tiruallikeni[2] or the lily-lake of Parthasarathi in modern Madras. There they performed Yajnas with the desire that a son might be born to them. The name of that locality of Madras is Triplicane, which is the English corruption of Tiruallikeni. What was reputed as Vrindaranya previously has now come to be known as Triplicane after the name of that lake.

The performance of Yajnas over, Kesavacharya had a vision of Parthasarathi in a dream. In his dream-state he heard the Lord address him and say, 'O Sarvakratu, I am much pleased with your good conduct and steadfast devotion. Be not anxious. I Myself shall be born as your son. Instigated by evil motives and unable to know the purport of the teachings of preceptors, men are considering themselves to be the Godhead and out of pride they are becoming wicked, wilful and perverse. So, unless I incarnate Myself as an Acharya, they are doomed. Go back home along with your wife. Your desire will be fulfilled.' Having dreamt such an auspicious dream, Kesavacharya's joy knew no bounds. He told his wife everything, and on the morrow they moved towards their own village.

About a year later, fortunate Kantimati gave birth to a son endowed with all auspicious marks who came to be known as Sri Ramanuja. He was born in 939 of the Saka era (4118 of the Kali era and 1017 of the Christian era) on Thursday, the 12th Chaitra, in the fifth day of the bright

1. यज्ञ एव परो धर्मो भगवत्प्रीतिकारकः ।
अभीष्टकर्मधुग् यज्ञस्तस्मात् यज्ञः परा गतिः ॥

2. Literally: Tiru=Sri, Alii=Water-lily, Keni=Lake.

fortnight, when the sun was in the zodiac of Cancer in the year Pingala. His natal star was Ardra, the sixth lunar mansion. He belonged to Harita lineage and Yajur Veda. Being so born, he appeared before all like the newly arisen sun dispelling the darkness of ignorance. As his birth caused destruction of evil-mindedness and brought about an efflorescence of right understanding in men, scholars ascertain his year of birth with the help of the word 'dhirlabdha' (which literally means 'knowledge has been attained'). In accordance with the rule *ankasya vama gatih*, that is to say, figures have to be valued from right to left, the word 'dhirlabdha'[1] presents three main letters, viz.

ध् *(dh)*, ल् *(l)* and ध् *(dh)*. The nine letters beginning with क् *(k)*, ट् *(t)* and य् *(y)* are indicative of the figures from 1 to 9. ध् *(dh)* being the ninth letter from ट् *(t)* indicates the figure 9. ल् *(l)* being the third letter from य् *(y)* indicates the figure 3, Hence by these three letters ध् *(dh)*, ल् *(l)* and ध् *(dh)* the Saka era 939 is understood.

About the same time, the younger sister Mahadevi too became the mother of a son. A few days after the confinement, she came to Sriperumbudur with her newborn babe to see the son of her elder sister Kantimati. Each was extremely glad to see the face of the other's child. In the meantime, the old Sri Sailapurna who came to know the news, also reached the place from Sriranga-kshetra with the intention of seeing the two newly born nephews. Both Kantimati and Mahadevi were immensely delighted to receive their brother after such a long time. The old Sannyasin too was very glad to see the two little infants endowed with all the auspicious signs. When he saw Kantimati's son marked with the various divine traits, he was reminded of what Nammalvar had foretold as the future messiah of

___

1. This expression is a chronogram decoded in the manner shown.—*Tr.*

Sri-vaishnavism in his *Tiruvoymozhi*.[1] He had no longer any doubt whatsoever that this babe was that incarnation of Lakshmana, the Anantadeva of Kali Yuga, about whose advent references are to be found in the thirty-second chapter of the *Brihat Padmapurana*, *Naradapurana*, twenty-third chapter of the *Skandapurana*[2] It is also stated in the fifth chapter of the eleventh Skandha of *Srimad Bhagavatam* that great devotees of Narayana will be born in the Dravida country in the regions through which rivers like Palar, Cauvery, Tamraparni, Periyar etc., flow. Accordingly, he named the child Sri Ramanuja. And Mahadevi's son was named Govinda. Afterwards Mahadevi became the mother of a second son who came to be known as Junior Govinda.

The great sage Valmiki, the ancient poet, writes:

> In the month of Chaitra under the ninth lunar mansion, when the sun had gone to the sign Cancer of the zodiac, Lakshmana and Satrughna were born.[1]

The month of birth and zodiac of Sri Ramanujacharya too are the same as those of the sons of Sumitra.

When the two babes were four months old, the mothers came out of confinement and taking the babes in their laps,

---

1. It is said that Nammalvar was once brooding with some melancholy on the failure of his own mission on earth to reclaim mortals from ignorance and sin, and God suddenly vouchsafed to him the vision of a distant glorious future when with the advent of a great Acharya the whole land would be ringing with the joy of a mighty spiritual awakening. This vision is described in a decad in Tiruvoymozhi, from which the following significant quotations have been selected: 'Behold even Kali (the dark age) shall perish' (5.2. 1). 'Kali Yuga disappears, and the Devas enter the kingdom of earth. The great Krita Yuga (the golden age) begins and the flood of Divine Bliss is flowing. The hosts of devotees serving the sea-hued and cloud-coloured Lord enter running and singing and occupy all places.' (5. 2. 3.)—Ed.

2. We have tried our best to verify these traditional references. But unfortunately we have been unable to trace them in the published editions of those Puranas. Probably those were found in some versions available only in manuscript.—Tr.

3. सार्पे जातौ तु सौमित्री कुलीरेऽभ्युदिते रवौ ।

Valmiki Ramayana, I. xviii. K.

made them see the sun. Afterwards, the ceremonies of rice-taking, the boring of the ear-lobes, the ceremony of the first tonsure, initiation in studies, investiture with the sacred thread etc., were also performed in due time. From his very childhood, Ramanuja gave proofs of the prodigious powers of his intellect. By hearing a lesson only once from the mouth of his teacher, he could grasp its meaning, however stiff it might be. For this reason he was the beloved of all teachers.

It was not that the power of his intellect was only directed outwards like the needle of a compass, showing him the north and the south representing Dharma and Artha, the first and the second of the four ends of life. The cultivation of righteousness and the association with holy men were also very dear to his heart. He missed no opportunity of associating with holy men.

At that time, a great devotee, by name Sri Kanchipurna, was widely known to be the best of devotees living in the city of Kanchi. He used to go every day from Kanchi to Poonamalle, a neighbouring village to worship the deity there. Sriperumbudur is midway between these two places. So he would, every day, pass by Ramanuja's house. Though a Sudra by caste, even Brahmanas used to revere him and pay him homage in view of his deep devotion to God. One evening, Ramanuja, on his way back home from his preceptor's house, accidentally met this holy man and, seeing the divine lustre of his face, quite naturally felt drawn to him. With great modesty, he requested him to take his meal at his house that night. At the sight of the celestial beauty and divine marks in the boy, he could not refuse the invitation. Finding this very holy man as his guest, Ramanuja could not contain his joy. After the guest had had his meal, Ramanuja went forward to stroke his guest's feet with his hands as a gesture of devoted service. But the guest would not permit it. He said, 'I am a low-born Sudra. Good God! How could you serve your servant? 'Saddened by this, Ramanuja said, 'I would consider it my bad luck if

I could not serve a noble soul like you. Pray, noble Sir, is it the wearing of the sacred thread that makes one a Brahmana? He who is devoted to God, he alone is a genuine Brahmana. You know very well how Tiruppanalvar, low-born though he was, came to be worthy of the worship of the Brahmanas.'

Struck by the devotion of the boy, Sri Kanchipurna could not consider him to be a mere human being. After long spiritual conversations, he enjoyed rest for the night in Ramanuja's place and proceeded towards his destination in the morning. Since that day, both of them were bound together by the love which each bore for the other.

It has been hinted above that the previous Acharyas cited the authority of the Puranas for regarding Ramanuja as the incarnation of Lakshmana. Even when we compare the character of the son of Kesava (Ramanuja) with that of the son of Sumitra (Lakshmana), we find many similarities. Lakshmana is indeed peerless in dutifulness, steadfastness to truth, devotion to Rama, mastery over the senses and righteousness. Sri Ramachandra was the only sovereign of the kingdom of his heart. He knew no other bliss than that of Rama. It is no wonder, therefore, that he stayed far away from the enticements of the world. We realise this when we bathe in the Ganga of the Ramayana which springs up from Valmiki the mountain and flows into Rama the ocean.[1]

When the golden deer, after deluding the daughter of Janaka, had also deluded Sri Ramachandra, Lakshmana cautioned the Chosen Ideal of his heart in the following manner:

> O Tiger among men, methinks the deer is none but the demon Maricha. When the kings go a-hunting merrily, this wicked one entices them by assuming many an illusive form

---

1. वाल्मीकिगिरिसम्भूता रामसागरगामिनी ।

From Valmiki Ramayana, Dhyana-sloka (of Smarta Sampradaya).

and thus brings about their ruin. This dazzling form of the illusive deer, like the imaginary city of the sky, is nothing but the ruse of that conjurer. O Ramachandra, there is no doubt that it is a phantom; for, where on earth is to be found a strange deer of golden lustre like this?[1]

The be-all and end-all of Lakshmana's life was only the service of Rama and Sita. After the killing of Ravana, his departed father Dasaratha, appearing along with the gods, blessed and admired him saying:

My boy, by serving Rama and Sita, the Daughter of Videha, unreservedly, you have earned both virtue and great fame.[2]

The *summum bonum* of Sri Ramanuja's life was the service of the Lord Narayana. When, out of conceit, the base-natured leaders of society had robbed the human hearts of devotion to God, even as Sita was kidnapped by Ravana, then Sri Ramanuja, like the true younger brother of Sri Rama, fought to the end with the heretics for the recovery of the Sita of devotion and was ultimately successful in his mission. By installing Sri on the flank of Narayana, he brought back the goddess of fortune into the unfortunate land of India. In establishing the eternal relation of Narayana with Sri, he has only proved the word of Maharshi Valmiki. The ancient poet sings through the mouth of a panegyrist:

1. तमेवैनं अहं मन्ये मारीचं राक्षसं मृगम् ॥
   चरन्तो मृगयां हृष्टाः पापेनोपाधिना वने ।
   अनेन निहता राम राजानः कामरूपिणा ॥
   अस्य मायाविदो मायामृगरूपमिदं कृतम् ।
   भानुमत् पुरुषव्याघ्र गन्धर्वपुरसन्निभम् ॥
   मृगो ह्येवंविधो रत्नविचित्रो नास्ति राघव ।
   जगत्यां जगतीनाथ मायैषा हि न संशयः ॥

   Valmiki Ramayana, III. xliii. 4,5,6,7.

2. अवाप्तं धर्माचरणं यशश्च विपुलं त्वया ।
   एवं शुश्रूषता रामं वैदेह्या सह सीतया ॥   *ibid.* VI. cii. 32.

O King of the Solar Dynasty, prosperity and righteousness ever abide in you.[1]

As Lakshmana was righteousness incarnate, so too was Sri Ramanuja. Like the son of Sumitra, the founder of Sri sampradaya also dwelt beyond the reach of fear and temptation.

---

1.   श्रीश्च धर्मश्च काकुत्स्थ त्वयि नित्यं प्रतिष्ठितौ ।

          Valmiki Ramayana, VII. xxxvii. 8.

3

Yadavaprakasa

As Sri Ramanuja stepped into his sixteenth year, his father Srimad Asuri Kesavacharya wanted to get him married. And he was soon wedded to an exquisitely beautiful girl to the great delight of his parents, relatives and neigh-bours. The poor were happy over the sumptuous feasts. The festivities continued for a week. Kantimati and her husband were very happy to see the countenance of the new bride. After a month of such worldly bliss, afflictions appeared in the wake of joy. Struck down by a severe illness, Kesava-charya reached the end of his life on earth. Like a full-moon night overcast by clouds, the Acharya's family passed from high delight to profound sorrow. Like the she-heron[1] that was the cause of the burning pain for the ancient Poet Valmiki, Kantimati suffered agony. At the loss of his father, Ramanuja was also plunged in grief for a while, but by the strength of his wisdom he soon rallied himself. He regained calm and began to console his mother.

The funeral obsequies and the Sraddha ceremony were performed in due time, after which they lived at Sriperumbudur for a short time only. As both his mother and he himself missed peace there, they decided to shift their residence to Kanchipuram. Accordingly, after constructing a house, Ramanuja together with his family came to reside there.

At that time in the holy city of Kanchi there lived a renowned professor, Yadavaprakasa by name, holding the doctrine of non-dualism. His scholarship captivated all and he had many disciples. Driven by his intense yearning for knowledge, Ramanuja too became his disciple. Yadava-

---

1. See Appendix A.

prakasa was pleased with the graceful appearance of his new disciple and the lustre of genius in his countenance. In a very short time, Ramanuja grew to be counted his chief disciple and a great favourite.

But this affection did not last long. Yadavaprakasa was a rare genius. The doctrine of non-dualism as enunciated by him is even today renowned as 'Yadaviya Siddhanta'. He was a rigid Advaitin of the type that would not acknowledge God with form. The universe is the changeful, ever-perishable cosmic form of God. But that imperishable Reality which is Existence-Consciousness-Bliss Absolute, beyond time, space and causation, which is at the back of cosmic form, is His supreme reality—that is what is to be accepted and known. Unlike the great Sankaracharya, he would not regard Virat as Maya or unreal appearance caused by nescience or snake-transformation (Vivarta) of a rope, or the cognisance in one thing of something else. In his eyes the universe was not as unsubstantial as a mirage and totally insignificant. It is one kind of God's own form which is ever changeful. It is unacceptable because it is perpetually unstable and the Supreme Form being eternally steady is acceptable. The Virat-seeing Atman is Jiva and the self-luminous (Svarat) Atman is Brahman.

Sri Ramanuja was all devotion, a personification of the attitude of service to God. So the doctrines of Yadava could not be pleasing to him. Out of respect for his Guru, he would never make bold to show the defects in his teachings. He often wished to do so, but would as often check himself.

One day, when the other disciples had gone home for their midday meal after finishing their morning lessons, Yadavaprakasa asked his dearest disciple Ramanuja to massage his body with oil. Even then another disciple who had stayed back was putting questions to the teacher for the clarification of some abstruse passage in the morning lesson. While studying the *Chandogya Upanishad*, he had failed to grasp properly the meaning of the word *'kapyasam'* which occurs in the earlier portion of the seventh Mantra of the sixth part of the first chapter. The portion of the verse reads as follows: *tasya yathā. kapyāsam pundarīkame-vamakshinī.* Taking the word 'kapyasam' to mean the 'nates of a monkey' as interpreted by the venerable Sankaracharya, Yadavaprakasa explained the passage as follows: 'The two eyes of that Golden Purusha are like two lotuses which are red like the nates of a monkey.' On hearing this interpretation with the unbecoming and low simile, Ramanuja's soft heart, tender by nature and softened by devotion, melted, and, as he was massaging, tears rolled down from the corners of his eyes like flames of fire and fell on the thigh of Yadava. Looking up at the touch of hot tears, Yadava understood that something troubled his dear disciple Ramanuja. When he asked in surprise as to what might be the cause of his affliction, Ramanuja replied, 'Revered Sir, I have been sorely grieved to hear such an unbecoming explanation from a noble soul like you. How sinful it is to compare with the posterior of a monkey the eyes of the Supreme Godhead—who is endowed with all gracious qualities, who is the repository of all the beauty of the universe! From the mouth of a wise person like you I never expected this! 'My boy, I am also very much grieved at your audacity,' said Yadava. 'Well, can you interpret the passage in any better manner? 'By your blessings everything is possible,' said Ramanuja. With a smile of derision the teacher said, 'Fine, very good, then speak out your novel exposition. I see, you like to climb higher than even Sankaracharya.' 'Revered Sir, by your blessings everything may be possible,' replied Ramanuja with great humility. 'Instead of deriving the meaning 'the nates of a monkey' from the word '*kapyāsam*', we can construe it as follows: *kam jalam pibatīti—kapih*, *sūryah*: he who drinks water, i.e. the sun; and the verbal root *as* being indicative of 'blossoming', the word *āsa* may well mean 'blossomed'. In this way the entire word '*kapyāsam*' comes to mean 'blossomed by the sun.' So, that part of the Mantra will mean, 'The eyes of that Purusha within the golden solar orb are as lovely as the lotuses blossomed by the rays of the sun.'

Hearing this exposition Yadava said, 'It is not the direct meaning, but only a derived one. However, you have here shown much skill in exegesis.'

Since this incident, the preceptor took Ramanuja to be a staunch devotee of dualism and hence his affection for him waned a little.

Another day when expounding the Mantra *satyam jnanam anantam brahma*, which occurs in the *Taittiriyo-panishad* (II.l), Yadavaprakasa said that Brahman is Truth, Intelligence and Infinitude. Ramanuja objected to that and explained the verse as follows: 'Brahman is endowed with the quality of truth, is not endowed with untruth; intelligence is His attribute, not nescience; He is infinite, i.e., is not finite. He is endowed with the qualities of truth, intelligence and infinitude. It is by no means reasonable to hold that all these qualities are He Himself. These are His, but not He, as the body is mine, I am not the body.' On hearing this exposition, the preceptor flared up in extreme wrath, 'You presumptuous lad! if you don't want to accept my exposition, why then come here in vain? Why not go home and open a school of your own? 'After collecting himself a little, he continued, 'Your exposition is not in accordance with the views of Acharya Sankara or with those of any other previous master. So don't trot out your impertinence again.' Ramanuja was naturally very humble and also devoted to the teacher. During the hours of study he would always try to be mute as far as possible. To contradict was not his intention at all. But what could he do, when he found truth being misrepresented? He had to contradict his preceptor, for truth was his very life. Though in the presence of other disciples Yadava used to make light of his refutations, gradually there began to grow in him a sort of fear of Ramanuja. He thought, 'This boy may in time establish the doctrine of dualism. Now, how to get rid of him? He should even be killed for the preservation of the age-old doctrine

of non-dualism.' It was not due to his excessive affection for
the doctrine of non-dualism but out of intense jealousy that
he came to that brutal resolution. The poet has said:

> Not to bear the prosperity of others is the nature of the
> (so-called) great.[1] The lion echoes only the thunder of the
> clouds and not the howls of the jackals.[2]

Needless to say that this cannot be the trait of a truly
great one. To such a person 'censure and praise are equal;
he is silent and content with anything'.[3] He has neither
friend nor foe. He wishes the good of all. He is ever
contented. He is full all around. The poet has spoken here
about the worldly great whom we popularly call 'big men',
who being driven by Tamas think about themselves, 'Who
else is there like me?'.[4] Yadavaprakasa was a big man of
that category. No wonder, therefore, that out of malice he
longed to see Ramanuja done away with! Though with the
help of his great intellect, he had mastered all the intricate
argumentations of the Vedanta and could clearly prove before
all that 'Brahman alone is real and the universe illusory',
though the whole of Kanchipuram was aglow with the lustre
of his name and he used to be worshipped as a second
Sankara by his disciples, yet for want of spiritual practices,
his knowledge was mere verbosity and so he could not save
himself from slavery to desires.

One day, Yadava called his other disciples in secret
and said: 'Look here, my children, you don't find any fault
in my exegesis. But this impudent Ramanuja every now and
then contradicts my expositions. What does it matter if he
is intelligent? His mind is full of the heresy of dualism. How
to get rid of this heretic?'

---

1. प्रकृतिः खलु सा महीयसः सहते नान्यसमुन्नतिं यथा ।

    Bharavi's *Kiratarjuniya,* II. 21, second half.

2. अनुहुंकुरुते घनध्वनिं न तु गोमायुरुतानि केसरी ।

    Magha's *Sisupalavadha,* XVI. 25, second half.

3. तुल्यनिन्दास्तुतिर्मौनी सन्तुष्टो येन केनचित् ।   *Bhagavad-gita,* XII. 19.

4. कोऽन्योऽस्ति सदृशो मया ॥   *ibid.* XVI. 15.

R 7

'Revered Sir, it is enough if he is not allowed to come to the school,' one of the disciples proposed.

'Then, what our teacher is afraid of, that will come to pass,' opposed another disciple. 'That is to say, Ramanuja himself will open a school and propagate the doctrine of dualism there. Have you not heard that he has already refuted the doctrine of non-dualism by writing an elaborate commentary on the Mantra *satyam jnanam anantam brahma.*'

It was a fact that meanwhile Ramanuja had grown to be an object of great affection in the circle of the elite by writing a lucid commentary on the above Mantra. After exchanging words in the above manner for some time, it was decided that there was no other alternative to putting an end to Ramanuja's life. They began to conspire as to how it could be effected with ease and without anybody's knowledge. In the end, Yadava said, 'Let us all start on a pilgrimage to wash off our sins in the Ganga, the destroyer of sins. Intimate this our intention to Ramanuja and take good care to persuade him to accompany us; for the purpose of this pilgrimage is to get rid of this heretic. After doing away with him on the way, we can wash off the sin of murdering a Brahmana by bathing in the waters of Bhagirathi. And thus this thorn in the side of non-dualistic doctrine could be removed.'

Thus instructed by their preceptor, the disciples set out to induce Ramanuja to go with them for the holy bath in the Bhagirathi (Ganga).

It has already been mentioned that Ramanuja had a cousin by name Govinda. He used to love Ramanuja better than himself. When the Acharya's family left Sri-perumbudur and came to live in Kanchipuram, Govinda also came over there and was living with them. Both Ramanuja and he were of the same age. So when Ramanuja became the disciple of Yadavaprakasa, Govinda also followed suit. They would very often go to, and return from, the school together. Ramanuja agreed to go on the pilgrimage.

It is superfluous to say that Govinda also consented very eagerly to go with them.

At an auspicious moment, the band of disciples headed by Yadava started on the pilgrimage. Kantimati could not object to this meritorious act of her son, though separation from him was well-nigh unbearable. After a few days' steady travel, Yadava came with his disciples to the Gondaranya at the foot of the Vindhya ranges. It was a totally unfrequented place. Thinking this time and place to be the most convenient, this villain of a preceptor asked his disciples to get ready for the savage task. Somehow Govinda came to know of this. Simple-natured Ramanuja, however, had no inkling of this devilish conspiracy. How could his pure, affectionate and tender heart ever entertain the possibility of such a horrible idea? A holy man thinks every one else to be so.

One day when Ramanuja and Govinda happened to go alone by themselves to some wayside tank for washing their feet, Govinda communicated to him all that he knew of the evil designs of their preceptor. He made it clear to his cousin that on the pretext of going on a pilgrimage, this band of rogues had resolved to murder him and said, 'These villains will very soon kill you in this desolate forest. Therefore, leave them and hide yourself somewhere.' So saying, he took leave of him and joined the other disciples. When on enquiry Yadavaprakasa discovered that Ramanuja was not to be found in the group of disciples, all busied themselves in searching him out. But none found a trace of him in that deep and lonely forest. They began to call aloud his name in all directions; but there was no response. At last, taking it for granted that Ramanuja must have been killed by some wild animal, they were well pleased. But knowing Govinda to be his relation, they began to show outwardly marks of great mourning. Yadavaprakasa delivered sermons on the evanescence of life and consoled Govinda with the words, 'None is none's'. Thus malice made Yadavaprakasa the preceptor into something worse than a beast.

4

The Fowler Couple

After hearing the heart-rending news from Govinda, Ramanuja at first did not know what to do. The world seemed all darkness. When he looked around after some time, he saw that his dear friend Govinda too was hastening to join the disciples of Yadava, leaving him behind. It was scarcely half an hour then for the nightfall. This young man of eighteen, helpless, friendless, knew not what to do. He mused, 'Let me call Govinda near me.' He thought again that then the other disciples would come to know of it. Govinda became gradually invisible behind the trees. Then, all on a sudden, a great strength never experienced before, braced him up, as if some one from within spoke, 'Why be afraid? The Lord Narayana is there.' To save himself from the designs of his fellow-students, Ramanuja promptly left the path and entered into the deep forest southwards. Without looking back even once, he went on walking at top speed for about an hour. Now and then, when he thought he heard some one calling his name, he would quicken his pace all the more. At last, unable to proceed any further owing to hunger, thirst and exhaustion, he sat down under a tree. When it grew difficult even to keep sitting, he lay down there and forgot the entire world in the embrace of sleep, the remover of all pains. When he woke up he saw it was afternoon and the sun was declining to the west. But his hunger and exhaustion had left him. Feeling himself very vigorous, he thanked God. After washing his hands, face and feet, he was thinking where to go, when he found a fowler couple approaching him. The fowler's wife came near him and asked, 'Ah! my child, is it because you have lost your way that you are sitting alone in this lonely forest? You look like the son of a Brahmana. Where's your home?'

'My home is very far off from here. Have you heard of Kanchipuram in the South? I come from that place,' replied Ramanuja.

'How could you happen to come to this dangerous forest infested with robbers? No party of wayfarers dare frequent these parts even during the day-time. Apart from that, wild animals move about here fearless. I know Kanchipuram. We are also going in that direction,' said the fowler.

'Where is your native place, and pray, wherefore are you going to Kanchipuram?' enquired Ramanuja.

'We were born in some forest-village at the foot of the Vindhyas,' replied the fowler. 'Having lived all our lives as fowlers, my wife and I have set out on a pilgrimage for the good of our souls. We wish to go to Rameswaram via Kanchipuram. It is good we got a companion so good as you, who, it seems, have lost your way. Be not afraid. It would seem the Supreme Lord, who is the refuge of all, has brought us here for giving you protection.'

Though Ramanuja was at first a little unnerved to view the appearance of this dark, tall and red-eyed fowler, yet the sobriety and affection in his face, the sweetness of his words, and the candid and affable speech of his wife, gradually dispelled all suspicions from his mind and he agreed to follow them. Not much of the day-time was left. The fowler said, 'Let us quickly cover this forest region and find our resting place for the night on the banks of the broad subterranean river which flows by not very far from here.' About an hour's walk brought them to the banks of the river. The fowler collected some pieces of wood and kindled a fire. Then he levelled a piece of the uneven ground and asked Ramanuja to rest there. His wife and he then retired to the other side. The wife told the husband, 'My dear, I am feeling very thirsty; can you look for some water near about?'

'The night is almost come,' said the fowler. 'Now it isn't advisable to quit this place, dear. Tomorrow you will quench

your thirst with the limpid water of a good well near by.
There are beautiful steps in the well.'

Early the next morning, Ramanuja got up and after
finishing his morning duties, followed the fowler couple on
their trek. Shortly, they came near the well mentioned above.
Ramanuja got down the steps, washed his hands and face
and quenched his thirst with the cool limpid water. Then
he brought up handfuls of water for the wife of the fowler
to drink. But, when he found that even after doing so thrice,
the thirst of the fowler's wife was not assuaged, he went
down the well and brought up water for the fourth time. But
lo! the couple had disappeared. He looked here and there,
but nowhere were they to be seen. He could not make out
how within a few minutes they went out of sight. Then it
struck him that they were not human but divine beings.
Lakshmi-Narayana had become his guide and protector in
the guise of the fowler couple.

On seeing the towers of the temples and a cluster of
houses in the vicinity, he thought that it might be some city.
He enquired of a passer-by, 'What is the name of this place,
Sir?'

Looking at his face with wonderment, the passer-by
said in a tone of surprise, 'Are you descended from the
clouds, eh? Can't you recognise the reputed city of Kanchi?
Your appearance shows that you belong to these parts; but
you are talking like a stranger. Aren't you the disciple of
Mahatma Yadavaprakasa? I have seen you many a time in
this Kanchipuram itself. Of course, you may not know of the
well wherein you have washed your hands and face and by
the side of which stands that big and venerable *sal* tree. Its
water assuages all kinds of misery pertaining to the flesh.
So people from various places come here, as they would do
to a place of pilgrimage, with a desire to drink of its water.'

Saying this, the passer-by went away without caring
for a reply, and Ramanuja, like one awakened from sleep
and unable to make out anything, looked awe-struck.
The next moment he remembered the fowler couple and

understood clearly that the limitless grace of Lakshmi-Narayana alone was the cause of his deliverance. With his heart overwhelmed with love, and tears rolling down his cheeks, he sang in adoration of the lotus feet of the blessed Lord Narayana:

> Again and again I salute that Brahmanyadeva, that Govinda, that Krishna, who is the doer of good unto the cows and the holy ones and the universe at large.[1]

---

1. नमो ब्रह्मण्यदेवाय गोब्राह्मणहिताय च ।
   जगद्धिताय कृष्णाय गोविन्दाय नमो नमः ॥

   —*Sri Vishnu Purana*, I. xix. 65.

5

Among His Own People Again

Intoxicated with love of God, Ramannuja repeatedly circumambulated the well beside the *sal* tree and, perhaps in the hope that Sri and Her Consort might again bless him with their vision in the form of the fowler couple, he cast his glances hither and thither. About an hour had elapsed after the dawn. One or two women with water pots on their flanks were coming from the city for the limpid water of the well, from where Kanchipuram was just a mile away. With forests on the east, north and west, the place was sequestered. Hence with open heart Ramanuja sang the endless glories of the Lord of his heart. He hymned the Lord in the words of Kunti:

> Again and again do I salute Krishna, Vasudeva, who is the son of Devaki and the darling of Nanda and who is Govinda. I salute the One of lotus navel; I salute the One wearing the lotus garland; I salute the One of lotus eyes; I salute the One of lotus feet.[1]

Like Kunti, he prayed to the lotus feet of the Lord:

> O World-teacher, may distress always befall us, for it is during times of distress alone that Your vision, which makes another birth impossible, is made possible. Those who, by birth in high families or possession of wealth, beauty or erudition think themselves to be immensely glorious, have no right to take Your name, for it is Your indigent devotees who see

---

1. कृष्णाय वासुदेवाय देवकीनन्दनाय च ।
   नन्दगोपकुमाराय गोविन्दाय नमो नमः ॥
   नमः पङ्कजनाभाय नमः पङ्कजमालिने ।
   नमः पङ्कजनेत्राय नमस्ते पङ्कजाङ्घ्रये ॥

Srimad Bhagavatam, I. viii. 21, 22.

You face to face. O Lord, You are the only treasure of the devotees who have nothing whatsoever in this world to call their own. You being beyond Dharma, Artha and Kama, are ever in supreme communion with Yourself. There being no urge of desire in You, You are all-quiet; You are the giver of deliverance to all the Jivas; I adore You.[1]

As Ramanuja, lost in love of God, was filled with the Sattvic marks of tears, perspiration and tremors, there appeared near the well three housewives with pitchers on their hips. At the sight of them, he checked his emotions and proceeded towards Kanchi.

Sorely sad at the separation from her son, Kantimati was weeping at home. She could not at first believe her eyes when all on a sudden she found her son standing before her. Her doubts were dispelled only when Ramanuja postrated himself at her feet and humbly addressed her, 'Here I am come, mother. All is well with you, I hope.' After blessing him and offering him a seat, she enquired: 'My dear child, how is it that you are returning so soon and alone? Where is Govinda? I am told it takes six months to return after the holy bath in the Ganga.' When Ramanuja had narrated all from beginning to end, she was shocked to hear of the evil designs of Yadavaprakasa. Yet she was beside herself with joy, remembering the grace of the Lord and seeing the face of her son.

She immediately entered the kitchen to prepare offerings for the Lord Narayana. But so great was her joy that she did not know what to cook or what to do. As she went near the hearth, she discovered that there was no

1. विपद: सन्तु न: शश्वत्तत्र तत्र जगद्गुरो ।
   भवतो दर्शनं यत्स्यादपुनर्भवदर्शनम् ॥
   जन्मैश्वर्यश्रुतश्रीभिरेधमानमद: पुमान् ।
   नैवार्हत्यभिधातुं वै त्वामकिञ्चनगोचरम् ॥
   नमोऽकिञ्चनवित्ताय निवृत्तगुणवृत्तये ।
   आत्मारामाय शान्ताय कैवल्यपतये नम: ॥

Srimad Bhagavatam, I viii 25, 26, 27.

firewood left. For, two or three days earlier, the stock was over. Ramanuja was not at home and, since his going, the new daughter-in-law also was living in her paternal home. For whom then was she to cook? She would pass her days taking some fruits or roots offered to God. Thus she had forgotten all about procuring firewood. Especially this day, her mind had grown very restless for Ramanuja and so she was sitting in a corner, shedding tears. Nothing of the household did she remember. She should now herself go to the shop to purchase firewood, for the maidservant had not yet come. She would not give any trouble to her son who had just returned after a long journey. When she was so musing, there appeared by the other door of the house, her younger sister Diptimati accompanied by her daughter-in-law, and after saluting at her feet, enquired, 'Dear sister, is it not all well with you? The maid-servant told us that you had abandoned food and sleep and were simply weeping day and night for your son. So we have come to see you. Why do you worry? There is Lord Narayana. He will protect the boys. Many are the persons who are coming back after ablutions in the Ganga. Be at peace, dear! Until Ramanuja and Govinda come back, I shall stay here with you. I have brought our daughter-in-law also with me. After purchasing firewood from the shop, the maid-servant ...' Before she could finish, Ramanuja came and bowed at the feet of his mother's sister. Diptimati was beside herself with joy to find her nephew before her. She lifted Ramanuja up from the ground and blessed him. Then on enquiry she came to understand everything about Govinda. Kantimati's joy was at its zenith to receive her sister and daughter-in-law. At the unexpected return of her beloved, the shy bride out of great joy fell at his feet and washed them with tears. It seemed as if the Acharya's house was transformed into a heaven for the nonce.

In the meantime, after the maid-servant had brought ghee, sugar, rice, greens, salt and firewood, the two sisters cooked a variety of offerings for Lord Narayana. As Ramanuja came out after making the offerings to Lord

Narayana, he found Sri Kanchipurna waiting at the door to see him. He had heard of Ramanuja's return from some people and so came to see him. Just as the sea, swelling with joy at the sight of the full moon, raises its high waves as arms to clasp the moon's rays, so did Kanchipurna, with horripilation of joy, hold Ramanuja in his arms, and as the young man tried to bow before him forbid him to do such an act contrary to custom. Ramanuja then requested him, 'Great one, I am very fortunate to have your Darsan. Do kindly dine with us today. Everything is ready.' Sri Kanchipurna agreed.

After the passing away of his father, Ramanuja's home had never known such delight. Diptimati had, however, some reason to be distressed, for Govinda was away. But she loved Ramanuja as her own son, and such was her faith in the Lord's unfailing grace that, instead of feeling distressed in the least, she was the happiest person in that house.

6

The Princess

Sri ramanuja continued his studies at home. He spoke
to both his mother and her sister about the Yadavaprakasa
affair but asked them to keep it a secret. He himself did not
reveal this to anyone else. After three months, Yadavaprakasa
returned to Kanchipuram, along with all his disciples but
Govinda. On enquiry about her son, Diptimati came to know
as follows: After the disappearance of Ramanuja in the forest,
the pilgrims continued their journey to Varanasi, and reaching there, had the Darsan of Viswanatha and bath in the
holy Ganga. They stayed there for a fortnight. One day, on
going for bath in the Ganga, Govinda got from under the
water a beautiful round symbol of Siva (Banalinga). Seeing
this Yadavaprakasa congratulated him many a time and
said, 'My child, the Consort of Parvati has been immensely
pleased with you. So He has come to you as this invaluable
symbol in order to accept your service. By serving Him with
the utmost care, you will attain both devotion and liberation.'
According to the words of his teacher, Govinda engaged
himself in the service of Siva from that very day. Gradually
his devotion grew so firm that coming near Kalahasti, he
said addressing his preceptor and brother disciples, 'I want
to pass the rest of my life in the service of the Consort of
Uma. This place is very pleasant and lonely. I shall live here
and meditate on my Chosen Ideal. Please communicate this
to my mother and her sister.' So saying, Govinda took leave
of them and went to the neighbouring village, Mangalagrama.
He purchased a plot of land there, installed his Chosen
Deity, and by consecrating his life and mind to His service,
got rid of all the fetters of the world.

Diptimati was overwhelmed with joy to hear of her
son's good fortune. She was not morbidly attached to her son

94

like ordinary women. She too had very deep love for God. So, instead of feeling distressed for her son, she felt blessed, knowing herself to be the mother of a worthy son. With the consent of her sister, she went to Mangalagrama to see her son. Her joy knew no bounds at the sight of her son's devotion to God. She held the son in her arms, blessed him and then returned to her sister.

Yadavaprakasa again started his work of teaching. At the sight of Ramanuja he was at first a little frightened. But taking it for granted that he did not know anything about his murderous designs, he expressed feigned joy and told him in the presence of his mother, 'My child, it is the greatest joy to me to see you once again. How to put into words the suffering we underwent for you in the Vindhya forests? 'Ramanuja bowed at his feet and said, All by your grace!'

Yadavaprakasa had many virtues, but clinging fanatically to the doctrine of non-dualism, he was totally blind to the beauty and sweetness of other doctrines. But today, seeing Ramanuja's humility and remembering his own monstrous behaviour, he felt mortally ashamed. Then he told Ramanuja affectionately, 'My child, from today you should come to study with me. May God do good unto you! 'From that day onward Ramanuja resumed going to Yadava's place for studies.

A few days later, the venerable Alavandar, accompanied by many disciples, came to Kanchipuram to have the Darsan of Sri Varadaraja. One day, while returning after the Darsan, Alavandar saw Yadavaprakasa, the lion of the doctrine of non-dualism, coming by the way, with his hand resting on the shoulders of Ramanuja and followed by a retinue of his other disciples. At the sight of Ramanuja's spiritual lustre and incomparable beauty, the venerable Yamunacharya felt intensely attracted towards him, and on enquiry, came to know that the young man was the author of that elaborate commentary on the Mantra *satyam jnanam anantam brahma* (Brahma is Existence, Intelligence and Infinity). Alavandar was exceedingly pleased at this, but felt very much concerned to find him living in the company of the dry polemic that Yadava was and prayed to Sri Varadaraja in the following strain:

I take refuge in that boon-giving Deity by a fraction of whose grace the deaf hear, the lame move swiftly, the dumb speak, the blind see and a barren woman becomes the mother of a son.

O Lotus-eyed One, O Lord of Lakshmi, do You bring Ramnnuja to your faith by bestowing Your grace upon him.[1]

Yamunacharya was pained to see the gracious form which gladdens the heart of the beloved of Vishnu by the side of the dry-hearted Yadava. Though he longed to talk with Ramanuja, he was forced to avoid him like sweet food smeared with poison. Old alike in wisdom and years, being now more than a hundred years old, the venerable Alavandar, the crest-jewel of the Vaishnavas, consoled himself with the thought that, if Providence chose, He would one day have an opportunity of seeing Ramanuja by himself. He then returned to Srirangam.

Apart from his erudition in Vedanta, Yadavaprakasa was a great adept in magic science (Mantra-sastra). He could cure people possessed by ghosts and Brahmarakshasas. In this regard he was widely famous.

Once the princess of Kanchipuram came to be possessed by a Brahmarakshasa. Exorcists were brought from all quarters. But none was able to cure the princess. Then, with great honour, was brought Vedantacharya Yadavaprakasa. But at his sight, the princess possessed by the Rakshasa burst into a loud laughter and said, 'Ah Yadavaprakasa! your Mantras will be of no avail here. You

---

1. यस्य प्रसादकलया बधिर: श्रृणोति पङ्गु: प्रधावति जवेन च वक्ति मूक: ।
अन्ध: प्रपश्यति सुतं लभते च वन्ध्या तं देवमेव वरदं शरणं गतोऽस्मि ॥
लक्ष्मीश पूण्डरीकाक्ष कृपां रामानुजे तव ।
निधाय स्वमते नाथ प्रविष्टं कर्तुमर्हसि ॥

Anantacharya's *Prapannamritam*, VII. 30, 31.

are wasting your pains. Go back home.' Disregarding her, Yadava uttered various Mantras for a long time, but was totally unsuccessful in producing any result. Thereupon the Brahmarakshasa interposed, 'Why take pains in vain? You are inferior in strength to me. If you are resolved that I should be driven off from this shrine of the body of the princess, so tender and delightful to touch, then bring here your youngest disciple, the blessed Ramanuja, whose arms reach down to his knees, who has broad forehead and large eyes, who is the pleasure resort of the goddess of genius, and the choicest blossom in the garden of youth. As the thick darkness of the clouded new moon night is removed at sunrise, so at the advent of that great soul, I too shall be driven away; otherwise not.'

At the behest of Yadava, Ramanuja was instantly brought there. When he asked the Brahmarakshasa to get off from the body of the princess, it replied, 'I won't go unless you graciously place your blessed feet on my head. Do please fulfil this desire of your slave.'

At the behest of his preceptor, Ramanuja placed both his feet on the head of the princess and said, 'Now, relieve the princess and go, leaving behind some proof that you have left her.'

'Look, there I quit', said the Brahmarakashasa. 'As a proof, I go instantly breaking the topmost branch of the neighbouring banyan tree.'

At once the topmost branch of the banyan tree broke with a crash and the princess began to look around like one just awakened from a slumber. Afterwards, when she regained full consciousness and could grasp her plight a little, she hung her face in shame and went away to another apartment, surrounded by maid-servants.

When the king of Kanchi came to know of the recovery of his daughter, he hastened to worship the feet of Ramanuja and express his deep gratitude. From that day on, Sri Ramanuja's name became famous in the Chola kingdom. We hear of similar incidents in the story of

Jesus's life also. Even now one hears, in many places in Bengal and other parts of the country, of women being possessed by spirits. Western doctors say that such persons suffer from a disease called hysteria, caused by nervous debility. Women being constitutionally delicate, it is they who generally become hysteric. It is the nerves which constitute the manliness in man. A man is weak or strong according as his nerves are weak or strong. By following such contentions one has to reach the conclusion that the annihilation of the nerves means the annihilation of the man. The followers of Charvaka in our land too reached the same conclusion a long time ago. But it is a wrong conclusion. The soul protects the body, not the body the soul; only from the presence of the soul are derived the liveliness and sanctity of the body. Through the body man experiences the pleasure and pain of the world. The desire-nature in man is ever eager to enjoy pleasure with the help of the body. This self when endowed with a gross body appears as man, animal, bird, worm, insect, etc. and, when bereft of it, assumes the forms of Devas, demi-gods, Brahma-rakshasas, goblins and ghosts. The forms of the latter, being subtle, cannot be grasped by the five senses. What cannot be grasped by senses also exists. Isvara-krishna, the great author of *Sankhyakarika*, has settled the issue in a fine manner. He says:

> (Non-perception may be) because of extreme distance, (extreme) proximity, injury to the organs, non-steadiness of the mind, subtlety, veiling, suppression and blending with what is similar. The non-perception of that (Primal Nature) is due to its subtlety, not to its non-existence, since it is perceived in its effects.[1]

---

1.   अतिदूरात्सामीप्यादिन्द्रियघातान्मनोऽनवस्थानात् ।
     सौक्ष्म्याद्व्यवधानादभिभवात्समानाभिहाराच्च ॥
     सौक्ष्म्यात्तदनुपलब्धि: नाभावात्कार्यतस्तदुपलब्धे: ।

Sankhyakarika, 7, 8 (first half).

The subtle body, when dominated by Sattva, becomes the body of a Deva, when by Rajas, the body of a demigod, and when by Tamas, the body of a Brahma-rakshasa, a goblin or ghost. That is why it is possible for men of Sattvic temperament to go under the possession of Devas, for men of Rajas to go under the influence of demi-gods, and for men of Tamas to go under the spell of ghosts.

After this incident, Yadavaprakasa continued as before his work of teaching. Every day Ramanuja and the other disciples would enjoy listening to his subtle expositions of the sacred texts. One day while expounding the two portions of two Mantras from the Upanishads, *sarvam khalvidam brahma*[1] 'All this is verily Brahman' and *neha nanasti kinchana*[2] 'There is no diversity whatsoever here', Yadava-prakasa was going to propound very beautifully, and with considerable eloquence, the oneness of Atman and Brahman. All the disciples but Ramanuja were simply captivated by the dexterity of his exposition. After the discourse was over, Ramanuja expressed his own reflections over these two parts of the two Mantras in the following manner: 'The interpretation of *sarvam khalvidam brahma* would have been 'the entire universe is Brahman' had not the following word *tajjalan* qualified the said meaning. As the universe is born of Brahman, is sustained by Brahman, and dissolves into Brahman, so it may surely be said to be permeated with Brahman. Fish is born in water, lives in water, and dissolves into water; so it may surely be said to be permeated with water. But as fish can never be water, likewise the universe too can never be Brahman. And *neha nanasti kinchana* does not mean that 'there is no diversity whatsoever here'; but, as 'the things of this Samsara are not existing severally, but as pearls strung on a thread form a garland, so the various objects threaded in Brahman have formed this universe'. Many have united and have only assumed the semblance of oneness; but by this the manifoldness has in no way been impaired.'

1. *Chandogya Up.*, III. xiv. 1.   2. *Katha Up.*, IV. 11.

On hearing this exposition, Yadava expressed great annoyance and said, 'If you don't like my expositions, then don't come to me any more.' 'As you wish, Sir,' said Ramanuja, and after worshipping the feet of his preceptor in great humility, he took leave of him and abstained from going there again.

7

Sri Kanchipurna

Next day shortly after dawn, when Ramanuja was en gaged in discussing the Sastras at his own place, Sri Kanchipurna appeared there. At the sight of him who was, so to say, an embodiment of 'servitude to God', Ramanuja's joy knew no bounds.

He got up and, offering him a seat, said, 'Your coming here to-day is due to my good fortune. Boundless is the grace of Varadaraja. Finding this ignorant boy of His, lost and wandering helplessly in this forest of Samsara, He has sent you as my guide. Perhaps you have heard that the learned Yadavaprakasa has deprived me of the shelter of his feet; but now I see that it happened so only because I was to enjoy the cool shade of the great sandal tree that you are. You are my Guru; do accept me as your disciple.'

'Ramanuja, my child,' said Kanchipurna, on hearing this, 'I am a Sudra, and what is worse, an ignorant man. You are a Brahmana and a great scholar. True, I am old in years, but you are old in wisdom. Not being versed in the Sastras, I am passing my life in the service of Sri Varadaraja. I am your servant; you are my Guru.'

'Sir, you alone are really wise,' Ramanuja replied. 'If the knowledge of the Sastras only brings about pride of erudition instead of devotion to God, then it is false knowledge; better is ignorance than this. You have verily tasted the real essence of the Sastras; other scholars merely carry the burden, like the ass that carries the load of sandalwood. Please do not forsake me; I take refuge at your feet.' So saying, Ramanuja suddenly fell at his feet and began to weep.

Kanchipurna instantly raised him up from the ground and, embracing him in deep love, said, 'My child, I am blessed to-day by seeing your devotion to God. From to-day,

101

you will fetch a jarful of holy water from the well for the worship of Sri Varadaraja. Very soon will Varadaraja fulfil your desire.'

'I shall carry out your behest most willingly,' said Ramanuja, and after getting a new jar from within the room, started towards the *sal-well*. Kanchipurna went towards the temple for the worship of the Lord.

Who is Sri Kanchipurna? He was born in Poonamallee. From his very boyhood, he had engaged himself in the service of Sri Varadaraja, who alone was his beloved, son, family and everything. He used to be always busy, his only concern being the service of Varadaraja. On summer days he would be ever engaged in serving his most Beloved One with the soft, cool breeze of a fan dipped in water. He knew very well where the best flowers had blossomed and most delicious fruits had ripened. He would buy or beg them for the Lord of his heart. Most men believed that he was the eternal servant of Sri Varadaraja, come from Vaikuntha.

The people of Kanchi used to hold him in high regard and love. Humble and childlike, he was ever smiling. Whoever saw him had his own face enkindled by the light of joy. Misunderstanding, afflictions of heart, misery and indigence, fled at his sight. As the spring showers sweetness wherever it appears, so he radiated joy and peace wherever he went. Everyone took him for a friend, but found in him some transcendental qualities as well. He was always accompanied, as it were, by some invisible person. While converging with anyone, he would forget himself and listen to the person talking, and smile on him with such sweetness that the beholders were wonder-struck. But none could call him insane, for his face was sweet and serene all the time. Who was that invisible person? Everyone would say in unison, 'It is Sri Varadaraja Himself. He (Kanchipurna) converses with Hastigiripati[1] and is, as it were, the mouth

---

1. Another name of Lord Vishnu who is worshipped as Sri Varadaraja in Kanchipuram.

of the Blessed Lord. Through him Sri Varadaraja reveals His own intents.' And yet, he called himself a Sudra and greatly revered the Brahmanas. Most Brahmanas would greet him with' veneration and take good care of him. Only the few who fancied themselves to be very learned and who were professional expounders of Sastras held firmly that he was insane and an imposter. Yadavaprakasa was one of them.

8

Stotraratna

Since seeing Sri Ramanuja, Alavandar was ever thinking of him and praying for his welfare. The old man would every day supplicate at the feet of the Lord so that Ramanuja, whom he loved like a son, might give up his discipleship to Yadava and resort to the supreme path of Vaishnnavism. One day, praying for his welfare, Yamuna-charya presented an offering of lovely verses to the lotus feet of the Lord of the three worlds. The fragrance of this poetic flower is still unfaded. It expresses his heartfelt ardour of deep devotion, of intense love. It has the purity and coolness of the waters of the sacred Ganga that springs from the feet of Vishnu and every letter of it is, as it were, soaked in nectar. The first few slokas are composed in adoration of the blessed feet of his own Guru and grand-father, Sri Nathamuni.

> Adoration of God is more tasteful when done after the adoration of the blessed Guru, for, milk, though naturally sweet, is sweeter still when sugar is added to it.[1]

The entire hymn[2] is as follows:

> 1.   Obeisance to the saintly Nathamuni, who is an unfathomable ocean of divine love and a storehouse of knowledge and renunciation, unimaginable, marvellous and spontaneous.

> 2.   Obeisance to that Master, Nathamuni, whose feet are my eternal refuge in this world and in the next, and whose life marks the farthest limit in the field of man's achievement of genuine knowledge and love for the lotus-feet of this Lord.

---

1. भगवद्वन्दनं स्वाद्यं गुरुवन्दनपूर्वकम् ।

   क्षीरं शर्करया युक्तं स्वदते हि विशेषतः ॥

—opening sloka of Sri Vedanta Desika's *Stotraratna-Bhashyam* (Kanchipuram edition of *Works of Vedanta Desika,* Vol. IV, p. 26).

2. For the original Sanskrit hymn see Appendix B.

3. Obeisance again to Nathamuni, the paragon amongst holy men, who has become the source of, and the sole authority on, the genuine traditions of Bhakti Yoga through his sacred precepts, which are verily the overflow from the ocean of knowledge and love of Achyuta that he himself was.

4. Obeisance to Parasara, chief among philosopher saints, who graciously composed the gem of Puranas (Vishnu-purana) in order to give a correct presentation of the categories of the sentient, the non-sentient, and Isvara together with their real nature, as also to expound the course and the means of the Jiva's attainment of the two destinies awaiting it—namely, the life of involvement in the enjoyments and sufferings of Samsara and the path of freedom from it.

5. I reverently bow down my head to the blessed feet of Parankusa (Nammalvar), the first patriarch of our family, whose feet are bedecked with offerings of Bakula flowers, and who is eternally united to us and all members of our clan with a bond of love dearer than everything else in life—be it father, mother, wife, sons or wealth.

6. I shall praise the lotus-feet of the Lord, which illumines my understanding and which gives significance to the Vedic revelation as its final meaning. They are the confluence of all aspirations, the treasure of our family, and the tutelary Deity of our lineage.

7. And lo! obeisance be to me, the impudent fool of a poet, who is intent on singing the praise of His oceanlike glory, a single particle of whose spray it is not possible even for Siva, Brahma and the like to measure truly!

8. Or, in spite of my incapacity, I shall praise Him to the limit of my strength and to the best of my knowledge; for verily, even they, the Vedas and the four-faced Brahma, praise Him only thus! Pray, what difference is there between an atom and a mighty mountain range when both are submerged in the great ocean?

9. Moreover, this psalmist deserves Thy pity, not for an enhancement of poetical gifts, but for his great exertion in praising Thee. And exertion for the purpose is quite natural to me, who am dull-witted. So, O lotus-eyed One, being sure of Thy compassionate aid, I feel this effort of mine to be on the right lines.

10. O Lord! If Thou dost not cast Thy glance at these worlds, they cannot even exist, much less can they have any activity. It is not strange therefore that Thou, O Master, who art the natural friend of all creatures, cherishest those who have sought shelter in Thee.

11. O Narayana, who among the learned adherents of the Vedas does not admit Thy intrinsic Godhood endowed with unsurpassable excellences? For, even Brahma, Siva, Indra and the supreme liberated souls are but drops in the ocean of Thy glory.

12. Who else but Thee is the splendour of even Lakshmi? who else, the asylum of perfect Sattva? who else, the 'lotus-eyed' par excellence? who else, the supreme among the Purushas? In a subdivision of a billionth of Thy part, the wonderfully differentiated universe is complete with its two-fold division of the sentient and the non-sentient.'

13. Who else but Thee preserves Prajapati (Brahma) and Pasupati (Siva) from adversities such as loss of the Vedas, heavy guilt and harassment by demons; bestows upon them the greatest of benefits; and renders Siva really Siva (the auspicious) with the sacred waters (Ganga) flowing from Thy feet on to his head?

14. In whose abdomen does the universe headed by Siva and Brahma rest? from whose navel has it sprung? in whom does it find protection? who else but Thee sucks it up and projects it again? and who else is there that can even by mistake be taken as equal or superior to Thee?

15. Men of demoniac nature are not able (because of their depravity) to recognize Thee even through Thy easily accessible disposition, loveliness of form and divine deeds; through Thy supremely excellent Sattvika nature; through the scriptures authoritative on account of their being Sattvika in character; and through the precepts of the famous knowers of the truth of God.

16. Some, who are inseparably united with Thee in thought and feeling, perceive and realise Thy sovereign nature, which transcends the threefold limits (of time, space and circumstances), which can equal or surpass, and which Thou dost keep shrouded from the view of all by the power of Thy Maya.

17. The cosmic sphere, all that is within it, its enclosures which are more than ten, the three Gunas, the Prakriti (primordial matter), the individual self, the Supreme Abode, and the transcendental Divine Form—all these are manifestations of Thy splendour.

18. Submissive to devotion, bountiful, benevolent, guileless, pure, tender, merciful, blissful, firm, impartial, self-fulfilled and responsive to love and worship, Thou art by nature a veritable nectar-ocean of auspicious qualities.

19. The Vedas in their enthusiasm to ascertain the utmost bounds of each of Thy attributes, take but one of them,

namely Bliss, and seek to describe it by hundred-folding its manifestation in beings in an ascending order from Brahma onwards. But they do not progress much in expounding even that one attribute, in spite of their incessant efforts.

20. It is for the benefit of those that have taken shelter in Thee that Thou engagest Thyself in Thy sportive cosmic activities of creation, preservation, destruction and redemption, and hast given out the teachings of Vedic revelation that are an expression of Thy unfathomable wisdom.

21. Obeisance again and again to Thee who art beyond the reach of speech and mind! Obeisance again and again to Thee who art the sole ground of speech and mind! Obeisance again and again to Thee of infinitely great powers! Obeisance again and again to Thee, the one ocean of infinite compassion!

22. Without steadfastness in right living, without knowledge of the self, and without devotion to Thy lotus feet, I am stricken with absolute spiritual poverty, and am wellnigh a lost soul. I, therefore, seek shelter in Thee, the most worthy refuge of sinful man!

23. There is not a despicable deed which I have not committed a thousand times. The time of fruition of these misdeeds having come, I—that heinous sinner responsible for them—am helplessly weeping and wailing in the dread of their consequences before Thee, O redeemer of men!

24. O Infinite Being! Drowning as I am in the expansive sea of Samsara, I seem to have at last reached a shore on resorting to Thy feet. And in me, the most helpless of beings, Thou too hast found an object most suited for the exercise of Thy mercy.

25. The future cannot have in store for me any new form of misery that the past has not already inflicted. And besides, I can put up with my suffering, since suffering has become natural to me. But, O Lord, it does not befit Thy divine status that defeat and downfall should overtake one like me who has taken shelter at Thy feet!

26. O Supreme Lord! Even if Thou rejectest me, I can never relinquish Thy lotus feet. A baby eager to suck at its mother's breast, will not leave her, even if she pushes it off in anger.

27. How can any other desire attract a soul that is absorbed in the bliss that Thy lotus feet afford? A bee settled in a honey-laden lotus feels no attraction for the (thorny and odourless) Ikshuaraka flower.

28. Whosoever joins his hands to supplication to Thee at any time, for any reason, even once, that act of supplication

dispels at once all his misfortunes and fosters immense good; never does it go in vain.

29. A drop from the nectar-ocean of love to Thy lovely lotus-feet extinguishes in an instant the blazing forest fire of transmigratory existence and bestows supreme bliss.

30. When shall I perceive with my eyes those lotus-feet of Thine, my dearest treasure, which covered the worlds high and low in one sportive stride, and which await eagerly the moment of the devotee's surrender for destroying his afflictions.

31. O Trivikrama! When will Thy lotus-feet, bearing the marks of conch, discus, the wish-fulfilling tree, banner, lotus, hook and thunder-bolt, adorn my head?

32. Thee who art beautifully clad in shining yellow raiment, whose pure splendour is like that of a blooming flax flower, who art endowed with a depressed navel, slender waist, high stature and the characteristic resplendent mark of Srivatsa adorning the broad chest;

33. Thee who shinest with four auspicious arms, which reach the knees and have the rough scars of the bow-string, and which bespeak their contact with the crest-lily, the ear-ornament and the loose curls of Thy beloved's braids;

34. Thee whose conch-like neck is adorned with curls of hair and ear-rings hanging over lofty and large shoulders, and whose face puts to shame by its lustrous beauty the brilliant splendour of the spotless full moon and of the lotus flower in bloom;

35. Thee who hast a pair of charming lotus-like eyes, gracious creeper-like brows, splendid lips, pleasant smile, soft cheeks, prominent nose, and curls hanging up to the forehead;

36. Thee who art handsome with ornaments like the shining diadem, bracelets, garland of pearls, necklace, the (Kaustubha) gem, girdle, anklets and the like; with weapons like discus, conch, sword, mace and the excellent bow (Saranga); and with decorations consisting of garlands of wild flowers and beautiful Tulasi;

37. Thee who hast assigned Thy breast as the abode for Thy Consort Sri, whose birthplace (the ocean) is Thy beloved abode, in whose side-glance the entire universe takes refuge, and for whose sake the ocean was churned and spanned;

38-40. Thee who art seated with Sri—who, though eternally comprehended in Thy Cosmic Being, continually generates in Thee uprecedented waves of Joy, and who is well-matched with Thee and Thee alone in virtue, beauty and gracious deeds—on the great serpent Ananta, who is the sold repository of excellent knowledge and strength, within Thy

Divine Abode (Vaikuntha), the inside of which is illumined by the circle of rays emanating from the clustered gems on that Ananta's hoods—Ananta who is aptly designated by devotees as 'Sesha' (appendage) on account of the different forms he has assumed for serving Thee in different capacities such as residence, couch, seat, sandals, raiments, pillow and umbrella to keep out sun and rain;

41. Thee who hast at hand for Thy service Garutmat, who is Thy servant, friend, vehicle, seat, banner, a canopy and fan, and whose figure is made up of the three Vedas, and who shines with the scar-sign produced by friction of Thy feet;

42. Thee who approvest with gracious glance whatever communication is brought by Thy beloved chief of hosts. (Vishvaksena), who partakes of the remnants of Thy food, and to whom Thou hast delegated the charge (of Thy sovereign authority);

43. Thee who art duly served by Thy companions who are suited to Thee, who are free from all the impurities arising from afflictions (such as nescience, egoism, etc.), whose sole delight consists in being spontaneously devoted to Thy service, and who (constantly) wait upon Thee with the appropriate means of service;

44. Thee of powerful arms, who dost exhilarate Thy queen (Sri) with lovely and skilful sports which are enlivened by diverse new sentiments and emotions and which make time measurable in aeons pass like a fraction of a moment;

45. Thee who art the nectar-ocean of beauty and eternal youth, unthinkable, divine and wondrous; who art the splendour (Sri) of Lakshmi, the sole sustenance of the devotees, the possessor of all powers, the friend of the distressed, and the wish-fulfilling tree of the suppliants—

46. When shall I delight Thee of *such description* with my service as Thy constant and exclusive servant for all time, having my mind freed from every other thought and filled with the satisfaction that my life is at last under the protection of a real Master?

47. O Supreme Lord! Fie upon me—an impure, immodest, audacious, impudent and self-willed fellow, yet desiring the rank of Thy servant, which even such spiritual worthies like Brahma, Siva and Sanaka will not even dare to conceive!

48. O Hari! Pray, make me Thine own out of sheer grace—me who am the repository of a thousand iniquities, who am fallen into the depths of the terrible ocean of worldly

existence, and who in utter helplessness have sought refuge at Thy feet.

49. With the quarters overcast with the clouds of ignorance, with the rain of sorrows constantly pouring, I have swerved from the right path, caught up as I am in the inclement weather of Samsara. O Lord! Achyuta! Deign to take notice of my predicament.

50. Hearken to this, my only entreaty before Thee! What I say is absolute truth without the slightest shadow of exaggeration. If Thou failest to show pity on me, Thou shalt perhaps never get a man hereafter to show pity on (or never get one more worthy of pity).

51. Therefore, without Thee, I am without the protection of a real Master; and without me, Thou art without a worthy recipient to bestow Thy compassion upon. Maintain this relation ordained by destiny, O Lord, and spurn me not.

52. Whatever might be my circumstances with regard to the body and worldly conditions; whatever might be the type of character I am endowed with—I dedicate here and now to Thee that self of mine which is denoted by the term 'I'.

53. O Lord! Whatever is mine, and whatever I am—all that is verily Thine own. O Madhava! my intellect being awakened, I perceive them all to be Thy property already. That being so in the very nature of things, what have I got to offer unto Thee?

54. As thou Thyself hast awakened in me this consciousness of being eternally Thine, so too, O Lord, grant me out of compassion, that type of Bhakti which makes one care for nothing else except for Thee and Thy service.

55. May I be born, be it as a worm even, in the homes of those who are solely devoted to the joy of serving Thee; but let me not be born, even if it be as the 'four-faced Brahma, in the abodes of those who are otherwise disposed.

56. Grant unto me that fitness to be regarded with favour by those great souls who in their eagerness to have a single glance at Thy divine Form have abandoned as lightly as a blade of grass even the greatest of worldly enjoyments as also liberation from Samsara—men who are so dear to Thee that Thou brookest not even a moment of separation from them.

57. O Lord! I cannot even for a moment put up with anything that fails to subserve the purpose of Thy glorious service—be it body, life, happiness, the very self, or any other values universally sought by men. Such in truth is my

feeling, such indeed my submission to Thee, O slayer of Madhu.

58. A repository of great sins—ominous, beginningless and irremediable, and a veritable brute without any sense of purity or good conduct, I pray to Thee none-the-less as above. For, remembering again and again Thy unique excellences, I am free from all fear about the fulfilment of my prayer.

59. Steeped in Rajas and Tamas, now enthusiastic and now careless, I have willy-nilly made this pretentious composition of a hymn. Accepting even this crude collection of words, may Thou, O support of all the worlds, deign out of sheer mercy to educate even such an imperfect mind as mine!

60. To me and to all the worlds, Thou art the father, mother, beloved son, dear friend, well-wisher, teacher and the goal. I for my part am Thine—Thy servant, Thy attendant and a refugee at Thy feet. Having offered whole-hearted surrender to Thee, I am now Thy sole responsibility.

61. Though born in the exalted lineage of those who are pure and devoted, who have grasped the truth about the distinction between matter and spirit, and who are therefore naturally endowed with wholehearted and unswerving devotion to Thy lotus-feet, yet, O Giver of shelter, the evil-minded man that I am, I keep sinking deeper and deeper in the darkness of ignorance.

62. I have been a transgressor, vile, fickle-minded, the breeding ground of envy, ungrateful, arrogant, lascivious, deceitful, cruel and most wicked. How shall I get out of this boundless sea of misery and serve Thy lotus-feet?

63. O the greatest of Raghus! Thou hast been, in Thy reputed way, kind to such a (villianous) crow, because he humbly bowed down before Thee. And O Krishna! Thou hast granted the blissful state of union with Thee to the king of Chedi, who had wronged Thee birth after birth. To one so merciful as Thee, say, what sin is there that is not forgivable?

64. If a man begs for shelter in Thee, saying even once 'I am Thine', he is worthy of Thy mercy. For, O Lord, remember this is Thy vow. But pray! am I alone excluded from the scope of this vow of Thine?

65. Having in view my grandfather, the self-possessed Nathamuni, who is the noblest example of pure and guileless love for Thy lotus-feet—pray, bestow on me Thy grace, regardless of my own conduct.

9

Alavandar

A few days later, the aged Alavandar fell ill and became bedridden. Though overpowered by illness, he did not for a moment stop chanting the glories of service to God. Addressing his disciples again and again he said: 'As the essence of the flower is the honey, and of the cow, ghee, so the substance of the three worlds is Narayana. By taking refuge in Him one attains the four main ends of human life, viz., virtue, wealth, enjoyment and final beatitude.' For the clarification of their individual doubts, the disciples— Mahapurna, Tirukkotiyur Purna and others—requested Nyasi-chudamani Tiruvaranga Perumal Araiyar, who was of the same age as Alavandar, to ask some questions of him on their behalf. At this, Tiruvaranga asked, 'Revered Sir, Sriman Narayana is beyond mind and speech. How should then one serve Him?'

Yamunamuni replied, 'One serves the Lord by serving His devotees. The devotee of God has no caste or race. He is the visible image of God. If you worship the image of Tiruppan Alvar, who came from a low family, that will be service unto Narayana.' He further added, 'The best among the devotees always worship the images of Narayana and His devotees with steadfastness and love. Notice how Tiruppan Alvar passed his life in single-minded service to Sri Ranganatha. Notice the supreme steadfastness of Kanchipurna in his service to Varadaraja! They are great men. By living like them you will earn felicity. "The way the great ones trod, that is the path." [1]

---

1. महाजनो येन गतः स पन्था ।

Mahabharata, Vanaparvan, cccxiv, 119.

Then he looked at Tiruvaranga and said, 'Tiruppan Alvar, the devotee of Ranganatha, is my only refuge; he will be my helmsman across this ocean of life.'

Hearing these words Tiruvaranga asked with an afflicted heart, 'Have you resolved, Sir, to discard your body?'

Yamuna said, 'Even if by the will of the Lord I am to give up the body, a wise man like you should not be sorrowing. Whatever happens by the will of the Lord is for the supreme good. After offering the ego at His lotus feet as a sacrifice, be free of all care for ever. Ego is the root of all miseries. Egolessness is the source of all bliss. Adopt the attitude, 'I am His servant'. When this attitude is firmly established in the mind, one gets rid of the ego. Then a man can understand that he is not subject to birth and death, but is the eternal servant of Narayana. Then he no longer prays 'O Lord, save me'; then he serves Him without any desire and his devotion becomes disinterested. Only then he becomes a real servant of God.'

On coming to know of Tiruvaranga's absolute stead fastness in his service to Tiruppan Alvar, Yamuna was pleased and said to him, 'You will soon attain disinterested devotion and become blessed.'

Mahapurna and Tirukkotiyurpurna were resolving mentally that as soon as Alavandar gave up his body, they would commit suicide. At that time another disciple said, with tears in his eyes, 'In whose shelter can we live after your disappearance? Who will give us such encouragement in sweet words?'

To console him, Yamuna said, 'My child, none of you need be anxious. Sri Ranganatha is there; He has given, is giving, and will always give you shelter. Have His Darsan always. And now and then visit Sri Venkatesa (Balaji) of Tirupati and Sri Varadaraja of Kanchipuram. Srirangam is the abode of Narayana; Tirupati is the supreme Sloka that leads one to the lotus feet of Narayana; and Kanchipuram is the liberating Mantra.'

When Tiruvaranga asked whether they should cremate or bury his body, he did not give any reply, for by then his mind had merged in the lotus feet of God. Many of his disciples resolved to commit suicide after his death.

The next day, when Sri Ranganatha along with his innumerable devotees came outside the temple, the men and women of Srirangam thronged to see the Lord. The crossing of two roads was thick with people. The disciples of Yamuna too came to have the Darsan of Sri Ranganatha. At that time, a servant of the Lord, being divinely possessed, said addressing Mahapurna and Tirukkotiyurpurna, 'Give up your resolution to commit suicide. It is not approved by Me.' So saying he put them in charge of Tiruvaranga, who brought them to Yamunacharya and told him all that had happened. Thereupon, the noble man of great wisdom said, 'Committing suicide is a great sin. God is immensely gracious to you; so He Himself has forbidden you.' After a short silence, he again said, 'My last advice to you is this: You should offer flowers at the lotus feet of the Lord and follow the instructions of your Guru. You should attain the goal of life by destroying the ego through service to the devotees.' So saying, he gave charge of all his disciples to Tiruvaranga.

Alavandar recovered once again and himself joined the festival of Sri Ranganatha one day. After taking the prasad of the Lord, he returned to the Math along with his disciples and, as usual, inspired all by expounding the scriptures. One day, while he was thus engaged, there came in two Brahmanas from Kanchipuram. Hearing of his illness they had come to see him. He was very glad to meet them and enquired about Ramanuja. The two Brahmanas said, 'After giving up his discipleship to Yadavaprakasa, Ramanuja is now studying the scriptures by himself and, according to the behest of Sri Kanchipurna, he every day fetches a jar of water from the *sal-well* for the worship of the Lord.' Yamuna's joy knew no bounds on hearing this. Then and there he composed eight hymns of salutation to the Lord. And addressing Mahapurna he said, 'My child, without any delay, please bring Ramanuja

here. It is good to have him included in our group.' On
hearing this, Mahapurna saluted the holy feet of the Guru
and started for Kanchipuram.

After a few days Alavandar fell ill once more and the
disciples again grew very anxious for him. This time his
illness brought him more suffering. Even in this state of
illness, he took his bath and went to the temple, had the
Darsan of Sri Ranganatha and after taking prasad returned
to the Math. After the disciples had finished their noon
meal, he sent some of them to fetch his householder devotees. When they had all assembled, he begged pardon of
them all for any offence he might have committed. 'If it is
possible for God to commit any offence,' said all of them,
'then it is possible for you too.' After giving over the charge
of Tiruvaranga and other disciples to their hands he said,
'You should every day attend the service of Sri Ranganatha
and take the consecrated flowers. As a result of this, your
mind and intellect will become purified. And very soon you
will have the vision of God. Be always devoted to your Guru
and serve the guests.' As they took leave of him, they were
surprised to see this new mood of Alavandar.

After the householder disciples had taken leave,
Alavandar sat in the lotus posture (Padmasana). He with-
drew his mind and concentrated it on his heart. At that time
his disciples were sweetly singing the glories of the name
of God. The sound of the flute and other musical instruments made the singing sweeter still. A kind of heavenly
bliss flushed the face of all, who were lost in devotion to God.
Gradually, Alavandar raised his mind from the heart to the
point between the eye-brows. Tears of joy began to flow from
the corners of his eyes. The hair stood on end and the entire
body trembled with joy. At last, by giving up the slough of
the body through the aperture at the crown of the head, he
got dissolved in the Supreme. The singing stopped all on a
sudden. Tirukkotiyur Nambi and other disciples burst into
loud lamentation. Some of them swooned and fell on the
ground.

After a while, when the poignancy of grief had abated
a little, the disciples along with Purna the junior, the son
of Alavandar (before he became a monk), prepared for the
obsequies. The body of the deceased was washed in cool pure
water and fresh clothes were put on it before it was placed
on a decorated bier. Then all started in slow pace carrying
the body towards a spot close by the bank of the Kaveri. All
men and women of Srirangam followed the body which was
interred duly at a spot close to the southern bank of the
Coleroon river in the north.

10
Seeing the Body

After taking leave of his revered Guru, Mahapurna started for Kanchipuram. He walked all day long, stopping at some house only for taking alms, and passed the night on the outer verandah of some fortunate householder. Thus he reached Kanchipuram in four days. After having the Darsan of Sri Varadaraja, he saw Mahatma Kanchipurna, when it was already evening. Coming to know of the purpose of his going there, Kanchipurna asked him to take rest there in his Ashrama for the night. They passed the night in various agreeable talks and at daybreak set out for the *sal*-well.

On the way, from a distance they saw Ramanuja coming with a pitcher on his shoulder. Kanchipurna said, 'I shall have to go to the temple now; so I take leave. Go yourself to Ramanuja and reveal your intentions.' With these words he left. At the sight from afar of Ramanuja carrying a pitcher of water on his shoulder—a divinely lustrous god in human form—Mahapurna was delighted. Words in praise of God spontaneously came out of his mouth:

> You are by nature powerful, magnanimous, good, guileless, pure, gentle, compassionate, sweet, sedate, impartial, blessed, beholden and a nectar-ocean of all auspicious qualities.[1]

Gradually Ramanuja came near. In joy, Mahapurna did obeisance to the lotus feet of God with the hymn:

> Salutation again and again to You who are beyond speech and mind; salutation again and again (to You) the only ground of speech and mind; salutation again and again (to You) of infinitely great superhuman powers; repeated salutation to the only ocean of boundless mercy.[2]

1. *Stotraratna*, 18. See Appendix B.   2. id., 21.

He chanted a few more hymns of Yamuna. Ramanuja stood motionless, like a portrait drawn on canvas, and listened intently to the chanting of the hymns.

Then, very politely and in very sweet words, he asked the adorable and aged Sannyasin, 'Sir, who is the composer of these incomparable hymns? I salute him again and again. And you too have made this morning propitious for me; for, hearing these sacred verses from your pure mouth, I deem myself blessed. I salute you.'

Mahapurna said, 'These slokas were composed by my master, Sri Yamunacharya.'

Hearing the name of Yamunacharya, Ramanuja asked with concern, 'Sir, I heard that the Maharshi was ill. Is he better now? How long is it since you left the blessed shade of his feet?'

'Right now I am coming straight from him. He had just recovered when I took leave of him,' replied Mahapurna.

'May I know what brought you here, Sir?' Ramanuja enquired. 'Pray, where do you intend to take your alms today? If there is no objection, do kindly make this humble one blessed by taking alms at his house.'

'Who is more blessed and fortunate than he of whom Maharshi Yamunacharya is thinking? O noble one, to you alone have I come at the behest of my master,' replied Mahapurna.

'That godly man has remembered one like me, meaner than the meanest!' Ramanuja exclaimed in wonder.

'My master wishes to see you,' informed Mahapurna. 'For that alone he has sent me to you. His health has been much impaired by the repeated attacks of illness. For the present, he is a little betted. So, if you wish to fulfil his desire, you should start immediately for his darsan.'

Ramanuja's joy knew no bounds at this happy news. He said to Mahapurna, 'Please wait a little; I shall place this pitcher of water in the temple and join you. We shall then set out for Srirangam.'

So saying, Ramanuja hastened towards the temple. Mahapurna was surprised to witness Ramanuja's natural and deep devotion to Yamunacharya. He thought himself blessed for having conversed with this pure-souled devotee and sang:

> May I be born even as a worm in the family of those who are attached only to the delight of servitude to You, but let me not be born even as the four-faced Brahma in the family of those who are otherwise disposed.[1]

Presently Ramanuja returned. He came ready to start on the journey. Mahapurna asked,' Should you not send word to your home? Should you not make arrangements for the smooth running of the house during your absence?'

'First obedience to the behest of God and His devotees, then household duties. I am eager to see Sri Yamunacharya. Let us start right now,' replied Ramanuja.

Mahapurna was overwhelmed with joy to hear these words. With deep love he embraced Ramanuja warmly. Very eager as they both were to see the great soul, they began to walk very fast towards their destination. During daytime they would take alms and after nightfall would rest on the verandah of someone's house. In this way they arrived at Tiruchirappalli on the bank of the Kaveri in four days. Without any delay they crossed the river and were about to proceed towards the Math situated near the temple of Sri Ranganatha. Just then, seeing a great crowd in front of them, they asked, 'Well, why such a crowd?' Someone answered, 'Sir, I don't know what to say. The earth has been deprived of its most precious ornament. Mahatma Alavandar has attained the supreme abode of the Lord.' Hearing this Ramanuja fell down unconscious and Mahapurna began to wail aloud, beating his forehead with his palm: 'Ah, my Lord, to deprive a slave of yours like

1. *Stotraratna, 55.* See Appendix B.

this! Is this why you sent me to Kanchipuram?' A short
while after, when he regained a little composure, he looked
at Ramanuja who was lying unconscious on the ground.
Controlling his own grief a little he then fetched some water
and sprinkled it over the young man's face. When he slowly
opened his eyes, he heard these words of consolation, 'My
child, what can you do? What was to happen must happen.
All is but the will of Narayana. The great man for whose
passing we are grief-stricken,—he said, 'All is but for
the good.' He told us ever to obey the will of Narayana.
Let us go and have the last darsan of that pure form, before
it is interred.' Gaining self-control, Ramanuja followed
Mahapurna. They saw the noble one in eternal sleep.
Mahapurna fell at his feet and began to wash them in
his tears. Ramanuja stood still. Tears rolled down from his
eyes.

With fixed gaze Ramanuja began to see that supremely
pure and blessed form of the greatest among the Vaishnavas.
The face was full of serene beauty. No black shadow of death
had fallen on that pure frame. Ramanuja, with his eyes
transfixed, kept gazing on that great one, as if the two were
exchanging thoughts. All stood mute; no one in that great
crowd uttered a word. With amazement, they beheld the
communion of the living with the dead.

After a while, Ramanuja asked, 'I find that the three
fingers of the Maharshi's right hand are folded and clenched. Were they like that during his lifetime?' The disciples
who were close by said, 'No, his fingers used to remain
straight. We cannot guess why they are so now.' On hearing
this Ramanuja declared aloud:

Remaining always in the fold of Vaishnavism, I shall protect
the people deluded by ignorance, bestowing upon them the
five samskaras, making them versed in the Dravida Vedas
and devoted to the religion of surrender (i.e., by making them
refugees of Sriman Narayana).[1]

---
1.   अहं विष्णुमते स्थित्वा जनानज्ञानमोहितान् ।

As soon as he declared this, one of the fingers became straight. Ramanuja declared again:

Taking into consideration all the interpretations, I shall, for the well-being of the people, write the *Sri Bhashya* which will usher in good and establish the knowledge of Reality.[1]

As soon as he said so, another finger relaxed and got straightened. Ramanuja said again:

In order to pay off the debt to that gracious Muni Parasara, who out of compassion wrote the gem among the Puranas (*Vishnu Purana*) in which he clearly lays down the nature of Isvara, jivas, the world and the way of their progress— I shall name one greatly learned Vaishnava after him.[2]

No sooner had he said so than the remaining finger relaxed and became straight. All were exceedingly amazed to witness this. It was clear that this young man was going to hold the position of Alavandar in times to come.[3]

पञ्चसंस्कारसंपन्नान् द्राविडाम्नायपारगान् ।
प्रपत्तिधर्मनिरतान् कृत्वा रक्षामि सर्वदा ॥

Prapannamritam, ix. 68 (second half), 69.

1. संगृह्य निखिलानर्थान् तत्त्वज्ञानपरं शुभम् ।
    श्रीभाष्यं च करिष्यामि जनरक्षणहेतुना ॥

    ibid. ix. 71 (second half)-72 (first half).

2. जीवेश्वरादीन् लोकेभ्यः कृपया यः पराशरः ।
    संदर्शयन् तत्स्वभावान् तदुपायगतीस्तथा ॥
    पुराणरत्नं संचक्रे मुनिवर्यः कृपानिधिः ।
    तस्य नाम्ना महाप्राज्ञवैष्णवस्य च कस्यचित् ।
    अभिधानं करिष्यामि निष्क्रयार्थं मुनेरहम् ॥   *ibid. ix.* 74, 75, 76.

3. According to a slight alteration in the version, the three vows taken by Sri Ramanuja on this occasion were: (1) to show gratitude to Vedavyasa and Parasara by giving those names to suitable persons, (2) to pay a tribute of love to Saint Nammalvar by arranging for a commentary to be written on the Alvar's hymns *Tiruvoymoli* and (3) to bring out a Visishtadvaitic commentary on the *Brahma-sutras.* All these vows were fulfilled by him in his later days.— *Ed.*

Before the body was interred in the grave, Sri Ramanuja set out for Kanchipuram. When the disciples of Alavandar requested him to visit Sri Ranganatha, he replied, in tearful pique, 'I don't want to see that cruel God who did not fulfil my cherished desire and who has taken away the idol of my heart.' After saying so, Ramanuja, absorbed in his own thoughts, started for his place without casting a look towards anyone, and without heeding any request. From that day on, the lingering smile on his naturally bright face disappeared. He reached Kanchipuram in due time.

The thoughtful seriousness of a grown-up took possession of him in place of boyish fickleness. He spent most of his time in solitude. He would not speak any more with his wife so open-heartedly, always trying his best to avoid her company. He found some joy only in the company of Kanchipurna.

11

Initiation

About six months before this mishap, Ramanuja had had to undergo another severe mental agony. Kantimati whose life was centred in her son Ramanuja, shook off her body and rejoined her husband. Rakshakambal, wife of Ramanuja, now became the mistress of the house. Very beautiful to look at and devoted to her husband, she had greater devotion to the observance of external cleanliness and ritual. But she took care to please her husband as far as possible by service and attendance.

Rakshakambal was not happy at heart, because of Ramanuja's utter indifference towards his household duties since his return from Srirangam. But she tried hard to keep her innermost feelings a secret. She gave no expression to the anger flaming in her heart.

Ramanuja spent most of his time in the company of Kanchipurna. His face was ever serious, his mind unhappy. Seeing his plight, Kanchipurna once told him,. 'My child, be not afflicted in mind. Be devoted to Sri Varadaraja. Continue to serve Him, as you have been doing, by fetching water for His worship. By His grace great good will follow. When the mission of Alavandar was over, he attained eternal peace at the lotus feet of Sri Vishnu. Now exert yourself to fulfil what you promised before him.'

'Please make me your disciple,' Ramanuja supplicated. 'Allow me to be at peace in the shadow of your feet.' So saying, he prostrated himself on the ground.

'Don't you be so restless,' said Kanchipurna picking him up. 'You are a Brahmana. I am a Sudra. A Sudra has no authority to initiate a Brahmana or to receive his prostrations. The blessed Narayana will before long send an

appropriate Guru for you. Have no worry.' So saying,
Kanchipurna proceeded towards the temple.

Ramanuja thought within himself: 'Taking me to be an
unworthy aspirant, he is refusing to bestow his grace upon
me. However, I shall purify my soul taking the leavings of
his meal. What is caste or sect to him who communes with
Sri Varadaraja day and night? A glance of his can transform
a pariah into one greater than a Brahmana.' So thinking,
he called on Kanchipurna in the evening and after much
importunity persuaded him to agree to have a meal with
him the following noon at his house. While accepting the
invitation, Kanchipurna said, 'Tomorrow I shall sunder the
veil of Rajas and Tamas by taking food from a great devotee
like you. Ah me! My great good luck!'

Back home, Ramanuja asked his wife to cook nice things
the next morning; for he had invited Mahatma Kanchipurna
for dinner. After getting up very early in the morning and
finishing her bath, Rakshakambal began cooking. Before
the sun was quite up, she had prepared rice and various
curries. Ramanuja was very much pleased to see this, and
set out towards Kanchipurna's Ashrama for fetching him for
dinner.

The servant of Varadaraja, on his part, came to know
of Ramanuja's intentions and, reaching his home by another
way, said addressing Rakshakambal, 'Mother, today I have
to go to the temple very quickly. Be pleased to serve this
son of yours with whatever you have cooked by this time.
I can't tarry a moment. Where is your husband?'

'Revered Sir, he has gone to your house to fetch
you. He will return right now; please wait a little,' said
Rakshakambal.

'No mother, I can't wait a moment,' Kanchipurna said.
'I can't neglect the service of the Lord in order to gorge
my stomach.'

At this Rakshakambal arranged a seat and drinking
water without a word, lest the guest should go away un-

served; and then, serving item after item, fed the invited
guest with great care. After he had finished his meal,
Kanchipurna himself threw away the leaf-plate at a great
distance, cleaned the place with cowdung-water,[1] took some
spices, and after prostrating himself on the ground before
Rakshakambal, took leave. The housewife gave away the
remaining portion of the food to a Sudra, had the cooking
vessels cleaned, and after cleaning the kitchen, started cooking afresh for her husband.

Ramanuja returned home and found that his wife had
started cooking afresh after taking bath for the second time
and that not a particle of what was cooked already was to
be seen. In surprise he asked, 'Did Sri Kanchipurna come?
Why are you cooking again? Where are those things you
cooked in the morning?'

'Mahatma Kanchipurna came,' Rakshakambal replied,
'I requested him to wait for you; but he did not agree to wait
for a moment, as he had to go to the temple without delay
for the service of the Lord. So, without waiting for you, I
served him with all that I had cooked. After his meal was
over, he himself cleaned the place and I gave away the
remnants to a neighbouring Sudra woman and am cooking
for you again after due ablutions. How can I feed you with
the remains of what was served to a Sudra?'

Ramanuja, sorely grieved at this, said, 'Ah, you foolish
one! How could you behave towards Mahatma Kanchipurna
as you would towards a Sudra? I was not lucky enough to
partake of the Prasad of that great one. I am really very
unfortunate.' So saying, he slapped his head in despair and
sat down at the foot of a tree outside.

Kanchipurna, for his part, while fanning Varadaraja
addressed the Deity, 'O Lord, what kind of action is this of
Yours, pray? While I want to be left alone to pass my life in
serving You and Your devotees, You are making a 'big man' of
me! Ramanuja, the incarnation of Lakshmana, the younger

1. A sanctifying Hindu custom obtaining even today, specially
in rural parts.

brother of Ramachandra, prostrates himself before me. Eager to take the leavings of my food, he invited me today to his place. While I should worship You and Your devotees incessantly, I myself am going to be made an object of worship! Permit me to go to Tirupati and serve the Balaji[1] image of Thine.'

Varadaraja gave him leave. Kanchipurna went to Tirupati and spent six months there in serving Balaji. Afterwards, one day Lord Narayana told him, 'I am suffering from extreme heat in Kanchipuram. Why don't you go there and fan Me?' At this Kanchipurna came back to Kanchipuram.

In the meantime, on one oil-bath[2] day, when a Sudra servant, lean and emaciated, came to rub oil on Ramanuja's body, he was moved to pity at his sight. He said to his wife. 'If any cooked rice is left over from yesterday, please give it to this poor servant. It looks as though he has not had anything for the last three or four days.'

'There is no rice left. Wherefrom am I to get rice at this early hour of the morning?' replied the wife and left for taking her bath.

Ramanuja went into the kitchen and found that there was a large quantity of cooked rice left. He at once gave the servant all the rice and asked him to rub oil on his body after he had eaten it.

On hearing that Kanchipurna had returned from Tirupati, Ramanuja went to see him, and was extremely glad to meet him after such a long time. The two friends experienced supreme peace of mind at the sight of each other. After some talk, Ramanuja said to the servant of Varadaraja, 'Noble soul, a few doubts have been agitating my mind for long. If you will please remove those doubts after asking Sri Varadaraja, I shall attain peace. To whom but you shall I tell the tale of my woes?'

_____

1. The image of Lord Vishnu worshipped in the famous shrine of Tirupati.

2. In South India the time-honoured practice is to take a special weekly bath in hot water after anointing the body from head to foot with oil. This is what is known as oil-bath.

'I shall apprise the Lord of this,' replied Kanchipurna.

When Ramanuja went to Kanchipurna, the next day, the latter said, 'My child, last night Sri Varadaraja told me this for telling you:

1. I am the absolute Brahman, the cause of Prakriti which is the cause of the universe.

2. O large-minded one, the distinction between Jiva and Isvara is axiomatic.

3. Self-surrender (at the lotus feet of God) is the only cause of liberation of those who strive after final beatitude.

4. The liberation of My devotees, even though they fail to remember Me at the last moment of their life, is sure to take place.

5. As soon as My devotees give up their bodies, they attain the Supreme Object.

6. Take refuge in Mahatma Mahapurna who is endowed with all virtues! Go soon to Ramanuja and tell him what I have told you.[1]

On hearing this, Ramanuja began to dance like a mad man. He fell prostrate towards the temple of Varadaraja. The six doubts which had long troubled his mind were now destroyed altogether. He had told none of these doubts to Kanchipurna. This great man was really the mouthpiece of Varadaraja. Notwithstanding all remonstrances, he lay prostrate at the feet of this Mahatma. And after getting up, without returning home, he straightaway set out for Srirangam to have his initiation from Mahapurna.

---

1. अहमेव परं ब्रह्म जगत्कारणकारणम् ।
   क्षेत्रज्ञेश्वरयोर्भेद: सिद्ध एव महामते ॥
   मोक्षोपायो न्यास एव जनानां मुक्तिमिच्छताम् ।
   मद्भक्तानां जनानां च नान्तिमस्मृतिरिष्यते ॥
   देहावसाने भक्तानां ददामि परमं पदम् ।
   पूर्णाचार्यं महात्मानं समाश्रय गुणाश्रयम् ॥
   इति रामानुजार्याय मयोक्तं वद सत्वरम् ।

   Prapannamritam, x. 66, 67, 68, 69 (first half).

It so happened that, after the disappearance of Alavandar, no one else in the Math at Srirangam could explain the subtle import of the Sastras in such an exquisite manner. Tiruvaranga was in charge of the monastery. He was a great devotee well versed in the sacred lore; but he had not the old master's dexterity in expounding the scriptures. He passed most of his time in worship; his devotion to the Lord captivated all. Though anxious to obey the biddings of others, he by his godly nature, commanded the obedience of all.

Both married and unmarried devotees used to reside in the Math. The wives of the married ones stayed outside the monastery, in the city. Sometimes they would come to the Math to worship the devotees of the Lord. Those residing in the monastery used to pass the day in the worship of the Lord and in singing His name. Almost a year rolled off in this manner. Afterwards, one day when all the devotees had assembled at his request, Tiruvaranga addressed them, in the following words:

'Friends, it is one year today since Mahatma Yamuna-muni, who was our very life, attained the final beatitude. Since his disappearance no one could sing of the glories of God in such exquisite language or expound so well the subtle purport of the holy texts. Though that great soul had given the charge of looking after you to this insignificant servant of his, I realise that it is an extremely difficult task for one of so meagre strength. You may perhaps remember that, before giving up his body, the master wanted to see Sri Ramanuja of Kanchipuram and sent Mahapurna there to fetch him. It is that great man of pure Sattva, erudite, beloved of Kanchipurna and chosen by Yamunamuni himself, who alone is competent to bear this responsibility. Let some one among us go there and, after initiating him with the five purificatory rites (Samskaras), bring him here. He will propagate the doctrines of Yamunacharya through-out the land of Bharata. It is as if I see before me even now the scene of his taking vows and the slackening of the sage's fingers at the place of burial.'

The assembled devotees unanimously approved of his proposal. Mahapurna was commissioned for initiating Ramanuja and bringing him to Srirangam. He was told, 'If you find him reluctant for the time being to part from Kanchipurna, do not press him to come here. By the will of Sri Ranganatha, he is bound, to come here sooner or later. Teach him the Tamil Prabandhas so as to make him proficient in the lore. For this you may have to stay there for a year. Take your wife along with you. He need not be told that we have sent you there for fetching him here.'

Thus instructed, Mahapurna and his wife started for Kanchipuram. After travelling for four days, they reached the town of Madurantakam. In front of the Vishnu temple there is a very big lake. When he and his wife were taking rest on the banks of that lake, Mahapurna found that Ramanuja himself came and worshipped his feet. He was beside himself with joy. Locking Ramanuja in a warm embrace, he exclaimed, 'This is a most pleasant surprise, indeed! The grace of Narayana can accomplish anything. May I know what brings you here, my child.'

'Indeed, it is the supreme grace of Narayana,' said Ramanuja. 'It was in search of your lotus feet that I left Kanchipuram. Varadaraja Himself has selected you as my Guru. Be pleased to purify me by initiating me into spiritual life without any delay.'

'Let us go to Kanchipuram and perform the sacred ceremony in front of Varadaraja,' Mahapurna replied.

'Revered Sir, even a moment's delay I am unable to bear,' supplicated Ramanuja.

'A man may be asleep, taking food, moving on the road; he may be a young man or a boy,—death brings him under its control under all circumstances.'[1]

---

1. स्वपन्तं वापि भुञ्जानं गच्छन्तमपि वर्त्मनि।
    युवानमपि बालं वा स्ववशे कुरुते विधिः ॥

'You know death makes no distinction between timely and untimely. With what expectations I went with you to see Yamunamuni! But alas! The great Ordainer would not let me have my wish then. Why trust Him now? Hence, this very moment give me refuge in the shade of your feet, please.'

Mahapurna was glad beyond measure to hear these words full of the spirit of renunciation. He lighted a sacrificial fire under the spreading branches of the flowering and fragrant Bakula tree on the bank of the lake in front of Lord Vishnu, and placed in it two metallic seals. One was inscribed with the sign of the discus and the other with that of the conch. When the two seals got heated, Mahapurna, uttering the Vedic Mantras, pressed on Ramanuja's right and left arms the insignia of the discus and conch respectively. And at last, after meditating upon the feet of Alavandar, he uttered the Vaishnava Mantra in his right ear! Thus initiated, Ramanuja worshipped Mahavishnu and then started back to Kanchipuram accompanied by his Guru and his wife.

When Kanchipurna heard of the coming of Mahapurna, he went to meet him. There was great joy in the assembly of the devotees. At the request of Ramanuja, Mahapurna initiated Ramanuja's wife Rakshakambal too with the insignia of the conch and the discus. Thus both the husband and the wife, after being initiated by him, took the leavings of Mahapurna's meal. Ramanuja placed a half portion of his house at the disposal of Mahapurna for his residence and looked after all his comforts. And seated at the master's feet, he studied the Tamil Prabandhas every day.

12

Sannyasa

Six months passed by in this way. One day while both Mahapurna and Ramanuja were out on business, Rakshakambal was getting things ready for cooking at home. After making all preparations, she went to the nearby well to fetch water. In the meantime, the wife of Mahapurna too had gone to the same well to fetch water for cooking. Both of them lowered their pitchers into the well and began to draw them up by ropes after they were filled with water. While so doing, a few drops of water from the pitcher of Mahapurna's wife fell into that of Rakshakambal, who got wild with rage and said impudently, 'Have you lost your eyesight? Look what you have done by your carelessness. One pitcher of water is wasted. Do you think you can sit on my shoulders simply because you happen to be the Guru's wife? Don't you know to what superior lineage my father belongs? How can I use the water touched by you? But why blame you? Having fallen into the hands of this husband of mine, I have lost my caste and all.'

On hearing these harsh words, Mahapurna's wife, who was by nature calm and modest, begged pardon of her. Though she was deeply pained at heart, she restrained her feelings, and placing the pitcher on the ground, she cried silently. After a while, Mahapurna returned home. Seeing his wife in tears, he enquired and came to know everything. He said, 'It is no longer the will of Narayana that we should stay here. So He has made you hear unkind words through the mouth of Rakshakambal. Do not grieve. All that the Lord ordains is for our good. Let us without delay go to have Darsan of Sri Ranganatha. We have not worshipped His lotus feet for a long time. That is why He has spoken unkind words.'

So saying and without a word of anger, the great man immediately started along with his wife for Srirangam. He did not wait for Ramanuja; for when he remembered the lotus-feet of Sri Ranganatha, he had forgotten everything else.

After his initiation, all the mental troubles of Ramanuja disappeared. Sanctified by the five purificatory rites of Yajna, Ankana, Urdhvapundra, Mantra and Dasya-nama, he began to consider himself blessed. He had attained peace of mind by the grace of Mahapurna, his supreme benefactor. No wonder, he looked upon his Guru as Narayana Himself. He would never take his meal without first taking the Prasad of the Guru. After getting up from bed, he prostrated himself before him. Then after finishing his morning duties, he would sit at his feet and study the Tamil Prabandhas. Within six months, he completed the study of the following Prabandhas: 100 composed by Poigai; 100 by Bhuta; 100 by Pey; 473 by Periyalvar; 143 by Andal; 145 by Kulasekhara; 216 by Tirumalisai; 55 by Tondaradippodi; 10 by Tiruppan; 11 by Madhurakavi; 1,360 by Tirumangai; 1,296 by Nammalvar. In all, he studied with Mahapurna about four thousand supremely sacred verses, the *Nalayira*, which were filled with the sweetness of devotion, and had the power to destroy all afflictions. These hymns go by the celebrated name *Divya Prabandha.*

He had just finished the study of *Tiruvoymozhi* that day. So he went to the shop and purchased some fruits, betel-leaves, flowers, and a new cloth for offering to the Guru as respectful terminal fee. He came home with the resolution of worshipping the Guru and his wife with the sixteen articles (Shodashopachara). But on entering the Guru's quarters, he could find no one there. He searched everywhere, and finding no trace of them, enquired of a neighbour, who told him that Mahapurna had left for Srirangam with his wife. Anxious to know what might be the cause of such an abrupt departure, he went and asked his wife, who said, 'I had a quarrel with the wife of your preceptor this morning when we went to fetch water from the well. I did not say any very rude word. The great man was so much enraged even at that, that he left the place with his wife. I am told when one becomes a Sadhu, one sheds anger. It seems that he is a Sadhu of a new sort. Millions of salutations at the feet of your Sadhu.' On hearing this, Ramanuja could not control his anger. He cried out, 'O vile one, it is a sin even to look at your face.' So saying he walked towards the temple of Varadaraja, in order to worship the Lord with the fruits, betel-leaves, flowers and new cloth he had purchased.

Some time after Ramanuja had left, a lean and hungry Brahmana appeared at the door and begged some rice of the housewife. Rakshakambal had not yet recovered from the shock of her husband's words. She could not bear the oppressive heat of the hearth. Hence, she turned on the beggar with flaming eyes and cried out in a shrill voice, 'Get off. Go elsewhere. Who is going to give you rice here?'

Grieved at heart and cursing his lot, the poor Brahmana walked slowly to the temple of Varadaraja. On the way he met Ramanuja returning from the temple. Seeing the emaciated frame of the Brahmana, he asked, 'O Brahmana, it seems you have had no food today!'

'I went to your house and asked for food. But, your wife said 'No,' and I am still hungry,' replied the Brahmana.

'No, Sir, you are not to go back,' pleaded Ramanuja. 'Please go with me to a shop. I shall give you a letter, with some turmeric, fruits and betel and a new cloth. With these, you will go to my wife and tell her that you were sent from her father's house. Then you may be sure she will feed you with all attention.' So saying, he bought those things from the shop and handed them over to the Brahmana. Then, under the signature of his father-in-law, he wrote a letter in the following strain:

'My dear son,

My second daughter is to be married soon. Please, therefore, send Rakshakambal to my place along with this man.

If you have no pressing business there, then I shall be very happy if you too can come. If Rakshakambal cannot be sent your mother-in-law alone will have to bear the full brunt of looking after so many relations.'

With that letter, he sent the Brahmana to his wife. He went to her, handed over the letter and said, 'Your father has sent me here.'

Rakshakambal, filled with joy, received him with great courtesy and brought him water for bathing. In the meantime, Ramanuja too came home.

'Father has sent this letter,' said Rakshamhal very modestly and handed it over to him.

Ramanuja read it out to her and said, 'I have some urgent business on hand. I cannot now afford to go with you. Hence, you may go alone to your father's house with this Brahmana. If I finish my job, I too shall try to go there later on. Please convey my salutations to my father-in-law and mother-in-law.' Rakshakambal agreed.

After the meal, she bowed at the feet of her husband and set out for her father's place escorted by the Brahmana. And Ramanuja too left home and walked towards the temple of Varadaraja, praying, 'O Narayana, grant this servant of Yours refuge at Your lotus feet.'

Reaching the temple, he prostrated himself before Sri Varadaraja and submitted, 'My Lord, today I have become Yours in every way. Do please accept me.' So saying, he procured some ochre cloth and a staff touched by the feet of Varadaraja and went to the banks of the old lake in front of the temple. After ablutions, he ignited the sacrificial fire and therein made oblations of the desire for wealth and wife. At that time, Kanchipurna, as commanded by Varadaraja, addressed him as 'Yatiraja' (king among ascetics). He then accepted the triple staff (tridanda) of the Sannyasin as a symbol of keeping the body, mind and speech under control. Yatiraja, dressed in shining robes, now appeared as effulgent as the newly risen sun.

13

Yadava Accepts Discipleship

Ramanuja took Sannyasa after getting rid of his wife through a little dissimulation. Many may think that this was not right on his part. But it has been said:

> Wealth should be preserved for warding off calamity; the wife should be protected even by losing that wealth; the Self should be always preserved even by losing the wealth and the wife.[1]

In obedience to this dictum he renounced his wife for the preservation of the Self. But one may say that it was not proper on his part to mislead his wife in that fashion. In some exceptional cases, it has been argued it is not wrong to tell a lie. It is futile to try to make a dunce understand that the sun is stationary and the earth is revolving around it. So they say:

> One must bring under control an ignorant man by speaking in favour of his views and an erudite one by telling the truth.[2]

Sri Chaitanyadeva informed his mother Sachidevi alone and not Vishnupriya about his intended renunciation of hearth and home. The great Sakyasimha stole away from home, like a thief. He did not let his beloved wife know anything of his inner feelings. Both Vishnupriya and Gopa (Yashodhara) were exemplary in their devotion to their husbands. Yet, infatuated by selfishness they wanted to keep all to themselves the two great souls who were the

---

1. आपदर्थं धनं रक्षेत् दारान् रक्षेद्धनैरपि ।
   आत्मानं सततं रक्षेत् दारैरपि धनैरपि ॥

   Mahabharata: Udyoga Parvan, xxxvii. 18.

2. मूर्खं छन्दानुवृत्तेन याथातथ्येन पण्डितम् ।

   Hitopadesa, Section IV, 106 (second half).

135

common treasure of all, and who were born for the good of all. Then, Rakshakambal was not quite so devoted a wife. Thrice she failed to carry out the behest of her husband. Ramanuja could not have divulged his inner feelings to her. A proud, self-seeking woman wishes that her husband should always remain engaged in her service rather than in the service of God. Ramanuja tried hard to sow the seeds of devotion to God in the heart of Rakshakambal; but seeing that the soil was barren, he waited for the time when he could help himself and her by parting from her. He knew that tears alone could wash away the sands of selfishness from her heart and hence his renunciation of hearth and home. As a result of this, on the one hand his mind, so eager to serve God, could remain blissfully absorbed in His meditation day in and out; on the other, the tears of repentance would moisten and fertilize Rakshakambal's heart. So Ramanuja did nothing wrong in taking Sannyasa in the manner he did.

What was the tradition that Ramanuja followed in adopting the fourth Ashrama? He did not follow the Advaitic tradition; for, from his student days, he had differed over that doctrine with Yadavaprakasa, his own Guru. He did not accept as his Guru any Sannyasin of the Order of Sri Sankara. The Eternal Lord Varadaraja Himself became his Guru; single-minded and spontaneous devotion to the Lord was the reason for his taking Sannyasa. Immersed in single-minded meditation on God, it became difficult for him to pay any heed to household affairs. Hence, he may be called a Sannyasin of the path of devotion.

All were surprised to hear of his Sannyasa. The wife was youthful, and endowed with exquisite beauty, and he himself was quite young and extremely handsome. Many took him to be insane, but some began to compare him with the incarnations of God. From all directions people poured in to see him. The inmates of the monastery of that place made him their head. His personal endowments and erudition were well known. So, by ones and twos disciples began to gather round him. One Dasarathi, a nephew of his, was the first to take initiation from him. Versed in the Vedas and the Vedanta, he was devoted to Vishnu. A large-hearted young man by name Kuranatha or Kuresa, of the lineage of Harita, became his second disciple. The power of his memory was incomparable; he would never forget anything he had once heard. When, Ramanuja, wearing the Urdhvapundra and seated along with these two disciples, discussed the scriptures with visitors, the sight was uniquely beautiful.

One day, when the old mother of Yadavaprakasa came to have the Darsan of Sri Varadaraja, she saw Ramanuja at the Math. Captivated by his gracefulness and scholarship, she thought within herself that if her son were to acknowledge the discipleship of this magnanimous person, he would surely know supreme peace. Yadavaprakasa knew no peace of mind ever since he behaved in that treacherous manner with Ramanuja. And his mother knew it. Viewing the divine greatness of this young Sannyasin, she considered him as a manifestation of Sri Varadaraja Himself, and was convinced that if she could bring Yadavaprakasa to the feet of this high-minded person, it would do her son supreme good. Returning home, she expressed her feelings and importuned her son to act accordingly. Yadava, of course, would not dream of becoming the disciple of his own disciple. But he found no peace in this wrong decision. While absent mindedly loitering about, he suddenly came across Kanchipurna and asked him, 'Sir, my mind is restless. Please tell me how this could be remedied. You are the mouthpiece of Varadaraja and so all-knowing.'

'Go home today,' replied Kanchipurna. 'I shall tell you something tomorrow, after knowing the truth from the Lord.'

The next day, Yadavaprakasa heard from Kanchipurna of the uncommon greatness of Ramanuja and of the benefits that could be derived by accepting his discipleship. Yadava then resolved to see Ramanuja at the monastery and have a discussion on the scriptures with him. He wanted to make sure that he was not acting like a fool. The previous night he was told in a dream by some divine being to become a disciple of Ramanuja. And the same words he heard again from the lips of Kanchipurna! But he was not the man to be beguiled by what he heard in a dream or from some other person. So after lunch he went to the monastery, and was really charmed to see the transcendental effulgence of Ramanuja. Yet, who could easily place on the seat of the Guru him whom one has known as a disciple?

Seeing Yadavaprakasa, Ramanuja offered him a seat with great reverence. He was very much pleased at this courtesy. After some general conversation, Yadava said, 'My child, I am very much pleased with your scholarship and modesty. I notice, you have worn the Urdhvapundra and have been stamped on your arms with the insignia of the lotus and the discus, which indicate that you think the worship of Saguna Brahman alone to be proper. Well, can you show any scriptural sanction for that?'

Whereupon Ramanuja said, 'This Kuranatha is highly intelligent and has all the Sastras by heart. Please ask him. He can easily cite authority.'

As Yadava cast his glance at Kuresa, he said, 'Revered Sir, the authority of the Sruti is the best. So I will cite from the Sruti at the outset:

> The best among men wear the pure insignia of Vishnu's lotus and discus on their arms to cross the ocean of Samsara. Some wear those ancient insignia on the body.[1]
>
> Fire is pure; He is as beautiful as the thousand-petalled lotus. The lotus is like a circular instrument. He whose body has been burnt by the application of the said instrument heated red in fire has attained the state of the ultimate

---

1. प्र ते विष्णोर ब्जचक्रे पविन्ने जन्माम्भोधिं तर्तवे चर्षणीन्द्रा: ।
    मूले बाह्वोर्दधतेऽन्ये पुराण लिंगान्यंगे तावकान्यर्पयन्ति ॥

From *Rig-Bashkala-sakha* as quoted by Vedanta-Desika in his *Saccaritraraksha.*

absorption of soul in the Divine Essence and hence the right to live in Brahmaloka.[1]

Like those who go to the abode of Vishnu, being marked by the insignia of discus etc., we too shall be impressed by the emblems of Vishnu and gain affluence here and hereafter.[2]

The Brahmanas, particularly the Vaishnavas, should wear the marks of the conch and the discus as they do the sacred thread.[3]

He who for the good of himself, wears the insignia (Urdhvapundra) resembling the footprint of Hari with an orifice in the middle becomes a favourite of the Paramatman, virtuous and liberated.[4]

'Learned Sir, now I shall cite from the Srutis again to prove that Brahman is Saguna (with attributes):

Who (He) is all-wise and omniscient.[5]

He is endowed with various highest powers. Knowledge, strength and action are His natural attributes.[6]

---

1. पवित्रमित्यग्निः । अग्निर्वै सहस्रारः । सहस्रारो नेमिः ।

   नेमिना तप्तनुर्ब्रह्मणः सायुज्यं सलोकतामाप्नोति ।

From *Sama-Veda* as quoted by Vedanta-Desika in his *Saccaritra-raksha.*

2. एभिर्वयमुरुक्रमस्य चिह्नैरङ्किता लोके सुभगा भवामः ।

   तद्विष्णोः परमं पदं येऽधिगच्छन्ति लाञ्छिताः ॥

From *Atharva-Veda* as quoted by Vedanta-Desika in his *Saccaritra-raksha.*

3. उपवीतादिवद्धार्याः शङ्खचक्रादयस्तथा ।

   ब्राह्मणस्य विशेषेण वैष्णवस्य विशेषतः ॥

From *Vayavya Upa-Purana* (a section of *Brahmanda Samhita)* as quoted by Vedanta-Desika in his *Saccaritra-raksha.*

4. हरेः पदाकृतिं आत्मनो हिताय मध्ये च्छिद्रमूर्ध्वपुण्ड्रम्

   यो धारयति स परस्य प्रियो भवति स पुण्यवान् भवति स मुक्तिमान् भवति ।

From *Atharva-Veda* as quoted by Vedanta-Desika in his *Saccaritra-raksha*

5. यः सर्वज्ञः सर्ववित् ।   *Mundakopanishad,* I. 1. 9.

6. परास्य शक्तिर्विविधैव श्रूयते स्वाभाविकी ज्ञानबलक्रिया च ।

                                              Svetasvatara Up., VI. 8

He is devoid of any trace of sin; decrepitude, death, bereavement, hunger and thirst are not there in Him. Whatever He desires and determines never come to be false.[1]

Narayana is the Supreme Brahman. He is the Ultimate Reality.[2]

All these are nothing but Narayana Himself.[3]

He alone is free from blemish; is sinless, without change, without name, pure and revealer of everything.[4]

Narayana alone was. Then none of Brahma, Siva, Earth, Sky, Stars. Water, Fire, Death or Sun was there.[5]

We also read in our devotional literature:

Hari (Vishnu) is the Supreme Refuge, Hari is the Supreme Refuge. I say repeatedly, Hari is the Supreme Refuge.[6]

Thus Kuranatha continued to cite many a passage from the Vedas, Puranas and epics. Yadava was dumbfounded at the torrent of scriptural testimonies pouring forth from his mouth. And, even before this, he had felt drawn by their grace and modesty. Besides, remembering his previous outrageous behaviour, the words of his mother, and the wish of Sri Varadaraja spoken by Kanchipurna, he could not hold himself any more. All on a sudden he fell at

1. अपहतपाप्मा विरजो विमृत्युर्विशोको विजिघत्सोऽपिपासः

संत्यकामः सत्यसङ्कल्पः ॥   *Chandogya Up.,* VIII, 7. 1.

2. नारायणः परं ब्रह्म तत्त्वं नारायणः परः ।

Taittiriya Narayanopanishad, 93.

3. नारायण एवेदं सर्वम् ।   *Narayana-atharva-sira-upanishad,* 2.

4. निष्कलङ्को निरञ्जनो निर्विकल्पो निराख्यातः

शुद्धो देव एको नारायणः । *ibid.*

5. एको वै नारायण आसीत् । न ब्रह्मा नेशानो नेमे द्यावापृथिवी

न नक्षत्राणि नापो नाग्निर्न यमो न सूर्य इति ।   *Mahopanishad,* 2.

6. हरिः परायणं परं हरिः परायणं परम् ।

पुनः पुनर्वदाम्यहं हरिः परायणं परम् ॥

Hari-bhakti-suddhodaya, III. 52.

the feet of Ramanuja and, though prevented, clasped his feet firmly and said while weeping, 'O Ramanuja, you are really the younger brother of Sri Raghava. Blinded by nescience, I could not see the truth about you. Please pardon my offences. Be you my helmsman and save me from this terrible ocean of the world. Here I take refuge in you.'

Ramanuja, unable to bear this sight, instantly picked him up from the ground and embraced him and removed all disquiet from his mind.

After getting his mother's permission that very day, Yadavaprakasa took Sannyasa from his former disciple and considered himself blessed. Being purified by the five purificatory rites such as the wearing of the Urdhvapundra, Ankana and Dasyanama, he put on the ochre garment. And on being given the name 'Govinda Jeer' by his Guru, he experienced supreme bliss. His old aversion to the path of devotion was utterly gone. All his pride of erudition disappeared also. He became a different man altogether. His once dry eyes were now flooded day and night with tears of repentance. Instead of pride, humility now filled his heart. He became a really devoted Vaishnava. Seeing this superhuman power of Ramanuja, even those who had spoken ill of him now acknowledged him as an incarnation of God. The aroma of his fame spread far and wide. Noticing the change in his former Guru, Ramanuja told him one day, 'O large-hearted one, your mind has become free of dross. To wash out the sins of the past, you may write a work on the Vaishnava religion, delineating the duties of a real Vaishnava. Then you shall attain perfect peace.'

According to his behest, Yadava wrote in a short while the incomparable work, *Yatidharmasamuccaya*, and offered it at the lotus feet of his Guru. He was above eighty at that time. A little later, he ended the play of his earthly life.

Sri Ramanuja, now without a rival, began to reign supreme in the realms of devotion and scholarship.

❧

14

Ramanuja's Brother Govinda Accepts Vaishnavism

In truth, after the demise of Yamanucharya, the monastery at Srirangam was without a leader, so to say. Mahapurna and Vararanga were no doubt worthy disciples of that peerless Mahatma, but they and other disciples sorely missed the great soul, who knew the meaning of all the Sastras and was full of love for God. But in their hearts they cherished the fervent hope of filling the void. From the lips of their Guru they had all heard great praise of Sri Ramanuja. He repeatedly told them that Ramanuja was an Avatara-purusha. Mahapurna was commissioned to bring him to Srirangam. And this great devotee stayed at Ramanuja's house for a long time and made him highly proficient in the Tamil Prabandhas. But now Mahapurna had returned to Srirangam along with his wife. As he left Kanchi quite suddenly, he could not bring Ramanuja along with him. In the meanwhile, when he heard that his godly disciple had taken Sannyasa, his joy knew no bounds. At once he hastened to the shrine of Sri Ranganatha resting on Ananta and prayed with folded hands: 'O Protector of the helpless, Perfect One, Supreme Brahman, You bring about the perfection of all. Deign to bring Ramanuja to Your feet and fulfil our great want.'

When he prayed thus, his voice choking with emotion, he was commanded by the Lord Himself thus: 'Mahapurna, My child, send Vararanga who is an adept in divine songs to Varadaraja, the Lord of Kanchipuram, who is very fond of music. When He is pleased to grant a boon to the singer, let him beg for Ramanuja. Without His permission, Yatiraja will never leave the precincts of His lotus feet.'

Thus commanded, Mahapurna sent Vararanga to Kanchipuram without any delay. There, Vararanga so pleased Sri Varadaraja with his songs that when he begged for Ramanuja, the Lord granted his prayer, though He found it very difficult to bear the separation of His beloved devotee. When Vararanga brought Ramanuja to the feet of Sri Ranganatha, great was the joy of the pure-minded Vaishnavas and all the citizens. Sri Ranganatha bestowed on him two mystic powers, the power to assuage maladies of the sufferers and to protect the devotees of God. Endowed with these two mystic powers, Yatiraja began to shine with celestial beauty. Vaishnavas who came in numbers from distant places considered themselves supremely blessed by touching his feet. On hearing his exposition of the glories of Lord Vishnu, all knew him to be the ideal Vaishnava.

At this time, Ramanuja's mind grew restless for his dear cousin Govinda, who had saved him from the murderous plot of Yadavapraka; whose simplicity, devotion to God, and erudition captivated his fellow-students and his own preceptor; and whose love made Siva accept his service in the form of Banalinga. He was anxious to make his dear friend a sharer in his divine bliss. He thought how he could bring him down from Kalahasti. After some time he remembered that Sri Sailapurna, the great Vaishnava, was living in Sri Saila—not very far from Kalahasti—in the service of the Lord. If Govinda could be brought to the Vaishnava fold by him, then his purpose would be fulfilled. He wrote a letter to Sri Sailapurna, on receiving which that great devotee at once set out and encamped with his disciples beside a large lake near Kalahasti.

Govinda used to come there every day to bathe and gather flowers. When as usual he went there one day, he found a Vaishnava—white-bearded and of divine beauty—discussing Sastras with a number of disciples. Intending to hear what he said, he climbed upon the adjoining Patali tree to pluck flowers, and from what he heard of his talk, a great devotion towards that Vaishnava arose in his mind.

When he was proceeding for ablutions after getting down from the tree, Sailapurna addressed him thus 'Mahatman, may I know for whose worship you are picking flowers?'

Hearing that he was doing so for the worship of Siva, he said, 'Good Sir, how could those enjoyable things like flowers be dear to one who has earned the name Vibhutibhushana by smearing Himself with the ashes of all desires, which he burned down knowing them to be the root of all the miseries of the world, and who has made the cremation ground His home, being mad for the love of Narayana? These flowers shine well only at the feet of the beginningless Vishnu, who is the natural repository of endless auspicious qualities, from whose supremely pure heart-lotus was born this Samsara, the holy abode of all Jivas from Brahma to the blade of grass. I am surprised to see that you, an intelligent person, have picked flowers for the worship of Siva.'

'Revered Sir,' replied Govinda, 'what you have said may be true; but I have great doubts in this matter. By the service of the Lord, we do good only to ourselves; no good whatsoever is done to Him by that. What can we give unto Him, who is the ordainer of the entire universe? He already possesses everything. What things can Sankara, who is the source of supreme good and the image of calmness, who saved the entire world by drinking off the poison Himself, desire from His own servant? Devotion is the only thing that is dear to Him. He wants nothing else from us. When we worship His lotus feet with flowers sprinkled with sandal-paste, our devotion increases; hence the necessity of worship.'

'Mahatman,' said Sailapurna, 'I am pleased with your devotion and humility. What you said is true. Who can give anything to Him, who possesses all and is the Lord of all? Nothing but self-surrender can be done unto Him who in the form of a Dwarf destroyed the pride of munificence

of Bali, the king of the demons. This absolute self-resigna-
tion is the supreme worship. Through the strength of this
alone he has made a captive of God in the form of a Dwarf.
Behold this sport of God. You will be deprived of that sweet
elixir if, instead of worshipping playful Hari, you worship
Sankara, who is averse to play. Apart from that, you were
born of a Vaishnava family; so you should follow the
Vaishnava religion alone. Remember the words of the Lord:
"Better is death in one's own Dharma; the Dharma of
another is fraught with fear." [1]

'Revered Sir,' Govinda replied, 'why are you making a
difference between Hari and Hara? The devotion like that
a Ghantakarna[2] is never commendable; such is the verdict
of the Sastras.'

Every morning they would exchange words like this.
At last Govinda embraced the Vaishnava faith. Sailapurna
gave him initiation. After his initiation, Govinda went to
Ramanuja and continued to live with him.

In South India, the quarrel between the Vaishnavas
and Saivas is an every day affair. After seeing or addressing
a Vaishnava, a Saiva takes a bath to deem himself pure and
vice versa.[3] The root cause of this seems to be that, bent upon
practising steadfast devotion, many have gone to deplorable
lengths. The vision of God cannot be had without steadfast
devotion. This can be easily understood by reading the story
of Upamanyu in the *Mahabharata*:[4]

> Upamanyu was the son of a Rishi. One day while playing with
> his younger brother and children of other Rishis, he noticed
> the milking of a cow and at the sight there grew in him a
> desire to take milk-rice. Back home, he asked for milk-rice

---

1. स्वधर्मे निधनं श्रेय: परधर्मो भयावह: ॥   *Gita, III. 35 (second half).*
2. See Appendix A.
3. It may be said with some gratification that today, more than
half a century after this was written, the relation between the two
communities stands much improved, thanks to various wholesome
forces.—*Tr.*
4. Vide: Anusasana-Parvan, Chapter XIV.

from his mother. Though there was no milk at home, out of affection, the mother served him rice mixed with decoction of pasted rice and said that it was milk-rice. Missing the sweet taste of milk in that, he said, 'Mother, it is not milk-rice. I took milk with my father at a sacrificial ceremony. Ah, how sweet was that! This is not like that.' 'My child', said the mother, 'wherefrom shall we poor ascetics get milk? If you desire to take milk-rice, take refuge in Sankara, the Lord of all creatures, the God of gods. Through His grace one attains the four main objects of human pursuit, viz., virtue, wealth, enjoyment and liberation.' 'Where could I meet that Sankara,' enquired eager Upamanyu, 'and how does He look?'

'My darling,' replied the mother, 'one can see Him face to face by practising austerity in the deep forest. The entire universe itself is His manifestation. He rides on a bull; white is His body; and He is gracious-looking. Just by seeing Him you will know that He is Sankara, for He is self-revealed. As the sun reveals itself and the universe simultaneously so too He reveals Himself to His devotees.' Hearing this, Upamanyu at once took his mother's permission and after worshipping her feet left for the forest. He sought out a quiet, lonely spot having a supply of clean water and passed a year in severe austerity. Pleased with his single-mindedness, the God of gods appeared to him, assuming the form of Indra mounted on the Airavata and said, 'I am Indra, the king of gods. Pleased with your austerity I have come to grant you boons. Ask for the boons you desire.'

'O king of gods! 'said Upamanyu, 'I have been practising austerity with the desire of having the vision of Siva. I do not ask for a boon from anyone but Siva. My salutations to you; be pleased to go back to heaven. I am ready right now to be transformed into a tiny worm or a tree with many branches at the command of Sankara, the Lord of created beings; but I do not desire to get the sovereignty and the wealth of the three worlds through the grace of anybody else. I am ready to become a worm or an insect at the behest of Sankara; but, O Indra! I do not desire the sovereignty of the three worlds given by you.'[1]

1.   पशुपतिवचनात् भवामि सद्यः कृमिरथवा तरुरप्यनेकशाखः ।
अपशुपतिवरप्रसादजा मे त्रिभुवनराज्यविभूतिरप्यनिष्टा ॥

                    Vide: Anusasana-Parvan, Chapter XIV. 176.

अपि कीटपतङ्गे वा भवेयं शङ्कराज्ञया ।
न तु शक्र त्वया दत्तं त्रैलोक्यमपि कामये ॥   *ibid.* 182.

When, by thus putting him to test, the Lord or all creatures was convinced of the single-mindedness of his devotion, He appeared before him in His world-bewitching form and granted him the cherished boon. What is more, he blessed him with immortality, eternal youth and omniscience.

From this story one can easily appreciate the power of single-minded devotion. In the epics and legends, one comes across many tales like this. The devotion which is required for the worship of the formless, omnipresent, and indwelling Spirit of all is called the 'Jnanamisra-bhakti' (knowledge mixed devotion). That intense ardour which one feels to know about the essential nature of Him, who is the creator, sustainer and destroyer of the universe, is known as knowledge-mixed devotion. The Vedas and other Sastras have originated from Him and He is to be known through them alone. When one devotes oneself to meditative life while practising the study of the scriptures, austerity, purity, contentment, continence, and steadfastness in truth, in course of time one's delusion is removed and one feels oneself blessed by realizing God.

The devotion to God with attributes is of another type. It is known as 'Suddha-bhakti' (pure devotion). This 'Suddha-bhakti' is of two kinds, 'Vaidhi' and 'Raganuga'. The Bhakti (devotion) which gets unfolded through worship with various articles, Japa, Homa, and meditation, practised according to the injunction of the scriptures, is known as Vaidhi'. When this 'Vaidhi' devotion is inspired by deep love, it is known as 'Raganuga'. As this devotion develops, God appears to be dear and near. The devotee regards Him as his master, son, friend, or sweetheart. There is no greater devotion than this, the supreme state of which is known as Prema. When the heart of the devotee is illuminated by love, he gets the vision of the Chosen Deity. Yasoda is the ideal of the attitude of parental love; Maruti of the attitude of a servant; the boys of Vraja of the playmate; and the Gopi-maidens of the sweetheart. Through the strength of this love and devotion, God, who is omnipotent, omnipresent,

Existence-knowledge-bliss Absolute, assumes human form and acknowledges dependence on the devotee as a son, master, playmate, or lover. Single-mindedness and intense stead-fastness alone constitute its life-force. If the Sadhaka devotee is to become blessed, then he must control the vagaries of his mind and be absorbed in the contemplation of the Lord of his heart alone. This is the only way to attain the goal through love and devotion.

Owing to ignorance, people of one sect think that to hate another sect and subject its people to oppression constitute a part of their religion. Bhagavan Sri Ramakrishna realised and taught that religions are but different paths leading to the feet of God. It is the duty of the followers of the Sanatana-dharma to remember the words of Sri Krishna in the *Gita*:

> In whatever way men worship Me, in the same way do I fulfil their desires; it is My path, O Son of Pritha, that men tread in all ways.[1]

This is the significance of the teaching of Sri Ramakrishna. Now one may ask, if all religions are true, whether one may achieve the end by adopting any religion. In answer to this, Sri Ramakrishna says, like Sri Krishna, that observance of one's own religion is the duty. Through that alone one can reach the goal.

To make this easily comprehensible, he gives an illustration:

> A man is digging a well. When he has dug to a depth of ten cubits, another man comes and says, 'Why are you toiling in vain? You are not going to get water here even after you have dug a hundred cubits. Come, man, I shall point out another spot.' Accordingly the digger begins his work at the spot shown by him; but not a drop of water is to be seen even after digging twenty cubits. In the meantime another person appears and says, 'Brother, who has given you the foolish

---

1.   ये यथा मां प्रपद्यन्ते तांस्तथैव भजाम्यहम् ।
      मम वर्त्मानुवर्तन्ते मनुष्याः पार्थ सर्वशः ॥   IV. 11.

advice to dig here? Dig a whole lifetime here, yet there is hardly any chance of getting a little drop of water. Come, I am going to show you a fine spot, where you will succeed with but very little effort.' In pursuance of his words, he begins digging at the spot shown by him. The well has been dug thirty cubits, but where is water? At last, driven to despair and repeatedly cursing his own fate, the man desisted from digging. All was only fruitless labour. Had he done the digging of all these sixty cubits at a single spot, undoubtedly his toil would have borne fruit.

The same too is the law for striking the well-spring of religion. If one holds fast to one faith, in time, one will achieve one's end through that alone. It is good to take recourse to one's own religion (Svadharma), for that being ingrained in one's nature, one can easily make progress by that. But to single out blemishes in another's religion in order to follow one's own is small-mindedness. Out of pride and delusion, mean people deny efficacy to any sect but their own. These bigots are the cause of all the troubles in the world. How then should a sincere seeker after religion behave?

In reply to this Sri Ramakrishna says: 'Just as the daughter-in-law of a house respects and obeys her father-in-law, mother-in-law, brother-in-law and others, yet remains most intimately associated only with her own husband, so also a really spiritual man regards and recognises all other religions; but his relation with his own religion is a special one, which he cannot have with any other. By so doing alone, he will attain pure devotion (Suddha-bhaki), through which he will realize God and become blessed.'

It was only to get unfolded this single-minded, steadfast devotion in the heart of Govinda through the observance of his own religion (Svadharma) that Ramanuja made him re-adopt the Vaishnava faith through the good offices of Sri Sailapurna. Boundless was his joy to have Govinda by his side. Before long he plunged his friend in the nectar-ocean of bliss. The divine beauty of Sriman Narayana, the concentrated form of all that is beautiful in the entire universe, very soon dawned in Govinda's heart, purified through love and devotion.

The Srirangam Math became, as it were, the gate of heaven whence were sprinkled the waters of peace on countless afflicted souls. How intensely Sri Ramanuja yearned to do good to the Jivas, is well illustrated by the incident which follows.

15
Goshthipurna

After coming to Srirangam, Ramanuja was satisfied to look on Mahapurna as his Guru, and he thereby forgot the sorrow caused by the passing away of Sri Yamunacharya. By his own behaviour Ramanuja set an example of the conduct of an ideal disciple, as embodied in this dictum: None else but he who holds his body, wealth, knowledge, raiment, activities, merits and life for his Guru is a real disciple.[1]

Ramanuja, who was indeed such a disciple, studied the *Nyasatattva, Gitarthasangraha, Siddhitmya, Vyasasutra* and the *Pancharatragama,* under Mahapurna. Captivated by his student's incomparable genius, Mahapurna placed his own son Pundarika as a disciple under Ramanuja. To Ramanuja he said, 'My child, at some distance from here there is a prosperous town called Tirukkotiyur or Goshthipura, where lives one Goshthipurna, a very pious scholar. It will not be an exaggeration to say that in this part of the country there is not another Vaishnava like him. If you aspire to learn the Vaishnava-mantra with its meaning, none but he can teach it to you. Go and receive the Mantra from him without any delay.'

Thus advised, Ramanuja at once went to Goshthipura and met Goshthipurna. When, after worshipping his feet, Ramanuja submitted his petition, the latter said, 'Come another day, I shall see.' At this Ramanuja became dejected and returned to his own place. After one or two days Goshthipurna came to Srirangam for the worship of the Lord on the occasion of the great festival there. Tradition says that one of the priests of Sri Ranganatha told him at the behest of the Lord Himself, 'Give the Mantra with its

---

1. शरीरं वसु विज्ञानं वासः कर्मगुणानसून् ।
   गुर्वर्थं धारयेद्यस्तु स शिष्यो नेतरः स्मृतः ॥

   Prapannamritam, XXVII. 40 (second half), 41 (first half).

meaning to Ramanuja, for he is the most worthy to receive it.' At this Goshthipurna replied, 'O my Lord, You Yourself made the Law that, this is never to be spoken by thee to one who is devoid of austerity or devotion, nor to one who does not render service, nor to one who cavils at Thee.[1] Purity of mind cannot be attained without doing tapas for some time. How is it possible for the impure mind to have the power to hold the Mantra? 'At this the reply came, 'Purna, you do not know his purity. You will be able to know afterwards that he is the saviour of all humanity.'

Ramanuja came again and approached the feet of Goshthipurna, but did not succeed. In this way he was refused eighteen times. So he concluded that there must be some serious impurity in him, by reason of which this greatest among the Gurus was not bestowing his grace upon him. And he began to shed tears in utter dejection and despair. When some people informed Goshthipurna of this, pity moved his heart. He sent for Ramanuja and gave him the sacred eight-syllabled mantra with its mystic meaning and said, 'None but Sri Vishnu is aware of its glory. I know you to be a worthy recipient, and so I have given you this. I don't find a second person worthy of this in this Kali Yuga. Whoever hears this will, after his death, attain liberation and go to Vaikuntha. So, do not give it to anyone else.'

Sri Ramanuja was exceedingly glad to hear the words of the Guru. The desire of his heart was fulfilled. Through the power of the Mantra he attained the knowledge divine and his face shone with an unearthly beauty. Having attained supreme peace, he considered himself blessed. He prostrated himself again and again at the feet of his Guru and deemed himself the most fortunate among men.

He took leave of his Guru and proceeded towards Srirangam. All on a sudden a strange feeling arose in his mind. As he walked towards the high gates of the Vishnu

---

1. इदं ते नातपस्काय नाभक्ताय कदाचन ।
   न चाशुश्रूषवे वाच्यं न च मां योऽभ्यसूयति ॥ *Gita*, XVIII. 67

temple of Goshthipura, he invited whomsoever he met on the way with the words, 'Please come near the temple. I will give you a priceless jewel.' Attracted by his joyous countenance, his eager words, and his effulgent beauty, men, women and children followed him spellbound, as it were. Gradually a rumour spread in the town that a prophet had descended near the temple and was giving away to men whatever they wanted. Within a short time a large number of men and women of the town and the suburbs assembled there. At the sight of this vast congregation of people being swept by the wave of joy, the boundless ocean of love in Ramanuja's heart swelled and heaved. He shared his joy with the two disciples, Dasarathi and Kuresa, who had come there, by embracing them. Then he climbed to the top of the temple tower and in a mighty voice addressed the gathering:

'Brothers and sisters, you that are dearer to me than my life, if you want to get liberation from the torments and afflictions of this world for ever, then pronounce three times along with me the gem of the Mantra which I have procured for you. Do this and be blessed.'

At this all spoke out in a chorus, 'Please tell us the Mantra; make us blessed; we are ready.' Then Ramanuja,—the incarnation of Lakshmana, the only knower of the innermost feelings of the heart of Yamunamuni, the master of both the superhuman powers (Ubhaya-vibhutipati), the dispeller of afflictions, the beloved of all people, the ocean of the milk of kindness, the sun that destroys the darkness of despair—pronounced, in a stentorian voice from the depths of his joyful heart, the great Mantra 'Om Namo Narayanaya' (Om, Salutation to Narayana). This great assemblage received the Mantra as eagerly as hungry men receive a dole of food, and pronounced it all together in a thunderous voice. They uttered the Mantra twice more in unison with Sri Ramanuja and then all became quiet. At that time, the earth appeared like Vaikuntha!

The faces of the children, men and women, were all flushed with joy. It seemed as if all misery had left the earth forever. Those who came with the hope of gaining money or fulfilling their worldly desires, forgot all about it and the world. In their joy, they felt like one who suddenly got a diamond, having come to gather pieces of glass. As the crowd began to melt away, men and women prostrated themselves towards Ramanuja in profound thankfulness and took leave of him deeming, themselves blessed. Ramanuja then got down from the temple tower along with his disciples and proceeded towards Goshthipurna's residence with the intention of worshipping the redeeming feet of the Guru.

In the meantime, Goshthipurna had come to know of what Ramanuja had done and he grew extremely angry. When Ramanuja along with his two disciples approached him, he cried out in a shrill voice unable to control his rage: 'Off with you, you vilest of men! I have committed a great sin in entrusting the precious gem to an untrustworthy man like you. Why again have you come here to plunge me in the great sin of looking at your face? A devil like you will find it hard even to get a place in the purgatory.'

Without being in the least frightened, but with great humility, Ramanuja said: 'Mahatman, it was only because I was ready to suffer in hell that I transgressed your behest. According to your words, whoever might hear the said Mantra is sure to attain the highest end of life. Depending on that assurance, I have placed all the men and women of the city on the high road to liberation. All of them will be blessed by attaining the supreme goal of life. If an insignificant creature like me goes to hell and thousands of men and women are thereby enabled to go to Vaikuntha, this is a consummation that I, earnestly pray for. I have transgressed your behest, no doubt. May hell be mine for it. But as assured by you, may these thousands of suffering people attain the highest thereby! What could be more propitious and profitable than this?'

Just as all people are frightened when a mass of black clouds gathers overhead and it thunders and lightning flashes, but all fears vanish giving place to delight when a moment later a strong wind blows hard and clears the sky of the clouds—likewise all became alarmed at the sight of the angry Goshthipurna emitting fiery words, but when the closely reasoned and sweet words of Sri Ramanuja rendered the countenance of his Guru free of the slightest trace of anger, they regained peace of mind. On realising his own narrowness and the supreme magnanimity of Ramanuja, Goshthipurna embraced him in deep devotion. All who saw it were filled with joy and astonishment at the sudden transformation they witnessed and stood like painted figures, unable to utter a word. Goshthipurna then addressed Ramanuja with folded palms, 'O magnanimous one! from today you are my Guru and I am your disciple. Undoubtedly, he whose heart is so vast, is born of the part of Vishnu, the Father of the worlds. I am a common creature. How can I grasp your greatness? Pardon my offence.'

Clasping the feet of his Guru, and with his head bent low in modesty, Ramanuja said, 'O high-souled one! you are my eternal Guru. The Mantra has attained such high sanctity only because it emanated from your blessed mouth. Charged as the Mantra was with the power of your illumination, it has enough efficacy to save all humanity; already today miseries of hundreds of men and women were burnt down. Though I have committed the sin of transgressing the behest of the Guru, I have become eternally blessed by receiving your embrace, which even the gods might envy. My most earnest prayer is that, regarding me as your son, your servant, you may grant me sanctuary at your blessed feet for ever.'

Supremely pleased with Ramanuja's sweetness and humility, Goshthipurna entrusted to him his son Saumya-narayana as his disciple. With the permission of his Guru, Ramanuja along with his disciples started for Srirangam. After this incident, all began to look upon him as the incarnation of Lakshmana himself.

❈

16

Ramauja trains his Disciples and himself receives training from his Gurus

Returning to the monastery at Srirangam, Ramanuja, the chief among ascetics, stayed there for a few days. When, at that time, his disciple Kuresa expressed his eagerness to know the mystic meaning of the supreme sloka,[1] he said, 'Well, Kuresa, my Guru Sri Goshthipurna has advised me thus in this matter: 'To him alone, who, free of the taint of egotism and observing continence, will attend on his Guru for one year in a spirit of service, you may communincate the significance of the verse, and to none else.' If you spend a year in this way, I shall give you the interpretation of the verse.'

'Magnanimous Sir,' said Kuresa, 'life is uncertain. How should I know that I shall live a year more? Please, therefore, deign to make me competent to receive the interpretation of the verse even now.'

'It is laid down in the Sastras,' said Yatiraja, 'that one who fasts for a month attains the merit of observing Bramacharya for a year. Live one month on alms along, for living on alms and observing fast are the same.' By so living for a month, Kuresa gained the interpretation of the verse.

His second disciple Dasarathi too approached him for the mystic interpretation of the supreme verse. To him he said, 'My child, you are my relative, born of a good Brahmana family. So it is my wish that you receive the

---

1. Sri Krishna's supreme counsel in the *Gita* (XVIII. 66):

सर्वधर्मान् परित्यज्य मामेकं शरणं व्रज ।
अहं त्वा सर्वपापेभ्यो मोक्षयिष्यामि मा शुच: ॥

Relinquishing all Dharmas take refuge in Me alone; I shall liberate you from all sins; grieve not.

mystic interpretation from Sri Goshthipurna. Though
there may be many faults in you, I won't see them because
you happen to be my relative. Do what I have told you.'
Dasarathi was a great Pundit, and of that perhaps he was
a little proud. That was why Yatiraja directed him to receive
the interpretation from Goshthipurna.

As directed by Ramanuja, Dasarathi went to Goshthipurna. But even after he had been with him for six months,
Goshthipurna did not bestow his grace on him. At last out
of pity one day he addressed him: 'Dasarathi, you are my
relative and a great scholar; I know all that. But know for
certain that scholarship, wealth and birth in a good family
can bring pride in small-minded men alone. In a virtuous
man, these, being the causes of self-control, bring good
qualities, not blemishes. Understanding this fully well, take
refuge at the feet of your own Guru. He himself will give
you the interpretation of the verse.'

Thus instructed, Dasarathi hastened to Ramanuja
without any delay and reported all that had happened. At
that time, Attulai, the daughter of Mahapurna, reached
there and spoke to Yatiraja thus: 'Dear brother, my father
has sent me to you. I shall tell you the reason at length;
please listen to me. I have just come today from my father-
in-law's house. There, I have daily to fetch water for cooking,
both in the morning and the evening, from a far-off lake.
It is an impassable and lonely road; so fear and physical
exertion overwhelm me. On my submitting this to my mother-
in-law yesterday,—let alone her sympathising with me—
she, in a frenzy of extreme wrath, said,' Could you not bring
a cook from your father's house? I don't command such
means to employ a servant so that I may keep you sitting
idle with one leg upon the other.' Greatly aggrieved at
this and all the time weeping, I came away to my father and
told him everything. He said, 'My child, go to Ramanuja,
your spiritual brother. He will do what should be done about
it.'

Accordingly I have come to you. So tell me what I am
to do now.'

'Dear sister, grieve not,' said Ramanuja. 'Here I have
a Brahmana whom I am sending along with you. He will
do for you the work of fetching water from the lake and
cooking.'

So saying he glanced at Dasarathi. Knowing the wish
of the Guru, Dasarathi gladly followed Attulai to her father-
in-law's house and did the work in the kitchen with much
care and devotion. Six months passed in this manner.

One day, a Vaishnava was expounding a verse from a
scripture and the assembled people were intently listening
to him. Dasarathi too was present there. On hearing the
exposition of the verse, he saw that the exponent had fallen
into a dangerous error and that the listeners believed in his
interpretation. So he could not help contradicting the
exposition. At this, the expounder angrily ejaculated, 'Stop,
you fool, where is a jackal and where is heaven! For a cook
to speak on the scriptures! What authority have you to
speak on the Sastras? Go to the kitchen to demonstrate your
talents.'

Without feeling hurt in the least at this, Dasarathi, a
great soul as he was, went on calmly expounding the verse.
His exposition was done with such grammatical precision
and in such beautiful diction that all were captivated, and
the exponent himself begged pardon by touching his feet and
asked, 'Why this profession of a servant for a profound
scholar like you?'

He replied that he had become a cook to carry out
the command of his Guru. When they came to know that
he was Dasarathi, the great scholar-disciple of Yatiraja, in
a group they went to Srirangam and supplicated, 'O
Mahatman worthy to be remembered at dawn every day! It
is not needed any more that your worthy disciple be kept
employed as a cook. He has not the slightest trace of
pride in him. He is a veritable Paramahamsa. Please give

orders so that in great honour we may bring him to your feet.'

Yatiraja was so greatly pleased with their words that he himself went along with them, and after embracing Dasarathi affectionately, gave him his blessings. After he was brought to Srirangam, Yatiraja gave him the esoteric interpretation of the supreme distich and thus made him blessed. Dasarathi achieved his end through the service of the Vaishnavas; so he is renowned by the name Vaishnava-dasa.

After this, in obedience to the behest of Mahapurna, Ramanuja studied again the Tamil Prabandhas under Sri Vararanga. When he had finished this course, Goshthipurna came to Ramanuja accompanied by Maladhara, a disciple of Yamunamuni, and said, 'My child, he is a great scholar and a disciple of Yamunamuni, our Guru. He knows the meanings of *Satharisukta*, the 'Thousand Songs' of Sathari, profoundly well. Learn all this from him and become blessed.'

And so did Ramanuja according to the word of his Guru. It so happened one day that some interpretation of Maladhara did not seem quite proper to Ramanuja, who expounded the passage in a new way. The scholar, taking such conduct of the pupil to be audacity, left for his home. Coming to know of it, from hearsay, Goshthipurna went to Maladhara and asked, 'Could Ramanuja assimilate the entire meaning of the "Thousand Songs"?'

In reply to this, Maladhara narrated all that happened.

'Brother,' said Goshthipurna, 'don't take him to be an ordinary man. None of you or I know the core of Yamunamuni's thoughts so well as he does. The younger brother of Rama, Lakshmana himself, has incarnated as Ramanuja for the good of the Jivas. So, take his exposition to be the esoteric meaning coming out of the mouth of Yamunamuni himself, though you might not have heard it from his lips.'

Thus counselled by Goshthipurna, Maladhara again went to Ramanuja and continued teaching him. It so happened again another day that Ramanuja gave a different interpretation of a particular verse. But this time, instead of being annoyed, Maladhara listened to him attentively. He could never dream that even this verse could have such deep meaning. In great joy he circumambulated Ramanuja and prostrated himself before him. Maladhara then placed his son as a disciple under Ramanuja. After thus completing his studies of the 'Thousand Songs', Yatiraja resolved to learn the secrets of Dharma from Sri Vararanga. When Vararanga, the adept in divine songs, got tired singing and dancing before Sri Ranganatha, Ramanuja would remove his exhaustion and physical pain by massaging his feet and anointing turmeric powder on his body. Every night he would himself prepare condensed milk and serve that for his supper.

After six months had passed like this, Sri Vararanga cast his gracious look on him. One day when Yatiraja was massaging his feet, Vararanga said, 'My child, I know that you have been serving me with a view to take my all. Today I am much pleased with you. Come, I shall tell you my innermost feelings.'

So saying, he continued, 'My child, what you are doing is the supreme pursuit of man.

It is Guru himself who is the supreme Brahman;
Guru is the greatest treasure.
Guru is the highest among all desirable things.
He is the most secure refuge.
Guru is the embodiment of the knowledge of Brahman.
It is he who is the supreme goal.
He being your teacher, there is none greater than he.
Know that he is the means to realise God, and
God Himself too is he.'[1]

---

1.   गुरुरेव परं ब्रह्म गुरुरेव परं धनम् ।
      गुरुरेव परः कामो गुरुरेव परायणम् ॥

On hearing this esoteric truth, Ramanuja considered himself blessed. All the wants of his mind were removed. With all his desires fulfilled, Ramanuja now became full of supreme joy. In his great work *Gadyatraya* he gave some vent to that immense joy of his own heart. From this time onward, all began to worship him as Lord Ranganatha Himself.

Sri Vararanga had no issue. He had one younger brother, his dearest, by name Chotanambi. Him he made a disciple of Ramanuja. The great five—Kanchipurna, Mahapurna, Goshthipurna, Maladhara, and Vararanga—were the most intimate disciples of Yamunamuni. Trained by each and all of them, Yatiraja now became as it were the second manifestation of Sri Yamunacharya; for the great sage was present in five parts in his own five disciples. Now these five parts were made one in the frame of Sri Ramanuja. The abundance of superhuman powers manifested in Yatiraja is proof of that. He had the special power of seeing God face to face and talking to Him; what is more, he could draw afflicted souls—souls burnt in the flames of worldly miseries—to the feet of God and remove all their miseries. This is why he used to be called Ubhayavibhutipati.[1] The afflictions of even the most miserable souls would take to wings at the mere look of his lotus-face beaming with love.   ❋

गुरुरेव परा विद्या गुरुरेव परा गतिः ।

यस्मात् त्वदुपदेष्टासौ तस्मादगुरुतरो गुरुः ॥

उपायश्चाप्युपेयश्च गुरुरेवेति भावय ।

From *Satyaki Tantra* as quoted by Vedanta-Desika in his *Rahasyatrayasara*. Chapter XXVIII.

1. The tradition has it that Sri Ranganatha one day out of joy made Ramanuja the master of both the worlds (Ubhayavibhutipati)— the Leelavibhuti (this world) and the Nityavibhuti (the eternal world); so both were at his disposal and either could be conferred on any mortal by his sweet will.—*Ed.*

17

The High Priest of
Sri Ranganathaswami

As in South India the Muslim domination took place in a comparatively lesser degree, one finds here a larger number of temples than in the North. One might almost say that, compared with the South, the vast expanse of land at the foot of the Himalayas, served by the ancient Rishis and purified by the Ganga and the Sindhu, is devoid of temples.

But, even though this part of the land is gloriously rich in works of art and architecture, nonetheless, in comparison with the wondrous work of nature, the snowy mountain of lofty peaks, the resort of monks and ascetics, the glory of the South is like moonlight before the effulgence of the sun.

Be that as it may, if one wants to see the artistic skill of the ancient Hindus, one cannot possibly do better than go to the South, which was purified by the tears of Rama at the separation from Sita, the land which gave birth to the militia of Rama. Both in spaciousness and in height, the temples of this part of the country are mightily imposing. Sri Ranganatha's temple at Srirangam is so very spacious that the worshippers of the Deity live with their families within the walls of the temple itself. And their number is so great that, in order to maintain peace, police is housed on one side of the temple premises. On another side of its vast premises, there is a hall, the ceiling of which rests upon a thousand pillars. When the British and the French were engaged in war in South India, the entire French army took shelter in one corner of this big hall! From this one can easily guess the massiveness of the temple.

All the priests of the temple are subordinate to one high priest, according to whose directions all have to work. So he virtually reigns over all others. Though one comes across some very devoted souls among the priests, it cannot, however, be said that all the priests took to worshipping the Deity out of devotion to Him. In many cases the motive behind this service was money-making. This is why in society the priests were slighted as 'Devalas'.

The high priest who used to worship Sri Ranganatha at the time of Ramanuja was not a man of great devotion. He was a rich man who cared only for money. He was ready by hook or by crook to throw out any one who became an obstacle in the way of his making money. This high priest now found in Ramanuja such an obstacle. He noticed how the devotion and patronage of all people in Srirangam, high and low, was now going towards Ramanuja and not himself, and how people had come to look upon him as a manifestation of Ranganatha himself. He could not brook this inroad into the status and income he was enjoying as the high priest, and therefore began to think of ways and means of getting rid of this dangerous rival. After hatching a plan, he one day went to Ramanuja and invited him to take alms at his place. Back home, he said to his wife, 'Listen. I have invited Ramanuja for alms today. The idea of inviting this scoundrel is to poison him. If this wretch is allowed to live, we shall soon have to go about begging for a morsel of food. You know where the poison phial is kept. What more need I say? You are so clever; conduct the whole business cautiously.'

When with a smiling face she nodded understandingly, the gleeful priest kissed her and said, 'It is only through the grace of Sri Ranganathaswami that I could get a wife of your mental make-up. Today we shall get rid of this thorn. And then only we shall be able to sleep happily.' So saying, the wicked man went towards the temple.

At noon Yatiraja came to the house of the priest for alms. The wife of the priest received him with great courtesy, brought water for washing his feet, and after carefully wiping his feet with cloth, offered him a seat. The heart of this sinful woman was made of stone, as it were. Yet at the sight of the guileless face and transcendent beauty of Sri Ramanuja, she was filled with a motherly love so intense that when she appeared before him with the poisoned dish, she broke forth into tears unable to check herself and said, 'My child, if you want to save your life, go elsewhere and take your alms. If you take this food, you will die.'

On hearing this, Ramanuja sat for a time in a state of perplexity and thought within himself: 'What great harm have I done to the high priest that he should think of treating me so horribly?' Unable to decide anything, Ramanuja got up and proceeded towards the Kaveri with a vacant mind. It was nearing noon. The sands of the banks of the Kaveri were hot as fire itself. Seeing Goshthipurna before him on the banks of the river, Ramanuja went and fell prostrate on those hot sands at his feet, all the time weeping. After he had remained in that way for a long time when Goshthipurna himself raised him up from the ground[1] and enquired about the cause of his weeping, he narrated the whole story, and asked, 'O Master, I am weeping at the thought of the mental condition of the high priest. Tell me, how he could be freed from this great sin.'

'My child,' replied Goshthipurna on hearing all, 'when you long for the redemption of this sinful soul, then there is no more fear for him. Very soon he will relinquish evil ways and enter on the path of virtue.'

---

1. A very interesting variation of this is as follows: While Sri Ramanuja was lying prostrate on the burning sands for some time, Goshthipurna was only a silent spectator. But Kidambi Achan, a disciple of Ramanuja, enraged at the attitude of Goshthipurna, fulminated against his stony heart, and swiftly raised Sri Ramanuja from the ground. Looking at Achan with eyes beaming with approbation, Goshthipurna explained his apparently inhuman action by saying that he was simply looking for a person who truly loved Ramanuja, and immediately asked him to be Ramanuja's body-guard and cook food for him.—*Ed.*

The Guru and the disciple took leave of each other. On returning to the monastery, Ramanuja found a Brahmana waiting for him with various eatables. He took a little and distributed the rest among his disciples, and without telling anything about the day's incident to any one, continued to think of the priest and his welfare.

On the other hand, when, after returning home, the priest came to know that his wife had been unsuccessful in carrying out the plan, his perturbation knew no bounds. Considering that women's hearts are naturally soft, he excused his wife and instantly hatched another plan to achieve his end. Ramanuja was in the habit of going to the temple every day after dusk for the Darsan of Sri Ranganatha. According to his wont he went to the temple on that day too. The priest gave him the water that was used for the ablutions of the Deity. He drank it but understood that it was mixed with poison. But far from being frightened, he expressed great joy like one drinking something sweet and pure and addressing Sri Ranganatha said, 'O ocean of mercy! Great is Your affection for Your servant. How do I deserve this ambrosia? Blessed is Your grace.'

So saying, Ramanuja, mad with joy, went reeling out of the temple. The priest thought that the poison had begun to work on the victim and his steps were therefore faltering. His joy knew no bounds. He expected that on the next morning the smoke from his enemy's funeral pyre would rise in the sky. For, the poison which he had administered could promptly send ten stalwarts to the abode of death.

Instead of seeing smoke rising from the funeral pyre of Sri Ramanuja next morning, the high priest felt his heart pierced by a joyful chorus song[1] sung by a hundred voices and renting the sky. Rushing out of his home, he found that

---

1.   भज यतिराजं भज यतिराजं भज यतिराजं भवभीरो ।

O you scared of worldly existence, worship Yatiraja, worship Yatiraja, worship Yatiraja.'

Andhrapurna's *Bhaja-Yatiraja-stotra.*

all the men and women of Srirangam were singing this song and dancing around the person of Sri Ramanuja covered with flowers. From the two eyes of Yatiraja were flowing tears of joy. He had lost all outward consciousness, his mind and heart being given over to the lotus feet of the Lord. At the sight of his celestial beauty and superhuman lustre, the Sattva Guna in the heart of even that demon of a high priest came to life. Thinking about his own evil thoughts and regarding Sri Ramanuja as deathless even like the gods, he shot through the crowd and fell at his feet. All looked in wonder at the high priest. Weeping bitterly, the priest said, 'O Yatiraja, you are not a man; you are Vishnu Himself. You have assumed a body in order to destroy sinners like me. Why then delay, my Lord? Send me forthwith to the abode of Yama. I am the meanest among men, not fit to touch your feet. Inflict on me the due punishment for my dire sins and thus grant me expiation. Oh, refuge of the lowly! why any more delay? Throw me soon under the feet of an elephant or into raging fire. I do not desire to live a moment more.'

So saying he began to strike his head so hard on the ground that the place became soaked with blood. The people nearby tried hard to deter him. But he became all the more disconsolate and beat his breast until blood came out, and his entire body became smeared with blood. In the meantime, Ramanuja regained his consciousness and pacified him by placing his palm on his head. He said, 'Brother, do not behave in this inhuman manner. Sri Ranganathaswami has pardoned all your misdeeds.'

'So much of your grace even on such a depraved sinner like me!' exclaimed the astonished priest. 'Or it is natural for you to do so, as your form itself is made of mercy. To the vile Pootana[1] who sought to kill you by suckling you at her poisoned breast, you vouchsafed the same divine Abode as to your mother! Is it not then natural that

---

1. See Appendix A.

you should bestow your kindness on this murderous fellow too. O refuge of the lowly! This great glory of yours will be proclaimed by men for all times to come.'

Overwhelmed with affection, Yatiraja began to pass his hand over his body. By the touch of his blessed palm all the sufferings of the priest were removed. And a fiend though he was, he attained to divinity.

18

Yajnamurti

Yajnamurti, an all-conquering scholar from the South, returned home after defeating all the scholars of North India. He had taken Sannyasa on the banks of the Bhagirathi, and when he heard that one Vaishnava Sannyasin, Ramanuja by name, had been refuting the Mayavada and propagating his own views, he hastened to Srirangam. A cart, full of books, followed him; for he would not go anywhere without his books.

Appearing before Yatiraja, he challenged him for a discussion with him. At this Ramanuja, the very image of quietness, said with a smile, 'O Mahatman, where is the necessity for any wrangle? Here I accept my defeat at your hands. You are a scholar without a second. Victory follows you everywhere.'

'If you acknowledge your defeat,' rejoined Yajnamurti, 'will that mean that you are accepting the flawless Mayavada, relinquishing the illusory Vaishnava doctrine?'

'It is the Mayavadins themselves,' replied Yatiraja, 'who are made in the name of illusion. According to them arguments, reasonings, etc., are all Maya. How then can the doctrine of Maya be free from error?'

'Whatever is there within the jurisdiction of space, time and causation, all that is Maya,' Yajnamurti replied. 'This is why the Mayavadins say that before transcending these three, one can never reach the real truth. What we hold to be illusion, that very thing you call truth. So how could we be in error and not you?'

Thus the wrangle went on for seventeen days. On the last day, Yajnamurti refuted the arguments of Ramanuja. Sad at heart on account of defeat, Yatiraja returned to his own monastery. Standing with folded palms before the Deity in the Math shrine, he prayed:

'O Lord, those Vaishnava scriptures, which enabled the previous Gurus to attain your blessed lotus feet, have in course of time become wrapped in the cloud of Mayavada. With the help of their abstruse arguments, the Mayavadins are deluding themselves as well as the infatuated people. The network of their reasoning bewilders even the great Mahatmas. O Abode of Bliss! How long will You keep Your children away from the shade of Your blessed feet?'

So saying, Yatiraja began to shed tears. That night, he had in a dream the vision of Devaraja who encouraged him with the words, 'Yatiraja, be not anxious. The real .glory of the path of devotion will ere long be declared in the world through you alone.'

Up from bed in the morning, he felt great joy in his heart. After finishing his morning duties, Ramanuja walked to the monastery where Yajnamurti was staying. At the sight of the celestial lustre in Ramanuja's face, the Mayavadin was simply dumbfounded. He thought: 'Yesterday Ramanuja returned to his Math with a pale face. But today he is coming here like a god from the heavens. He comes here now, charged with some divine power. Futile it is to argue with him. It is better to take refuge in such a great soul. I have squandered my life in futile, dry reasoning. I have fattened my pride, and starved my heart. When purity of heart has not been achieved, the knowledge of Brahman is a far cry indeed. But how flawless is this great man! Wrath or pride cannot come near him. His face is beaming with some unspeakable transcendent beauty. Many harsh words I have used, but he is not enraged. Meantime, I have been scorched countless times in the fire of wrath and conceit. I shall atone for this sin of mine by becoming his disciple. I shall destroy my ego root and branch and strive to taste the elixir of purity.'

So resolved, Yajnamurti, fortunate as he was, saluted Yatiraja with great devotion by touching his feet. Being a little embarrassed by this, Yatiraja said,

'O Yajnamurti, does this conduct befit a great man like you? Why, again, are you delaying today to start the debate?'

'O large-hearted one!' replied the scholar, softened by modesty, I am no longer the wrangler who had tried in vain for so many days to pierce you with ironical words. I will argue no more with a magnanimous person like you. I stand here before you, your eternal slave. Be pleased to cast your gracious glance on me. I am your disciple. Illumine my dark mind with the light of purity. 'This Atman cannot be attained by mastering the Vedas; neither by intellect nor by much hearing.'[1] By indulging in the pride of erudition, I have only strengthened my ego. Kindly make this stupid servant of yours blessed by granting him refuge at your holy feet.'

Ramanuja was not surprised at this transformation of Yajnamurti; for he remembered the words of his Chosen Ideal, which he had heard at night in dream. He realised that it was by His grace alone that this overbearing Pundit had come to wear such celestial beauty, being adorned by the jewel of modesty.

He said in a soft, sweet voice, 'Blessed be the name of Sri Devaraja. His grace has melted even the stone! Yajnamurti, it is easy to give up all other vanities; but to get rid of the vanity of scholarship is not within human power. The grace of the Lord alone can make this impossible possible. By the power of that grace alone you have today got rid of pride, man's dire enemy. You are supremely fortunate.'

'When it was given to me to see such a magnanimous soul like you,' said Yajnamurti, 'I am indeed fortunate. Now, please order me what I should do. I am an ignorant child of yours.'

----

1.   नायमात्मा प्रवचनेन लभ्यो न मेधया न बहुना श्रुतेन ।

                                                    Katha Upanishad, II. 23

Yatiraja said, 'My child, it is said:

If an aspirant after perfect meditation is without sacred thread, all his actions will be fruitless; for him expiation is also prescribed. After receiving the sacred thread according to injunctions, he must observe Prajapatya (a kind of penance accompanied by regulated fasting) for six days with Gayatri. Till death he should not abandon sacred thread, the triple-staff, Kamandalu (water-vessel), strainer, loin-cloth and the waistband.[1]

'According to the above exhortation, your first duty is to put on the sacred thread.'

Yajnamurti instantly agreed to do that. According to the injunctions of the Sastras, he wore the sacred thread. Then after he had put on the Urdhvapundra, he was marked 'with the insignia of the conch and discus by Yatiraja. As he gained his illumination through the grace of Devaraja, he gave him the name Devarajamuni, and said, 'My child, now your incomparable scholarship, freed from the clouds of vanity, has gained a new charm. Engage yourself now in writing books of good counsel for the benefit of humanity.'

In obedience to his Guru's behest, Yajnamurti wrote two invaluable books in Tamil by name *Jnanasara* and *Prameyasara*, and became an object of everyone's affection. Ramanuja had a big monastery built for his stay.

A few days after this incident, four intelligent, quiet-natured, devoted young men, full of the spirit of renunciation, came to Ramanuja to be blessed with initia-

---

1. हीनो यज्ञोपवीतेन यदि स्यात् ज्ञानभिक्षुकः ।
   तस्य क्रियाः निष्फलाः स्युः प्रायश्चित्तं विधीयते ॥
   गायत्रीसहितानेव प्राजापत्यान् षडाचरेत् ।
   पुनः संस्कारमाहृत्य धार्यं यज्ञोपवीतकम् ॥
   उपवीतं त्रिदण्डश्च पात्रं जलपवित्रकम् ।
   कौपीनं कटिसूत्रश्च न त्याज्यं यावदायुषम् ॥

From *Vriddha-Jabali-smriti* as quoted by Sri Vedanta-Desika in his *Sata-dushanee*, Ch. LXIV.

tion by him. Yatiraja said to them, 'Go to Devarajamuni and become his disciples. He is a rare Pundit. But scholarship is not the only ornament he has; rarely does one come across one so full of devotion to God.'

Accordingly the four young men became the disciples of Devarajamuni. Far from thinking himself fortunate in thus being surrounded by disciples, he thought, 'What a new bother here again for me! When, with great pains, I have been struggling to rid myself of vanity, here comes again the idea of 'I-am-the-Guru' to make a fool of me!'

In his bewilderment, he appeared before his Guru and in great humility submitted, 'My master, I am, your child. Then why practise this cruelty on me?'

'Why, my child, what is the matter?' enquired Yatiraja.

'Revered Sir,' replied Devarajamuni, 'through your grace I have been trying to shake off the demon of vanity. Why, pray, again are you throwing this worthless fellow into the arms of vanity? Kindly do not ask me to become a Guru. I have not attained the detachment of a lotus leaf on water. Make me rather a servant of yours and grant me a little place by your side. I have no need for a new monastery.'

Greatly pleased with his words, Ramanuja embraced him warmly and said, 'My boy, I have done so only to test you. And you have passed the test. Stay by my side and pass your life in the service of Sri Devaraja, the tutelary Deity of the Math.'

Devarajamuni considered himself blessed to receive this order. He passed the remaining years of his life in the service of Sri Devaraja and Sri Ramanuja.

19

Yajnesa and Karpasarama

Ramanuja then began to teach his own disciples Nammalvar's Tamil Prabandha of 1,000 hymns, the *Sahasragiti*, which he had previously studied under Mahapurna and Maladhara. But, a superhuman genius as he was, to the amazement of his disciples, he very often began to give various new mystic interpretations. In one place of the Prabandha the glory of Sri Saila (Tirupati) is narrated as follows:

'This Sri Saila is as it were Vaikuntha on the earth. He who lives here throughout his whole life does verily live in Vaikuntha itself and in the end goes to Vaikuntha and finds refuge in the shade of the feet of Sriman Narayana.'

After finishing the study he asked his disciples, 'Who among you is prepared to go to Sri Saila, make a flower-garden and serve Srinivasa with flowers and live there till death?'

Anantacharya, a very quiet disciple, replied, 'My Lord, if you would kindly permit me, I shall go to the mount and make myself blessed.'

'You are indeed blessed, my child. You have become the cause of liberation for fourteen generations of your ancestors and progeny. And I too am blessed to have a disciple like you,' said Ramanuja, well pleased with the disciple.

After worshipping the feet of his Guru, Anantacharya proceeded towards Sri Saila.

After this Yatiraja studied thrice over the *Sahasragiti* with all his disciples. The study over, accompanied by his disciples, he started for Sri Saila. Singing the name of Hari served as their viaticum. On the first day of their journey they took rest after reaching Dehali, a town. Next day they walked towards a village called Ashtasahasra. In this village there lived two of his disciples, Yajnesa and Varadacharya. Intending to be a guest at the house of the former, a rich man, he sent ahead two of the disciples accompanying him to convey the news. When the two disciples hurriedly brought him the intimation, Yajnesa's joy knew no bounds. He at once ordered the inmates of his house to procure all things required for according a fitting reception to Yatiraja and himself entered the parlour for supervision, all the time totally forgetting to extend any service towards the two tired messengers. Being pained at such behaviour of the owner of the house, they returned to Ramanuja and reported all that had happened.

Extremely sorry to hear this, Yatiraja decided to be the guest of the other disciple named Varadacharya. This second disciple was poor and pure-natured like Vidura. Every morning he went out with a begging bowl in hand, and on returning home at noon from his round, worshipped Narayana with things got by begging. Thus he lived in perfect contentment with Lakshmi, his chaste, pious and exquisitely beautiful wife. Near about his house there were a few cotton trees and this was why people would jokingly call him 'Karpasarama'. When Ramanuja together with his disciples entered the house of Karpasarama as guests, the husband of Lakshmi was out on his round of begging. Finding there no male member in the outer apartments, Yatiraja went inside the parlour and announced his arrival. Wearing a torn rag after bath, Lakshmidevi was then drying her wet cloth spreading it in the sun. And so unable to appear in front of her Guru, she clapped her hands and thus apprised him of her state. Instantly Yatiraja threw in from outside his upper cloth. Covering herself with that, Lakshmi-devi came out in front of her Guru and was exceedingly delighted to see him. Even as one gone mad, she saluted him again and again, and said, 'Revered Sir, my husband has gone on his round abegging. Please, all of you, be seated comfortably. Please make me blessed by accepting this water for washing your feet. There is the tank in the front; please remove your weariness by taking your bath there. In no time I will prepare the offering for Sri Vishnu.' So saying she entered the room. But there was not a particle of rice in the store. She began to wonder what she could do then. How could she be blessed by serving her Guru?

In the neighbourhood there lived a wealthy merchant, who had become enamoured of the exquisite beauty of Lakshmidevi. He had tried, through woman messengers, to tempt her with money, but with no success whatever. Lakshmidevi now mused within herself: 'Why not I be blessed by serving my Guru, at the cost of this body of bones, blood and filth? It is said that a devotee by name Kaliyan served his Chosen Ideal by adopting the profession of a thief. God, being pleased with his service, said, 'Even sin committed for My sake amounts to an act of virtue,[1] Even an act of virtue done ignoring Me, amounts to a sin. Therefore, I shall now go to the merchant with the resolve 'I will fulfil his desire', and in return bring the things needed for entertaining the guests.' Accordingly, she went out of the house through the backdoor. She entered the merchant's big mansion with seven gates, crossed one door after another and then found herself in the private apartment of the owner. She saw him there and laid bare her heart in the following words: 'O merchant, tonight I shall fulfil your desire. My Guru and his disciples have been pleased to come to my house as guests. Send without delay to our house all things necessary for their entertainment.'

The merchant was surprised to hear this. What could be a greater wander! She, to win whom he had long attempted, she, whom he had given up as inaccessible, she had come to his house of her own accord! His joy was great.

1. मन्निमित्तं कृतं पापमपि पुण्याय कल्पते ।
मामनादृत्य तु कृतं पुण्यं पापाय कल्पते ॥
cf. a variant of the sloka, *Prapannamritam*, XXVII. 51.

And at once he sent various good things to his neighbour's house.

Lakshmidevi busied herself preparing offerings for Lord Vishnu out of those things. She then invited her Guru and the disciples for the meal. They took the good dishes with great relish and blessed her profusely for her hospitality.

On his return home from his begging, Karpasarama was overjoyed to see his Guru and his disciples actually at his own place. Afterwards, when he heard that his wife had accorded them a very fitting welcome and had provided them with various rich dishes, his surprise was very great indeed. He was a poor man. He could not make out whence his wife could procure the many things needed for such lavish entertainment. He went inside the house and asked her about it. Lakshmidevi told him all from beginning to end, and then with folded palms and downcast face, remained standing before her husband.

Far from being angry, Varadacharya danced with joy saying, 'O I am blessed, I am blessed.' Addressing his wife, he said, 'O faithful lady, today you have given the highest testimony of your chastity. Narayana in the form of the Guru is the only Purusha, and He is the husband of all Prakriti. What could be a matter of greater good luck than that you have in exchange of this body of flesh and bone been able to serve that supremePurusha? Oh, how fortunate am I! Who says I am poor? How fortunate is he who has a lady like you as his consort in Dharma!'

So saying he held her hands in his own and led her to the presence of his Gurudeva and remained prostrate at his feet for a long time. When humble Varadacharya apprised Yatiraja of his wife's action, Yatiraja and his disciples were surprised.

As enjoined by the Guru, the couple partook of the Prasada, rested for some time, and then carrying the remaining part of the consecrated food, both of them went to the merchant. Varadacharya remained outside, Lakshmidevi entered the room and entreated the merchant to partake of the Prasad. He accepted the consecrated food with great eagerness. After taking the Prasad, the merchant was a completely changed man. His sensual desires had completely disappeared from his mind. He regarded Lakshmidevi as his mother and said with tears, 'What a despicable act was I about to commit! As the hunter was turned to ashes when he went to touch Damayanti,[1] so I too would have met my doom; but through your great compassion I have been saved this time. O mother, forgive my many transgressions and make this beast a man. And, pray, make me blessed by showing me the lotus feet of your Guru.'

The lady was astonished and delighted at his words. All her troubles were now over. Witnessing this glory of her blessed Guru, her joy matched her devotion. When she recounted to her husband all that had happened, the poor but pure-hearted Brahmana also experienced the same joy. Both of them came to their Guru along with the merchant and prostrated themselves before him.

The disciples grew all the more devoted to Yatiraja after this manifestation of his boundless spiritual power. Sri Ramanuja touched with his blessed hand the Brahmana couple and also the merchant. This brought an end to all their miseries. When the merchant expressed a wish to become a disciple of his, Sri Ramanuja initiated him and thus made him blessed. With a view to making the Brahmana couple happy and secure, he entreated them to accept the huge amount of money given to him by the merchant. At this the poor Brahmana said with folded palms, 'Revered Sir, through your grace we have no want whatsoever. We are able to live by what we get by begging. Money is the root of all evil. It panders to the senses and draws the mind away from the lotus feet of God. Kindly do not order this servant of yours to accept money.'

Yatiraja was highly pleased with these words. He embraced this pure-hearted devotee and said, 'Today, I have

---

1. See Appendix A.

become pure by the touch of a Mahatma like you, so utterly desireless, so full of quietude.'

When every one present there was filled with this celestial joy, there came in Yajnesa, the wealthy disciple of Yatiraja. Having waited for his Guru at his house in great expectation, he became very much agitated when he learned at last that Yatiraja had accepted the hospitality of the indigent Karpasarama. In extreme excitement he thought: 'What offence have I committed that Gurudeva did hot accept my services? Some mistake must have been committed; otherwise, why should he, whose only aim in life is doing good to beings, forsake me and make some one else blessed? 'So thinking like one who had committed a crime, he came in a mood of depression before Ramanuja, and falling prostrate at his feet, began to weep. Yatiraja raised him up affectionately and said, 'My child, have you been mortified by my not becoming your guest? The reason was your offence to the Vaishnavas (Vaishnavaparadha). There is no greater Dharma than service to Vaishnavas. And in this you have failed. When my two disciples, tired and thirsty after their journey, communicated to you the news of my arrival, you gave them no water to wash their feet; you did not even ask them to take their seats. You were so thoughtless and discourteous. That was why I would not accept your services. And what heavenly dishes this indigent Brahmana has treated me with! Could I get such things had I become the guest of one like you, so vain of his wealth?'

Very much wounded at these words, Yajnesa said, 'O Gurudeva, this inhuman conduct of mine was not due to my blindness born of vanity of wealth; rather my exultation on hearing the news of your coming was responsible for it. I am indeed unfortunate.'

So saying, Yajnesa began to weep. Ramanuja consoled this repentant and simple-hearted devotee by promising to be his guest on his way back from Sri Saila.

❀

20

Seeing Sri Saila and
The Coming of Govinda

The next morning Ramanuja along with his disciples left the village Ashtasahasra for Kanchipuram. Reaching there at noon, they had the Darsan of Sri Varadaraja and considered themselves blessed. Then they met Kanchipurna and were much gratified. After a sojourn of three nights there, they went to the sacred Kapila Tirtha, where they finished their ablutions etc., and on that very day reached the foot of Sri Saila. At the sight of the Mount, Ramanuja's joy knew no bounds. For a long time he remained transfixed gazing at this Vaikuntha on earth, while tears of joy rolled down his cheeks. He thought: 'This is the holy place where Sri Hari Himself is residing along with His divine consort Lakshmi. Ah me! the heavenly beauty of this place! All the accumulated virtue of earth is here in the form of this hill. Upon this great mount of merit Narayana and Lakshmi are residing. I shall not defile it by climbing on it with this sinful body. I shall look at it from here and be blessed by thus purifying my body and mind.' Thus resolved, he stayed on at the foot of Sri Saila itself. Hearing of the coming of Ramanuja there, Vitthaladeva, the king of that part of the country, came to have his Darsan along with his courtiers. Yielding to his entreaties, the kind-hearted Yatiraja accepted him as a disciple after he had been put through the observance of the purificatory rites. As an offering to the Guru, Vitthaladeva made a gift to Ramanuja of a vast tract of land called Elamandiya, which in his turn Yutiraja gifted away to the poor Brahmanas.

In the meantime, all the Sadhus and ascetics of Sri Saila came o know of Yatiraja's presence there and were naturally very eager to see him. When they heard that for

fear of touching it with his feet, Yatiraja had resolved not
to climb the hill, they came in crowds to him and in, great
humility said, 'O pure-souled one, if great ones-like you do
not climb the hill for fear of touching it with their feet, then
common people also will behave in the same way. They will
say,' When such a pure soul as the great Ramanuja did not
climb the hill for fear of touching it with his feet, then what
of us?' Then even the priests too may not appear before the
Lord. Therefore, kindly make up your mind to climb the hill
without delay. Again, the hearts of great ones like you are
the real temples of Sri Hari. There He is being always
worshipped with the supreme nectar of devotion, which is
the only object dear to Sri Hari. Narayana is ever residing
in that heart where there is devotion. This is why
Yudhishthira says to Vidura:

> Revered Sir, devotees like you, themselves being holy,
> sanctify holy places with Vishnu dwelling in their heart.[1]

The places of pilgrimage attain purity only because
great ones like you go to them.'

Accepting these entreaties of the high souls as a
command, Ramanuja along with his disciples proceeded
to climb up the hill.

While climbing, he felt hungry and thirsty and became
tired. Presently there appeared the aged, serenely wise
Saila-purna, the great devotee, with Prasada and
Charanamritam (sacred water) of the Lord from the top of
the hill in his hand and entreated Yatiraja to accept them.
Seeing that this saintly person had carried the consecrated
food for him, Yatiraja exclaimed, 'O Mahatman, why have you
done this unbecoming act? How could a great teacher like you
take all this trouble for an insignificant servant like me? A
boy could have done it at your order.'

---

1. भवद्विधा भागवतास्तीर्थीभूताः स्वयम्प्रभो ।
   तीर्थीकुर्वन्ति तीर्थानि स्वान्तःस्थेन गदाभृता ॥

Srimad Bhagavatam, I. xiii. 10.

'Yatipati,' said Sailapurna, 'I too thought so and accordingly searched for a boy; but finding none less in attainments than I, I myself had to carry this.'

'Revered Sir,' said Ramanuja, exceedingly astonished at the humility of Sailapurna, 'today my inward eye has been opened. I am blessed to witness such humility.'

With a heart surging with intense devotion, he made obeisance at the feet of the illumined sage Puma, and then along with his disciples, partook of the Prasada, which served to remove the fatigue of travel. After some more climbing, they found themselves in front of the temple of Venkatanatha. Sri Anantacharya, one of his disciples residing at the Mount, came and prostrated himself before him. Ramanuja was very glad to see him and blessed him profusely. Then after circumambulating the temple he appeared before Sri Venkatanatha, the presiding Deity of the place, and while shedding tears of joy overwhelmed by love, he lost his outward consciousness. It took a long time for him to regain normal consciousness. With great reverence, the priests of the temple gave him the holy water and Prasada, which he shared with his disciples in great joy. Then he saw the other deities enshrined there and had ablutions in the holy lake. He felt very happy, and camped there for three nights.

In the meantime, Govinda, the most devoted disciple of Sailapurna and Ramanuja's own cousin, came and joined him. In great love and delight,, Yatiraja embraced his boyhood friend and the saviour of his life. It has been mentioned in an earlier chapter that after being reconverted to Vaishnava religion by Sailapurna, Govinda went to Ramanuja. While living there with him, Govinda felt so intensely the parting from his Guru that Yatiraja could rest only after sending him back to his Guru. From that time onward Govinda had been with Sailapurna. Intensely devoted to the service of his Guru, he was by nature as simple as a child.

Coming down from the top of the hill at the request of Sailapurna, Ramanuja lived at his house for a year.

Mahatma Purna would every day read the *Ramayana* with him, offering his own beautiful and profound exposition. During that one year he finished studying the entire *Ramayana* under the guidance of this great man and in so doing, deemed himself highly fortunate.

While residing there, he was much astonished on one occasion to observe Govinda's behaviour. He found Govinda arranging the bed of his Guru and then lying down upon it. Surprised and sorry, Yatiraja submitted the fact to Sailapurna. The latter at once called Govinda and asked, 'You lay down on my bed. But do you know what happens to one who lies on the bed of his Guru?'

'One who lies on the bed of the Guru suffers eternal damnation,' replied Govinda calmly.

'Why did you act like that, in spite of your knowing all this?'

'I lie on your bed only to make sure that the bed has been made comfortable and that you would easily fall asleep. If by my going to hell, a little of ease and comfort can be ensured to you, I consider it more desirable than ensuring a place in heaven for myself.'

Yatiraja was amazed at this devotion of Govinda to his Guru. Ashamed of his ignorance in misjudging his cousin, Yatiraja begged pardon of him.

On another occasion, Ramanuja found Govinda thrusting his finger into the mouth of a snake and then forcibly drawing it out, which made the snake almost dead with pain. When after so doing and finishing his bath Govinda came to Yatiraja, the latter enquired in surprise,

'Brother, why did you act like that? Is it not sheer madness to thrust your finger into the mouth of a poisonous snake? It is only through sheer luck that your blood has not become poisoned. By thus behaving like a lad you not only ran a grave risk but that innocent creature too is lying there almost dead. How could you inflict pain on any creature?'

'Brother,' replied Govinda, 'while eating something, the snake had a thorn stuck in its throat and it was tossing about in pain. So I thrust my finger into its mouth and pulled out the thorn. Now its pain is not so acute as it was formerly. Only because of exhaustion it looks lifeless. After some time, it will be quite all right.'

Ramanuja was surprised beyond measure by this compassion to creatures. After this incident, his love towards Govinda became profounder.

By the end of the year, when Ramanuja had finished studying the *Ramayana*, and wanted to pay proper presents to Sailapurna, his preceptor, before taking leave of him, the large-hearted Guru said: 'Ramanuja, my child, if you have any desire, please tell me. I will try to fulfil it, if it is not beyond my capacity.'

'O Mahatman,' said Ramanuja, 'please give unto me your godly disciple Govinda. This is my only prayer.'

Hearing this, Purna at once made a gift to Ramanuja of his own dearest disciple. At this regaining of Govinda, Ramanuja's joy was great.

Without any more delay, Ramanuja went to Sholingar (or Chola Simhapura) along with his disciples and was greatly delighted to have the Darsan of the Lord Narasimhadeva there. From there he went to Tirukkazhikundram where he visited the deities and had his ablutions and returned to Kanchipuram. After the Darsan of Varadaraja, Yatiraja went to Kanchipurna to whom he submitted an account of Govinda's devotion to his Guru and his acts of mercy to creatures, and then said, 'O Mahatman, kindly bless my cousin and make him all the more devoted to his Guru and beneficent to creatures.'

'Your desires will always be fulfilled. No harm can befall any one to whom you wish prosperity,' said Kanchipurna, his face lit up with a smile.

Noting the wanness of the face of Govinda who was nearby, Kanchipurna said, 'Yatiraja, for want of service to the Guru, the moon of Govinda's face has turned pale. Why don't you send him to Sri Sailapurna?'

At these words, Ramanuja asked him to go back to his Guru. Govinda took the shortest route and reached the residence of his Guru situated at the foot of the hill. On hearing of Govinda's return, Purna did not even for once cast his glance at him. It was past noon and all had finished taking their meal. Purna did not call Govinda to the meal. The third watch of the day passed away. Govinda was sitting unfed at the outer gate. Unable to bear this, the soft-hearted wife of Purna told her husband: 'You may or may not talk to Govinda; but ask the child to take his food.'

'I am not in duty bound to feed the horse that has been sold away. He should now be brought up by his new master only,' replied the husband.

On hearing this, Govinda, who was still unfed, came back to Kanchipura and clasping the feet of Ramanuja said: 'Yatiraja, don't you kindly address me any more as your brother; I heard from the lips of my previous master that you alone are my master now. Order me what I have to do.'

Finding him tired because of the day-long fasting and long journey, Ramanuja first removed his exhaustion by making him take his bath and food. From that time onward, Govinda began to render service to his new master with the same zealous care and profound devotion as he used to do to Sailapurna.

They passed three nights at Kanchipuram. Then they all reached the village Ashtasahasra and accepted the service of Yajnesa. After passing one night there, Ramanuja returned along with Govinda to Srirangam. He had the Darsan of Sri Ranganathaswami, saw his own Gurus, and then repaired to his monastery.

21

Govinda's Sannyasa

Govinda was not in the least aggrieved at the behaviour of his own maternal uncle Sailapurna. On the other hand, he came to understand that the idea behind such conduct of this great soul was to commit him fully to the charge of Ramanuja. Thenceforth he applied himself to the devoted service of Yatiraja. Within a day or two he found out the requirements of the new master. With this knowledge he would perform all work in such perfect order that the other disciples of Yatiraja would be struck with wonder at the sight. Once they praised him very highly for his efficiency in service. On hearing it, Govinda said, 'Yes, my qualities do really merit such adoration.' At this they took him to be conceited. When they brought this to the notice of Yatiraja, he called Govinda near him aid said: 'My child, they are praising your good qualities; but should you on that account become vain?'

'Mahatman,' replied Govinda, 'after passing through three hundred and twenty lakhs of births, this deluded creature has attained human birth, and even in this present birth, obtained after so many similar births as man, he went astray and was about to fall. Your excessive kindness alone was the cause of my redemption. Whatever good tendency I may have in me is due to you; for, I am naturally dull-witted and low-minded. Therefore, praise of any good qualities in me is praise of you alone. Hence it was I spoke like that.'

Another day, early in the morning, Govinda was sitting without finishing his morning duties, like one bewitched, at the outer gate of a prostitute's house. Scandalized at this, the fellow-students informed Yatiraja of his strange behaviour. He called Govinda near him and enquired: 'Why were you sitting at the door of a prostitute's house instead of attending to your morning duties?'

'The woman was singing the tales of *Ramayana* in a very sweet voice. I was listening to the entire piece with a view to reciting the whole. This is why my morning duties have yet not been done,' replied Govinda. All were captivated at his simplicity and natural devotion.

One day, Govinda's mother, the sister of Sailapurna, came and said to Ramnuja: 'My child, Govinda's wife has now come of age; so, please ask him to abide by the duty to his wife (Sahadharmini); for he won't listen to me. When I informed him earlier of this, he said, "You may bring my wife to me when I have finished my services to Yatiraja and have some leisure." But, my child, up to this day I have waited in vain for his leisure. He would always be busy with some work or other.'

Hearing this, Ramanuja called him by his side and said, 'My child, after relinquishing the quality of Tamas, lie down with your wife in the same bed.'

Govinda accepted the behest of his Guru. That night he lay down by the side of his wife and passed the hours in various spiritual talks. Dyutimati, Govinda's mother, heard all about their conversations from her daughter-in-law and went to Ramanuja and told him about it. At this Yatiraja took Govinda aside and said, 'I asked you to lie down with your wife in the same bed in order to preserve her Dharma. You didn't act accordingly and why?'

'Great one,' Govinda replied, 'you ordered me to lie down with my wife after relinquishing the quality of Tamas. I have acted accordingly. As soon as I relinquish Tamas, the Lord (Antaryamin) seated in the heart flashes forth. Where is the chance for sensuality and the like, born of Tamas, in the face of such manifestation?'

Ramanuja was amazed to hear that. He kept quiet for some time and then said: 'Govinda, if such be the state of your mind, it is your duty to take Sannyasa without any delay. For if you remain in an Ashrama, you have to behave like an Ashrami, that is to say, you have to observe the duties of the stage of life to which you belong; such is the injunction of the Sastras. So, if you have established mastery over the senses, then it is proper for you to take Sannyasa.'

Supremely happy to hear this, Govinda said, 'At this moment I am ready for it.'

Without any loss of time, Yatiraja, with the consent of Dyutimati, the mother of Govinda, first sanctified him with the fivefold purificatory rites such as stamping the insignia, Urdhvapundra, Nama, Mantra and Yaga. Then with the gift of the staff and the Kamandalu, he elevated him to the position of a Paramahamsa. Looking at the divine beauty of this new Sannyasin, with his face aglow with supreme knowledge, his lotus eyes filled with tears of love, a visible manifestation of pure knowledge and devotion, Yatiraja gave him the name Mannatha. Ramanuja himself used to be addressed by his disciples by that name. He gave to Govinda his own name because of his great affection for him. How can the loving Sannyasin Govinda the very embodiment of Dasya-Bhakti (devotion of servitude)—who was full of Sattva, and who was childlike like Sanaka, beautiful like the morning sun, pure like the dew drop, and fascinating like a full-blown flower,—how could he adopt the 'I am He' (Soham) attitude, relinquishing that of servitude? When he would not agree to be addressed by the name of his master, Ramanuja translated the word 'Mannatha' into Tamil as 'Emperumanar'; then joining the first and last parts of the word, made it Em-ar or Embar. And this came to be the new name for Govinda. The renowned monastery by the name Embar Math at Jagannatha-kshetra was built by Ramanuja and named after Govinda.

At that time, in all seventy-four disciples were staying in the Srirangam Math of Ramanuja. All of them were learned, all-renouncing and highly devout souls. They knew by heart all the Vedas and the Dravida-Prabandha-mala. They used to be called Simhasanadhipatis or Pithadhipatis. It would appear that the Gaudiya Vaishnavas gave the title Goswami to the disciples of Sri Chaitanya in imitation of them. We have mentioned before the names of Dasarathi, Kuresa, Sundarababu, Chotanambi, Saumyanarayana, Yajnamurti and Govinda who were his chief disciples. Surrounded by these disciples and expounding the essential principles of devotion as well as the Sastras, Ramanuja lived for some time in great joy in his own monastery.

❧

22

Writing the Sribhashya

One day, while describing the qualities of Yamunacharya to his disciples, Ramanuja remembered his own pledges. When by the side of the ground chosen for its burial, the dead body of that Mahatma was lying, there appeared Yatiraja and saw that three fingers of his right hand were clenched together. When Ramanuja took three vows, the three fingers gave up the clenched position and were stretched in the natural state. Recalling his vow, he said to his disciples: 'I have bound myself by a promise to Yamunamuni that I would write the *Sribhashya*; but till now, I have done nothing in this matter. If the book is to be written, we shall have to take the help of the *Bodhayana-vritti*. It is hard to get Maharshi Bodhayana's *Vritti* in this part of the country. In spite of much searching, I have not been able to procure a copy. I am told, however, that it is preserved with great care at the Saradapitha in Kashmir. Accompanied by Kuresa, I shall start for that destination even today. O devotees of the Lord, pray to Sri Vishnu that we may succeed in our search.'

Thus taking leave of the disciples, Ramanuja, accompanied by Kuresa, started for the Saradapitha, which they reached after three months of travel. He interviewed the scholars of the place and had long discussions on the scriptures with them. The scholars were amazed at his proficiency in the Sastras, his fluency, and the depth of his wisdom, and considering him to be a rare guest, accorded him great honour and care. When Ramanuja mentioned the *Bodhayana-vritti*, the scholars belonging to the doctrine of non-dualism thought that he should not be shown the book; for his conclusions had been approved by Maharshi

Bodhayana. Now, if this great man got hold of this work, he would be in a position to strengthen his own doctrine all the more and become a formidable danger to the doctrine of non-dualism. Thinking thus, they said, 'Revered Sir, the book mentioned, we did have here with us; but unfortunately, it has been eaten up by worms.'

Yatiraja was very much disheartened to hear this and thought that all his labour had been wasted. Tradition has it that when one day Yatiraja was lying down in a distressed state of mind, there appeared before him the Goddess Sarada, and presenting the book to him with Her own hands, said, 'My child, take this book and return home without any delay; for if they come to know of this, it will be impossible for you to take the book and go.'

So saying, She disappeared. Ramanuja considered himself blessed to receive the rare Darsan, grace and command of the Goddess of Knowledge Herself. Without loss of time, he took leave of the company of scholars and started towards the South.

After a few days the scholars of the Saradapitha, while rearranging the library, brought out the books one by one in order to scrutinise if any book was being eaten by worms. While thus examining the books, they failed to find the Bodhayana-vritti among them. They came to the conclusion that those two scholars from the South must have stolen it away. Some well-built men from among them at once set out to follow them. After walking day and night for a month, they overtook Ramanuja and Kuresa. When on enquiry they came to know that the Bodhayana-vritti was with them, without any word whatsoever, those small-minded men wrested the book from them and went away homeward. At this, the dismay of Ramanuja knew no bounds. But Kuresa said, 'Revered Sir, be not distressed. From the time we started from Kashmir, every night, when you were fast asleep, I used to study that Vritti and now I have got the entire work by heart. Even now I shall sit down to write it out. And I hope to be able to finish writing it out in five or six days.'

Great indeed was Ramanuja's joy on hearing this. Locking Kuresa in a warm embrace, Ramanuja said, 'My child, may you be immortal! Today you have bound me in eternal debt by recovering this lost treasure.'

When the writing of the book was over, they returned to Srirangam without any delay. After narrating the tale of their travel to his own disciples, Yatiraja said, 'Dear devotees of the Lord, through the strength of your devotion and the uncommon power of Kuresa's memory, the *Bodhayana-vritti* has been procured. I can now refute the doctrines of these wrong-headed persons who think that the mere intellectual understanding of the great Vedic statements like 'That Thou art'[1] and 'I am Brahman',[2] is enough for final beatitude of liberation. I have also to explode the views of those Jnana-karma-samucchaya-vadins who admit the great efficacy of Yajna, Dana, Tapas and Karma along with the understanding of these statements. I have to establish that the purport of the Vedas and the Vedanta is the attainment of liberation through Dhyana, Upasana and Bhakti. For all this, I shall begin writing the *Sribhashya*. All of you, kindly pray to God that this work may be accomplished without any impediment. Kuresa, my child, you will be my amanuensis. But when some argument does not seem proper to you, stop writing and sit quiet. From that I shall know that I have to reconsider my view. And if I find it erroneous, I shall change it immediately.'

Thus was begun the writing of *Sribhashya*. In the course of taking down the entire commentary, Kuresa had to stop writing only once. One day, while describing the true nature of the Jiva, Yatiraja said, 'In his essential nature, Jiva is eternal (Nitya) and a knower (Jnata).' In other words the soul is that which is conscious or that which has cognition alone as its distinguishing attribute.

---

1. तत्त्वमसि।   *Chandogya Upanishad*, VI. ix. 4.

2. अहं ब्रह्मास्मि।   *Brihadaranyaka Upanishad*, I. iv. 10.

On hearing this, Kuresa stopped writing. Notwithstanding his Guru's repeated behests to write, he would not obey. Expressing his annoyance at this, Ramanuja said, 'Kuresa, if you behave like this, you had better write the commentary yourself.'

But after this outburst, he thought again: 'If Jiva is by his true nature eternal and a knower, then what is the harm in saying that he is an independent actor and enjoyer endowed with body-consciousness? But when Sri Bhagavan says,' An eternal portion of Myself having become a living soul in the world of life....',[1] the Jiva is dependent and never independent. Because the Jiva lives, moves and has his being in Isvara, he is always dependent on Isvara. And Isvara is the soul of the Jiva, eternally related to Isvara as His liege. Hence Isvara is called the Whole (Amsin or Seshin), and the Jiva the part (Amsa or Sesha).' Thus concluding, when he propounded that the essential nature of Jiva is 'Vishnuseshatva 'along with 'Jnatritva',—that is to say, the most essential characteristic of the soul is its conscious dependence on God (Vishnu) like a property on its owner or master, for being appropriated solely for His own purposes—Kuresa began to write again.[2] Thus was written the commentary, *Sribhashya*.

After accomplishing this great work, Yatiraja wrote four more invaluable books,[3] viz., *Vedanta-deepam, Vedantasara, Vedartha-sangraha* and *Gita-bhashya*. By composing the *Sribhashya* he fulfilled the second desire of Yamunamuni. He had previously fulfilled his first desire by

---

1.   ममैवांशो जीवलोके जीवभूतः सनातनः ।   *Bhagavad-Gita*, XV. 7.

2. On another occasion he sent Kuresa to Goshthipurna with the question: 'What is the chief characteristic of the individual self (Jivatma)?' After some time Kuresa returned with the reply: 'Remind him of what Nammalvar had said: "The slave is and He is." Let him know that dependence upon the Lord precedes consciousness (Jnatritva) and every other characteristic of his.'—*Ed.*

1. For a complete list of Sri Ramanuja's works see Appendix C-I.

reading with his own disciples the Dravida-prabandha-mala and giving them the Dravidaveda which made it equal in rank with the Vedas. Now, naming his doctrine Visishtadvaita-vada,[1] he considered himself blessed.

23

The Conquest

After he had finished writing the *Sribhashya* and other works, mentioned above, Yatiraja, accompanied by seventy-four of his chief disciples and other numberless followers, set out on a campaign of conquest. He first entered the kingdom of the Cholas and reached Kanchipuram, its capital, wherefrom, after taking the permission of Lord Varadaraja, he left for Kumbakonam. There he defeated the local scholars in dialectics on the Sastras and brought them into his own fold. Then Ramanuja appeared in Madura, the capital of the Pandya kingdom. This city was, as it were, a fortress of the Dravidian scholars. He expatiated upon the Prabandha-mala before the assembly of the scholars as a result of which they all adopted his doctrine. There he visited the main shrine of the place where he experienced supreme bliss in having Darsan of the image of Sri Sathari. After a few days' stay here, he proceeded to the city of Kuranga (Tirukkurungudi). Unbounded was his joy when he saw the image of Vishnu enshrined in the local temple. Tradition has it that Sri Vishnu was very much pleased with Ramanuja's incomparable deeds. What is more, the Lord, in a sportive mood, became a disciple of Yatiraja and thought Himself blessed in receiving the name Sri Vaishnava-nambi given by His Guru. Next, he went to Kurukapuri (Kurukoor), the birthplace of Satharipu. There he visited the main shrine of the place and experienced great bliss in having the Darsan of the image of Sri Sathari and in reciting the great Vaishnava hymns.

Thence he went to Kerala, where in the capital Tiruanantapuram (Trivandrum) he saw Padmanabhaswami lying on Ananta and was filled with devotion. Next he moved northwards. Gradually he passed through Dwaraka,

Mathura, Brindavan, Salagram, Saketa, Badarikashrama, Naimisa and Pushkara, and at last reached the Saradapitha of Kashmir. It is said, the goddess Sarada was very much pleased to hear his exposition of the Mantra *'kapyasam pundarikaksham'* and gave him the title 'Bhashyakara'.

It is not to be supposed that the scholars of Kashmir gave in without a fight. They went so far as to try incantations for putting an end to Ramanuja's life. But the outcome was contrary; those who took recourse to incantations were themselves about to lose their lives. At this crisis, the king of Kashmir fell at Ramanuja's feet and begged his mercy and he cured them all. The king and scholars became his disciples forthwith. Here Ramanuja had a vision of God in the form of Hayagriva. At the command of the goddess Sarada, Ramanuja then went to Kasi, where he lived for some time and gathered many philosophers and scholars into his fold. Then he proceeded southwards.

Reaching Sripurushottama-kshetra (Puri) after a few days, he took rest for some time. He founded a monastery there and called it Embar Math after the name of Govinda, his own disciple. Out of fear of defeat the scholars of the place did not meet Ramanuja in any discussion, though the latter invited them. Ramanuja grew all the more eager to establish his doctrine there. He requested the priests of Lord Jagannatha to worship the Deity according to the Pancharatra Agama. When they refused to adopt any new doctrine, he appealed to the king for arranging a discussion. Being frightened at this, the priests took refuge in Sri Purushottama. It is said that, on that night, Ramanuja while asleep, was thrown by Jagannatha to Kurmakshetra, a hundred yojanas[1] away from that place.

When he woke up Ramanuja saw that he had come to a different place, where none of his numberless disciples was near him. On enquiry, he came to know that he was in Kurmakshetra. Knowing for certain that it was an artifice

---

1. A measure of distance equal to about nine miles.

of God, after his morning duties, Ramanuja went to the
temple of Sri Kurmadeva, and with deep devotion,
worshipped that image of the incarnation. Pleased with him,
the Deity commanded him through His priest to wait there
for sometime for his disciples and Ramanuja complied.
Reunited with his disciples after a few days, he went to
Simhachala. He stayed there for a few days after which he
went to the Ahobila temple situated on the Garuda Mountain and established a monastery there. Then he came to
Isalinganga and worshipped Sri Nrisimhadeva. From there
he came by stages to Venkatachala or Tirupati. At that time,
a quarrel was going on between the Saiva and Vaishnava
communities concerning the Deity of the place. Ramanuja,
by dint of his superhuman powers, established that the
image could be none other than that of Vishnu and both the
Vaishnava and the Saiva communities were satisfied. He
stayed there for some time and then along with his disciples
returned to Kanchipuram where, having the Darsan of Sri
Varadaraja, he considered himself blessed. From there he
came to Madurantaka en route to Viranarayanapuram, the
birthplace of Nathamuni. He made obeisance to the place
where the Mahamuni practised Yoga. At last returning to
Srirangam, he had the Darsan of Sri Ranganathaswami and
deemed himself blessed.

24

Kuresa

Uttamapurna, one of the worshippers of Sri Ranganatha, wrote a poetical work named *Lakshmi Kavya*. We are giving here an account of Kuresa's life as narrated by him in this work.

Kuresa was a wealthy Brahmana of the Vatsya lineage. He was a resident of Kuragrahara, situated a couple of miles west of Kanchipuram. As he was the landlord of the place, he came to be known as Kuranatha or Kuresa, the lord of Kura. After marrying one Andal, who was quite a worthy helpmate to him, he engaged himself in spending his immense wealth in the service of the lowly and the helpless. From his very boyhood he used to cherish great regard for Ramanuja. After Yatiraja had taken Sannyasa, Kuresa, along with his wife, became his disciple and would always be in the company of the master. He was a mighty scholar and had a prodigious memory, as we have heard before. Whatsoever he would hear or read once, he would remember for all time. It was with his assistance that Ramanuja defeated the great scholar Yadavaprakasa in the contest.

His spacious mansion would resound until midnight with the words, 'take, give and enjoy'. Then the huge iron, gate would be closed to be reopened early next morning. When Ramanuja left Kanchipuram and went to Srirangam, Kuresa lost all interest in wealth and possessions.

It is said that when once Lakshmidevi, the Consort of Sri Varadaraja and Mother of the universe, on hearing the sound of the closing of the gates of Kuresa's mansion, wanted to know the cause of that sound, Kanchipurna, describing the services of Kuresa to the poor, said, 'Mother, from morning till midnight, the services to the lowly, the blind, and the lame went on. After finishing all their work and with a view to taking rest for some time, the servants closed the gates of the Dharma-sala. Every night we hear their banging sound while being closed.'

Desirous of seeing Kuresa, Lakshmidevi said to Kanchipurna, 'My child, tomorrow morning, please bring this high-souled one to me. I would like to see him.'

Accordingly, early the following morning, when Kanchipurna saw Kuresa and told him the wishes of the Mother of the universe, he said, 'O noble one, where am I, an ungrateful, evil-minded, sinful and fraudulent man, and where is Lakshmidevi, the Mother of the universe, who is worshipped by even Brahma and Rudra? A Chandala, they say, has no right to enter the temple. I am more depraved than any Chandala. This filth of wealth has corrupted my heart and soul. How can I ever merit in this life the Darsan of Lakshmidevi?'

So saying and shedding profuse tears, Kuresa removed from his person all costly apparel and threw it away. Then wearing a tattered cloth, he walked out of his mansion, saying to Kanchipurna, 'Revered Sir, I cannot transgress the command of the Mother of the universe. I shall get ready to have the vision of Her lotus feet. But this body and mind, sullied as they are by the filth of wealth, must be purified by ablutions in that lake of immortality, the water touched by the feet of the Guru. There I am going for ablutions. I do not know how-long I shall take to wash off this dirt. Who knows, by the blessings of noble ones like you, I may merit the vision of the lotus feet of the the Mother of the universe, even in this very life?'

Kuresa proceeded towards Srirangam. Andal too followed him. The only thing she took with her was a golden cup, in which, when her husband got thirsty, she might serve him drinking water. After covering a distance, they entered a deep forest. When fear crept into her mind, Andal asked her husband, 'My lord, I suppose there is no cause for fear in this forest?'

'It is only the rich that have cause to fear,' replied Kuresa. 'If you have no money or wealth with you, you have nothing to be afraid of. Come away.'

On hearing this, Andal instantly threw away the golden cup. The next day they reached Srirangam. When Ramanuja knew of the couple's arrival, with great kindness he brought them to his monastery. When they had taken rest after bath and dinner, Yatiraja fixed up a separate house for their residence.

Kuresa began to live by begging. He considered himself blessed; for now he could always remember the gem of a Mantra given to him by his revered Guru, chant the name of God, discuss the holy scriptures, and see the lotus feet of his Guru. Andal, who was engaged in his service, was also passing her days in great joy without thinking even once of the immense wealth which they had left behind. She was happy in the happiness of Kuresa.

One day, because it was raining till noon, Kuresa was unable to go on his round of begging. Hence the husband and wife fasted all that day. Kuresa had no thought of his hunger. But Andal, whose only motive was service of her husband, finding her husband fasting, mentally prayed to Sri Ranganathaswami. A short while after, a priest came with various rich dishes of consecrated food, offered them to Kuresa and went away. Surprised at this, Kuresa asked his wife, 'Did you mentally pray for anything to Sri Ranganatha-swami? Else, why should He try to bind us again with those very enjoyments which we have left behind as we would the droppings of a crow?' When, with tears in her eyes, Andal confessed what she had thought, Kuresa said, 'We can't help what is already done. But never do so again.' So saying, he took a little of the Mahaprasad himself and then asked his wife to take the rest. He began to chant the *Sathari-sukta* again and again and thus passed the night.

Tradition has it that ten months after taking this consecrated food (under the star Anuradha, on the full moon night of the year Subhakrit of the Saka era 983) Andal gave birth to twins, both sons. Exceedingly glad on hearing this,

Ramanuja at once sent Govinda to perform the Jata-karma.[1] After the Jata-karma, he sanctified their body and mind by whispering into their ears the sacred couplet: '*sriman-narayana-charanau saranam prapadye*'; '*srimate narayanaya namah*' (I take refuge at the feet of Narayana with Sri; salutations to Lord Narayana with Sri). Yatiraja affectionately presented the two babies with the emblems of the five weapons of Vishnu—Panchajanya, Sudarsana, Kaumodaki, Nandaka, Sarnga—which he got made of gold so that by wearing them on their persons the babies might be protected from the evil influences of spirits and goblins. After six months Yatiraja named the elder one as Parasara and the younger, Vyasa. It was then also the time for naming the son of Balagovinda, the younger brother of Govinda. Ramanuja gave him the name Parankusapurna. Thus Yatiraja fulfilled his third vow.

From his very boyhood Parasara gave proofs of incomparable genius. One day, when he was five years old, Sarvajna Bhatta, an all-conquering scholar, was passing through the street along with his many disciples, ostentatiously proclaiming his fame by beat of drums. Along with his playmates. Parasara was then playing in the dust of the street. He heard the drummer proclaim: 'Here goes the universally renowned Sarvajna Bhatta accompanied by his disciples. All who dare to face him in polemics or wish to become his disciples may come to his feet without delay.' On hearing this, the boy, with smiling face, appeared before Sarvajna with a handful of dust and asked, 'Let me see if you can tell how many grains of dust I have in my hand? As you are a Sarvajna, you should know everything.'

The Pundit was much surprised to hear this question suddenly put to him by a boy. Discarding his conceit of all-knowingness, he took the boy on his lap, kissed his forehead and said.

---

1. A Hindu religious ceremony in connection with the birth of a child.

'My child, you are my Guru. Your question has brought me to my senses.'

Their birth being the result of partaking of the consecrated food of Sri Ranganathaswami, all believed that Parasara and Vyasa were His own sons. After the investiture with the sacred thread, while reading the Upanishads, Govinda was instructing them about God's qualities,— smaller than the smallest and bigger than the biggest.[1] Parasara, a mere boy, asked him, 'How is it possible for One to have those two contrary qualities?' Govinda was surprised, but could not answer. According to the wishes of Yatiraja, a few days after the investiture with the sacred thread, Parasara was married to the two daughters of a relation of Mahapurna.

---

1.   अणोरणीयान् महतो महीयान्।   *Katha Upanishad*, II. 20

25

Dhanurdasa

It was the day of the great festival of Garuda at Srirangam. Hundreds of men and women from various places had assembled there to have the Darsan of the Deity. At the huge temple-gate all were waiting for Sri Ranganathaswami coming out seated on the shoulders of Garuda. The tumultuous sound of drums had been proclaiming in all directions the victory of Lord Narayana. When all were very eagerly looking towards the spacious courtyard inside the temple, there was heard the chanting of the holy Dravida-vedas by hundreds of Brahmanas proceeding in rows. Thereupon all the uproar quietened down. The chanters of the Vedas were slowly proceeding from the inner courtyard to the temple-gate. A red streamer marked with the insignia of the conch, discus and Tilaka and supported on two bamboo poles was carried before them. The sounds of the Vedic chanting, which were as purifying as the waters of the onrushing Ganga, just freed from the chasm of the Himalayas, washed away the sufferings of the assembled men and women. The earth was, as it were, transformed into heaven.

After crossing the gate, the chanters of the Dravida-veda appeared on the street followed by gaily decorated elephants marked with big Urdhvapundras moving with majestic pace and waving their trunks. Behind them came a number of bullocks with long horns and fat humps, each carrying two drums slung across their backs. Then followed a number of beautifully caparisoned horses, also carrying double drums beaten by drummers. At their heels came a huge concourse of devotees singing sweetly the name of Hari to the accompaniment of various musical instruments. Behind them was seen Lord Narayana with His Consort Lakshmi mounted on the shoulders of Garuda, hymned by the Devadasis,

surrounded by priests, and carried by hundreds of devoted
bearers. The pious men and women filled the firmament
with shouts of joy. The Lord took rest for a while in the
pavilion in front of the gate. Following Him advanced with
steady steps a big crowd of Brahmanas chanting in a loud
voice the Sanskrit Vedas. When Lord Narayana was seated
in the pavilion, all movement stopped. During this time
hundreds of devotees worshipped the Lord and made
various offerings. Some broke coconuts and sanctified them
in the presence of Lord Narayana. Others offered bundles
of plantains, and yet others waved lighted camphor before
the Lord. After some time, the Lord left the pavilion and the
entire concourse, beginning from the red streamer to the
chanters of the Sama and the Yajur Vedas, surged forward
like a mighty current. All had their eyes fixed on the Lord
and His Consort, Lakshmi.

As the procession moved along the streets, the
housewives on either side handed over flowers, camphor,
fruits and betel leaves to the priests, who in their turn,
offered them in the proper way to the Lord. Then they gave
Prasada to the devoted housewives and afterwards touched
their bowing heads with the crown bearing the footprints
of the Lord. With folded hands and heart filled with devotion,
every one in that vast concourse fixed his eyes on the lotus
feet of the Lord. The power of devotion was felt everywhere
except in one spot where a contrary attitude was noticed.

A handsome man—stalwart and broad-shouldered—
was walking along, attracted by the current of men as it
were. He had a big umbrella in his left hand: but he did
not use it to protect his head from the rays of the sun.
The umbrella was held over the head of an exquisitely
beautiful, large-eyed young lady. It was her lily-like face
that he was shielding from the scorching rays of the sun.
In his right hand he held a fan which he moved to and fro
for her benefit. All his mind, heart and looks were so fixed
on her that he was not conscious of the rest of the
world. He never thought how people would regard such

behaviour. Though many whispered on seeing the couple, he did not notice this at all. Just as a bee sipping the honey at the heart of a lotus is absorbed in its own enjoyment and forgets the world, so too did this sturdy young man lose himself, drinking in with his eyes the beauty of this young lady. How then could shame, hatred or fear touch him?

After ablutions in the Kaveri and Darsan and worship of the Lord, and with his left arm resting on the shoulders of Dasarathi, Sri Ramanuja, the redeemer of the fallen, was then returning along with his disciples to the monastery by the same street. Suddenly his eyes fell upon this strange sight. 'My child,' he said to one of his disciples, 'go and call that man who is without shame and hatred and bring him to me.' The disciple went and called him several times before he could be made to take notice. Slightly perturbed, like one suddenly aroused from sleep, by the sight of a Brahmana in front of him, he said with folded hands, 'Sir, what is your behest to this servant?'

The Brahmana replied, 'There stands Yatiraja, and he wishes to talk to you. Please come with me for a few minutes.'

Hearing the name of Yatiraja, the young man took leave of his lady-love for a moment and followed the Brahmana. Presently he came before Yatiraja, prostrated himself before him and then stood in silence in front of him. Looking at him Yatiraja said, 'What nectar have you found in that young lady that, giving up all hatred, shame and fear, you have made yourself the laughingstock of this vast concourse of men?'

'Mahatman,' replied the young man, 'there are many beautiful things on earth; but of all these things the most beautiful are the bright eyes of that bewitching lady. When I look at them I go mad and cannot turn away my eyes.'

'Is she your wedded wife?' enquired Yatiraja.

'No, revered Sir,' replied the young man. 'Though she is not married to me, I have resolved once for all not to love any one else in my life.'

'What is your name?' asked Yatiraja.

'My name is Dhanurdasa. I come from Nichulanagara. I am an adept in wrestling. The name of my lady is Hemamba.'

'Dhanurdasa,' said Yatiraja, 'if I can show you a still more beautiful pair of eyes, then, tell me, will you give up this person and love the other one?'

'Revered Sir,' replied the young man, 'if indeed it is possible that there are more beautiful eyes, surely I shall leave these and adore those!'

'We shall see,' said Ramanuja, 'come to me this evening.'

'As you command,' said Dhanurdasa. He returned to the youthful lady and resumed his walk with her, holding the umbrella as before.

It was evening. Sri Ramanuja along with Dhanurdasa was crossing one after another the huge gates of the temple of Sri Ranganathaswami. Thus they passed through the five portals and appeared before the principal Deity. The priest received Yatiraja with reverence. Then with the burning of camphor he began the vesper services of Lord Narayana, the cloud-hued Consort of Lakshmi—who holds the world lotus in his navel, who is recombent on the couch of the serpent Ananta, the symbol of infinity, and who is the destroyer of the fears of all and the abode of peace and tranquillity.

In the light of that camphor flame, the two large lotus eyes of the blessed Lord shone, causing supreme joy in the hearts of the devotees. From the beauty of those eyes, Dhanurdasa who was standing by the side of Yatiraja could not turn away his eyes. Tears of love flowed in an endless stream from his eyes and he experienced supreme beatitude. Hemamba's eyes faded from the firmament of his mind like the stars at sunrise. After remaining thus immersed in beatitude for some time, he slowly regained his outward consciousness. Then, seeing Yatiraja by his side, he fell at his feet and said:

'O large-hearted one, through your supreme grace today you have made this lascivious beast enjoy the bliss that even the gods long for and rarely gain. I am now your slave forever. Up till now I had forgotten the ocean and like a frog in the well cherished great love for the well. Turning away from the sun, like an owl of night, I was infatuated with the glow-worm. You, who have opened my eyes,—you are my Master, my Master for ever!'

Sri Ramanuja, the redeemer of the fallen, raised up Dhanurdasa from the ground and embraced him in deep affection. Though a courtesan, Hemamba used to regard Dhanurdasa as her husband. When she came to know that her dearest one had seen the divine vision through the grace of Yatiraja, her joy knew no bounds. She too gave up her slavery to the senses and took refuge at the feet of Ramanuja. The boundless ocean of mercy, Yatiraja, graciously freed her too from the darkness of delusion, and removing the bond of lust between the two, bound them together with the bond of love. Though now they lived together like husband and wife, yet lust could no longer touch them. Leaving Nichulanagara, they settled in Srirangam where they dwelt in a rented house in the vicinity of Yatiraja.

Because of his devotion to the Guru, dispassion, modesty, frankness and sweet speech, all men and women honoured him and Hemamba as the recipients of Yatiraja's supreme grace. In order to uphold the excellence of his divine qualities despite his low birth, Ramanuja would hold the arm of Dhanurdasa with his hand, while returning to the monastery after taking bath, though, while going for bath, he would hold the hand of Dasarathi, a Brahmana disciple. At this his Brahmana disciples were grieved and some of them even hinted to him that his behaviour was unbecoming.

One night, when all the inmates of the monastery were fast asleep. Yatiraja tore off, from each disciple's cloth hung out on lines for drying, a strip sufficient for a loin cloth. When the disciples got up in the morning and noticed that their cloths had been shortened, they began to utter vile and vulgar words against one another and continued quarrelling for hours. At last, Sri Ramanuja himself had to intervene to calm them down.

That day at nightfall, he called some of his disciple and said, 'Look, today Dhanurdasa will be sitting here for a long time, talking with me. Meanwhile, some of you go and secretly steal away all the ornaments from the person of his slumbering lady-love. We shall see what effect the loss produces on Dhanurdasa and his beloved.' According to the words of their Guru, the disciples went to the abode of Dhanurdasa at dead of night and found the young woman apparently fast asleep.

As she was awaiting the return of her husband. Hemamba had not closed the door. So the Brahmanas could enter the house easily. Taking her to be in deep sleep, they began, very cautiously, to remove the ornaments from her person. Hemamba knew what was happening. But lest the Brahmanas should flee in fear if she moved she remained still. When the ornaments on one side were removed, in order to give away those on the other side. Hemamba pretended to change sides, as one sometimes does while in deep sleep. At this the Brahmanas thought she was waking up. They took with them the ornaments already secured, and going to Ramanuja, reported in secret all that had happened. Calling Dhanurdasa, Yatiraja then said, 'My child, the night is far advanced; you should go home now.' When the wrestler left for home with the words, 'As you order, my lord,' Ramanuja said to the disciples who had committed the theft, 'You may now follow him close on his heels, and listen to the words exchanged between the couple.' The disciples acted accordingly.

Entering the house, Dhanurdasa noticed her appearance and enquired. 'How's this? You have jewels on one side. Where are the others?'

'My dear,' replied Hemamba, 'owing no doubt to want at home, some Brahmanas have turned into thieves and have stolen some of my jewels. At that time, I was waiting for you, mentally repeating the name of the Lord, while lying on the bed. Thinking I was fast asleep, they carefully removed the ornaments from one side. In order to enable them to take the ornaments from the other side, I changed my side. But, thanks to my ill luck, they fled away in fear.'

On hearing this, Dhanurdasa felt sorry and rebuked her, saying, 'Ah, it was a mistake to have changed your side! Your ego has not left you. You still seem to think, "These are my ornaments; I shall give them." This wrong idea has deprived you of a good opportunity of getting rid of this filthy gold. Had you remained lying there still and steady, resigning yourself to the Lord, then taking you to be sound asleep, they would have removed all the ornaments. It is clear we are yet to root out entirely this sense of "I".'

Recognising her fault, Hemamba said in tears, 'O my dearest, bless me so that such egotism never more finds place in my mind.'

The Brahmanas returned to the monastery with this knowledge of the ego-less state of this divine couple and they reported everything from beginning to end to Ramanuja. As the night was far advanced, Ramanuja asked them to go and rest. The following day, finishing their morning duties, the Brahmana disciples assembled around Yatiraja for study. Then, addressing all, he said, 'You are adepts in the Sastras and proud of your Brahmanism. Tell me whose behaviour is more befitting a Brahmana—yours last morning when you found your cloths a few inches shorter, or that of Dhanurdasa and his wife last night when the jewels were stolen?' They hung down their heads in shame and said in one voice: 'Master, it was Dhanurdasa whose behaviour was worthy of a Brahmana. Ours was abominable.'

At this Yatiraja said, 'Therefore, my children, know this that it is the qualities of the head and heart

which are the causes of good, and not the caste.'[1]
'Relinquishing all your pride of caste, take pains to acquire
good qualities. If caste becomes the mother of conceit, then
there could not be a more formidable foe. But if it saves you
from evil, you cannot find a better friend.'

The Brahmanas—who afterwards came to occupy high
places in the monasteries—learned a lesson that day.

1.   न जातिः कारणं लोके गुणाः कल्याणहेतवः ।

26

Krimikantha

One day after this incident Ramanuja heard that Mahapurna, his Guru, had himself set fire to the dead body of a devotee who was a Sudra and all were speaking ill of him for that act not befitting a Brahmana. Desirous of knowing the truth of it, Ramanuja went to his Guru's house. There he came to know that all the relatives of Mahapurna had abandoned him and for that reason, Attulai, his daughter, had to come from her father-in-law's house and attend on him. When Ramanuja asked him as to why he acted like that, Mahapurna said: 'True, my child, that was not proper according to the injunctions of the Dharma-sastras. But what is Dharma? The path marked by the footsteps of the great ones is the real path of Dharma.'[1] Remember that Jatayu, though born a mere bird, was cremated by Sri Ramachandra. Yudhi-shthira, a Kshatriya, worshipped Vidura, a Sudra. Why did they act that way? The answer is that a real devotee of God has no caste. Such devotees are the crown of all castes. With the upholders of Dharma like Ramachandra and Yudhishthira, no unbecoming conduct is possible. The devotee whose body I cremated was a thousand times more devoted than I. And I felt blessed that I served him.'

Yatiraja, who was exceedingly glad to hear this, prostrated himself at his Guru's feet and begged pardon of him for his doubts.

One day when Mahapurna came and prostrated himself at the feet of Ramanuja, the latter did not show any embarrassment. The devotees seated by his side asked in

---

1. महाजनो येन गतः स पन्था । *Mahabharata*, Vana-Parvan, 314. 119.

amazement, 'Yatiraja, your Guru bowed before you and you did not prevent him; how do you explain this?'

'Sri Gurudeva behaved in that way,' said Ramanuja, 'in order to teach the traits of a real devotee; or, in other words, how a true disciple should behave before his Guru. So I shall take refuge only in that path that has been shown by him; I won't transgress it in any way.'[1]

When they asked Mahapurna about this strange conduct of his, he said, 'In Yatiraja I found my Guru Yamunacharya, and therefore I prostrated myself before him.' By saying this, Mahapurna revealed before them all the uncommon greatness of Yatiraja.

Ramanuja used to consider Goshthipurna as Narayana Himself. One day, seeing him meditating for a long time in a room with the doors closed, Ramanuja asked him when he had come out of his meditation, 'Revered Sir, what is the Mantra and who is the Deity that you are meditating on?'[2]

'The lotus feet of my Guru Yamunacharya—them alone I worship,' he answered. 'His name alone I repeat and it removes all sufferings.'

From that day onward, Ramanuja began to consider his Gurudeva superior even to Narayana Himself.

After a few days Mahapurna[3] passed away. Though Ramanuja himself was very much grieved at this, he assumed courage and pacified Attulai and others of the family.

---

1. गुरुणोक्तप्रकारेण वर्तनं शिष्यलक्षणम् ।

अतस्तेनोक्तमार्गेण वर्तेऽहं वै न चान्यथा ॥ *Prapannamritam*, LX. 35, 36.

2. को मन्त्र: किश्च ते ध्यानम् । *ibid.* XLII. 22.

3. According to a reliable version, Mahapurna did not die a natural death. He accompanied Kuresa while going to the court of Krimikantha and like Kuresa refused to sign the statement. 'There is none higher than Siva.' As a consequence his eyes too were plucked out by the king's servants and both the blind Vaishnavas were turned out. The old Mahapurna, unable to bear the pain, laid himself down on the way in the open, his head resting on the lap of Kuresa, and after speaking words of consolation to the sorrowing Kuresa, expired with his thoughts lovingly fixed on Yamunacharya, his Guru.—*Ed.*

At that time the Chola King, Krimikantha by name, while residing in his capital Kanchipuram, resolved to see that the entire Chola kingdom embraced the Saiva doctrine. In the annals of India there have been very few kings so narrow-minded and cruel-hearted as he. He mused that if Ramanuja could be brought to the Saiva fold, the entire Chola country would become Saiva. In case he did not give up the Vaishnava faith, then even by putting him to death the sovereignty of the Saiva faith was to be established in the Chola kingdom. Thus resolved, he sent a number of his stalwart emissaries to bring Ramanuja to Kanchipuram. When they came to Sri rangam and served the order of the king, Ramanuja at once agreed to follow them and went inside the monastery to get ready. But Kuresa said to him, 'The rumour is that it is only to put an end to your life that Krimikantha has sent these men to take you to Kanchi. Why should you go there? If your life is preserved, it will be for the good of the entire world. You show us the way to the feet of the Lord. For those like me who are scorched by the flames of the world, you alone can give shelter. Let me go instead of you. Let me put on your ochre cloth, while you wear my white clothes and make your escape from Srirangam. Please get ready at once.'

Hearing this, Ramanuja pondered for a moment and then acceded to the request of Kuresa. Without any more delay he dressed himself like Kuresa, and finding Kuresa dressed in ochre robes, went out of the monastery in quick steps towards the forest westward. Govinda and the other disciples followed him one by one.

In the meantime, Kuresa, dressed in the ochre robes of his great Guru and taking his staff and water-pot, appeared before the king's men, who thinking he was Ramanuja himself, took him to Kanchipuram and presented him to Krimikantha. The king received him well and took great care of him in the beginning. He knew that he was a man of great talents and of profound learning. For, when he was a boy of eight, while his sister was possessed by a ghost, it was Ramanuja who cured her. Therefore, considering Kuresa to be Ramanuja himself, the King said: 'Revered Sir, please be seated. I have brought you here with the sole intention of hearing good talks on religious matters. The scholars of my court are also eager to converse with you. Please tell us what is the duty of men like us.'

'O King and scholars!' said Kuresa, 'Lord Vishnu, the redeemer of all the worlds, is the only object of worship for all from the highest created being to the lowest.'

Krimikantha at once flew into a rage and said, 'I had an idea that you were a great scholar and a devotee. Now I see that you are an imposter; for, you worship Vishnu instead of Siva, the Guru of all and the destroyer of everything. Please give up this folly. With the help of the Sastras and reasoning, the Pundits here will teach you the supreme Saiva doctrines. Listen to them and be converted to the Saiva faith. Otherwise there is no escape for you today.'

When Krimikantha stopped, the Pundits of the king's court fell upon Kuresa, as a pack of well-trained hounds fall upon the leading elephant of a herd and try to tear him to pieces. Taking only one side of the Sastras, they talked at length. A long time passed in this way. At last, Krimikantha said, 'You pedant, if you want to save your life, then acknowledge that there is none greater than Siva.'

'Why, Drona is bigger than Siva,'[1] said undaunted Kuresa laughingly.

Here the words 'Drona' and 'Siva' mean units of weight. The weight of about thirty-two seers is known as 'Drona' and one half of that weight is 'Siva'. What Kuresa ridiculed was the Pundits' attempt to set limits to God, who is limitless, immeasurable, without a second and unknowable. In other words, they were trying to establish their

---

1. द्रोणमस्ति ततः परम् ।   *Prapannamritam*, XLIX. 16.

conclusions born of mean understanding, such as: God is this and nothing else; neither can He be anything else.

Kuresa's intellect equalled his devotion. He had totally surrendered all—mind, life, knowledge, intellect, strength, body and soul—at the feet of Ramanuja. And here was the supreme testimony of his devotion to his Guru. He knew that going to the king was walking into the jaws of death. But he deemed it his good fortune to be able to give up his own life in order to save his Guru's. The mind of a genuine Bhakta and Jnani is naturally free from all traces of fear. 'Knowing the bliss of Brahman, man fears nothing.'[1] Instead of being perturbed by the king's threats, Kuresa was at that time feeling keenly the immensity of his good fortune and mentally thanking God with the words:

'O Lord, remembering Your immeasurable grace on this poor child of Yours, I have partially grasped the import of the nectar-like words of Srimat Yamunamuni. Repeatedly do I bow down before you:

Salutation again and again (to You) who are beyond speech and mind;

Salutation again and again (to You) the only ground of speech and mind;

Salutation again and again (to You) of infinitely great divine powers;

Repeated salutation to You the ocean of boundless mercy.[2]

'Even this powerful king and these learned scholars are not aware of Your endless glory. But You have kindly revealed it to this insignificant creature so that he has shed pride and grown humble. What greater good fortune than this is there?'

Anger raged in the minds of Krimikantha and his courtiers when they heard the words of ridicule uttered by Kuresa. The King ordered Kuresa to be bound, and then said

---

1. आनन्दं ब्रह्मणो विद्वान् न बिभेति कुतश्चन । *Taittiriya Upanishad,* II. 9.

2. *Stotraratna,* 21 (See Appendix B).

addressing his courtiers, 'Take away at once from my presence this blasphemer against Siva and instantly pluck out his eyes. When my sister was possessed by a ghost, he exorcised her; for this reason, spare his life.'

According to the royal order, the king's men took Kuresa to a secluded place, and after subjecting him to varied tortures, plucked out his eyes.[1] But this great one, notwithstanding the extreme pain he was suffering, was neither displeased nor angry with them. On the contrary, he uttered prayers to the lotus feet of the Lord for the good of his tormentors. He rejoiced at heart that he could save, from these indescribable sufferings, his Guru, who was dearer to him than his own life.

When, instead of surrendering oneself to one's wife, son, body and home, one takes refuge at the lotus feet of Sri Hari, one enjoys bliss eternal. He who has succeeded in doing this has risen superior to all miseries. Kuresa had renounced all his immense wealth, knowing it to be the root of all miseries, and taken refuge at Sri Ramanuja's lotus feet. We have mentioned before that his wife—his partner in Dharma—too had followed him on this path. The treatment which he received at the hands of Krimikantha gave him joy rather than pain. Kuresa therefore prostrated himself before his tormentors and said 'Brethren, you are my true friends. Today through your grace I have got rid of those two rank enemies, the two eyes, which instead of taking the human mind towards its Creator, entangle it in illusory and perishable creation. May God bless you!'

Seeing his calm and joyous bearing, and hearing his words of blessing, awe and devotion were awakened in the

---

1. According to another current version, when the mandate to pluck out Kuresa's eyes was issued to his courtiers', Kuresa exclaimed to the astonishment of the king, 'You need not take this trouble. I will pluck out my eyes; for they ought not to remain after seeing a sinner like you and thus becoming unfit for seeing my holy Guru, Ramanuja.' So saying, he gouged out his eyes and contented himself martyr-like, with the thought that he was chosen by God to give his 'Darsan' (eye) for the sake of his 'Darsan' (philosophy).—*Ed.*

hearts of these fiendish men. They called a wayside beggar and ordered him, 'Take this Sadhu by the hand to Srirangam, Here is some money which you may spend on the way.' The beggar accepted the offer gladly and proceeded towards Srirangam with Kuresa.

It is said that a few days after this incident, Krimikantha died of some incurable disease. Though the king was a devotee of Siva, he persecuted Vaishnavas because he had not the knowledge that Hari and Hara were only different aspects of the one Godhead. Some Vaishnavas too were equally narrow-minded because of similar ignorance.

27

Vishnuvardhana

When, on his part, Ramanuja had found secret asylum in the spacious thick forest west of Srirangam, gradually, one by one, his disciples began to gather round him. When Govinda, Dasarathi, Dhanurdasa and others came, they moved quickly westward into the denser regions of the forest. For fear of being detected and arrested by the spies of Krimikantha, they walked incessantly for two days without halting anywhere and at last reached the outskirts of the Chola kingdom. Meanwhile, they had neither eaten food nor slept, nor taken rest on the way. Extremely tired, all of them sat down at the foot of a hill. Not only were they troubled by hunger, thirst and want of sleep, but their hands, feet and bodies were full of severe pain. The soles of their feet were pierced by thorns and were sore with blisters. They lay down on stones and fell into deep sleep.

Nearby was a village of the Chandalas. Though they belonged to a very low caste, their minds were not so low. Seeing the Brahmanas sleeping in that state, they understood that some untoward fate made them enjoy such blissful sleep at that place where no Brahmana was ever to be seen. Forthwith they collected various fruits from the forest and placed them in the vicinity of the sleeping party. Then they collected bundles of dry wood and kindled a fire and waited with attention and devotion for their getting up. After some time, when they woke up, Ramanuja and his disciples felt refreshed to a great extent. When they found a number of Chandalas standing with folded hands at a distance, a heap of fruits near them, and a pile of dry wood near the blazing fire, they understood that by the grace of the Lord they had come to a forest-hamlet belonging to these good-natured folk. Without any delay they took their bath in the nearby rivulet. They washed the fruits and offered them to Sri Hari

217

and were supremely glad to eat them after the starvation
of two days. While conversing with the people, Yatiraja
came to know that they had crossed the boundry of the
Chola kingdom.

After blessing the Chandalas, and with the guidance
of some of them, Yatiraja set out in search of some village
and in the afternoon reached the house of one Brahmana. The
master of the house was not present at home. But Chelan-
chalamba, his chaste wife, thought herself supremely blessed
at the coming of so many Vaishnavas to their house and,
notwithstanding the absence of her husband at home,
received them in the proper manner and then entered the
kitchen for cooking. On his return from begging, Srirangadasa,
the master of the house, was extremely glad to find so many
Vaishnava guests at his place. Soon his devoted wife prepared
the offering for Sri Vishnu and invited their guests to take
the consecrated food. They were only too happy to do the
fullest justice to the consecrated food. They halted there and
took rest for two days when Srirangadasa and his wife were
initiated into the Vaishnava Mantra.

Then taking leave of the Chandalas, they started from
there in the morning accompanied by Srirangadasa and at
nightfall reached a place by name Vahnipushkarini, and
camped there for two days for taking rest.

Thence Yatiraja took leave of Srirangadasa and came
with his disciples to a village called Salagrama, where they
became the guests of Andhrapurna, a Brahmana and a great
ascetic. Seeing the dispassion and devotion of Andhrapurna
and learning that he had not enmeshed himself in matrimonial ties, Ramanuja initiated him into Vaishnava faith and
made him his personal attendant. From that day onward,
Andhra-purna devoted himself entirely to the wholehearted
service of Yatiraja. He would follow his Guru like a shadow.
In him alone he perfectly realised his Chosen Ideal, his all
in all.

After a few days' stay at Salagrama, they all came to
Nrisimhakshetra. Desirous of seeing one Purna, a great

devotee in the village Bhaktagrama, of whom Ramanuja had heard from Andhrapurna, he went to that village with is disciples and became his guest for a day. Later, being invited by Vitthaladeva, the king of the country, he became his guest. This king was a Jain[1] and used to serve thousands of Sramanas every day. When his daughter became possessed by an evil spirit, he first brought many physicians. When they failed to show any result, he sought the help of the Jain monks, but they too failed to cure the princess. Meanwhile, when Vitthaladeva heard that a few Vaishnavas had come to Purna's house from the east, he sent some Pundits who duly invited and brought them to the palace, Ramanuja cured the princess by simply looking at her, at which Vitthaladeva was much amazed. Thenceforth he grew very devoted to Ramanuja. Wishing to hear of Vaishnavism from Yatiraja, the king prostrated himself before him and made his desire known. Now Ramanuja—who was all devotion, sweet-natured, ever eager to do good to he Jivas, endowed with superhuman powers, full of divine lustre, attractive to all hearts and like a thunderbolt to the rock of the Charvakas— expounded his doctrines with such easily comprehensible and captivating reasonings that the king repented of his own godless attitude and invited the Sramanas to enter into a discussion with Yatiraja. A great assembly was called forth on that very day. Thousands of Jains gathered there. As Ramanuja commenced expounding the Vaishnava religion, some mean-minded Jain Pundits resorted to booing and cat-calls, but they were turned out of the assembly hall at the command of Vitthaladeva. In a steady and serious voice, Yatiraja submitted all that he had to say before the assembly.

---

1. In Chapter XLVII of the *Prapannamritam,* Bittideva (or Vitthaladeva) is referred to as a Buddhist king. Perhaps in pursuance of this version, the author of this book in his original also refers to Bittideva as a Buddhist king. But in historical records this Hoysala king—who subsequently came o be known as Vishnuvardhana after being converted to Sri Vaishnavism by Sri Ramanuja—is referred to only as a follower of Jainism. Hence necessary alterations are made in the chapter.—*Tr.*

As he finished his discourse, the foremost scholar among the Sramanas rose up to contradict his doctrine. But, when without refuting the arguments of his opponent, he began attacking the Sanatana-dharma, Vitthaladeva said, 'Revered Sir, there is nothing so easy as speaking ill of others. You are a great scholar. Refute, if you can, with precise arguments the doctrine expounded by your opponent. And if you cannot, then give up your false faith and be initiated into Vaishnavism.'

No reasonable argument came into the Jain scholar's mind. He sat down pale-faced in the midst of the assembly. The other Jain scholars tried for some time to establish their own faith; but they too failed to do so. Then the king arose and addressed the assembly:

'Members of the assembly, today you have all seen for yourselves that the Jain scholars have been utterly defeated by the Vaishnavacharya. What is our duty under these circumstances? To fall into hell ridden with all sorts of miseries by taking recourse to a false religion, or to become blessed by earning supreme knowledge, which is the mine of all bliss, by taking refuge in a true faith? Any intelligent man will acknowledge that bliss is by far preferable to affliction; and knowledge, to ignorance. Let us all even today be initiated into the true faith by this large-hearted Vaishnava and become blessed.'

All but a few Sramanas commended his view. And all were blessed with initiation by Ramanuja on that very day. The few Jains who could not be persuaded left his kingdom. King Vitthaladeva was named by Yatiraja as Vishnuvardhana and was known thence by his new name.

28

Yadavadripati

Thus Ramanuja converted Vitthaladeva and thousands of other Jains to Vaishnavism. He lived in their midst for some time and then, accompanied by his disciples, went to Yadavadri. The present name of this place is Melkote. He set his foot on this holy ground in 1020 Saka era. In the morning of the fourteenth day in the month of Paush (Dec-Jan) in that year, Ramanuja, while taking a stroll in the Tulasi grove, came across an image underneath an ant-hill. Digging up the image and cleaning it, Ramanuja put it on a pedestal and all the assembled devotees there felt blessed to look at its life-like and captivating features. The old inhabitants of the place said, 'In our boyhood we have heard from our elders that of yore an image known as Yadavadripati used to be worshipped here. But when the Muslims overran the place and desecrated temples and images, the worshippers hid the image of Vishnu in some secret place and then went away somewhere else. From that time onwards, the Deity has not been worshipped or any festivals celebrated. It must be that Yadavadripati has again arisen on the advent of one like you, to accept the services of His devotees.'

'What you have spoken is right,' said Ramanuja. 'This is that Yadavadripati. At night He appeared to me in a dream and demanded service. Please join hands and see that a beautiful and magnificent temple is built and consecrated to Him. Let regular worship of Him be conducted from today.'

According to the behests of Yatiraja, his disciples and the village people built on that very day a spacious thatched structure, and after installing the Deity therein, engaged themselves heart and soul in the Lord's worship and service. A large and beautiful temple was built up there within a very short time. There was a big tank, by the name Kalyani near this temple, and its limpid water was used for the ablutions and offerings of Yadavadripati. One day, while walking on the northern side of the tank, Ramanuja was very glad to discover white earth there; for the Vaishnavas used that earth for marking the Urdhvapundra. Until then they used to collect this earth from Bhaktagrama. But by that time the particular kind of earth being already exhausted in Bhaktagrama, Ramanuja had sent many people to search for that kind of earth at different places. But none had succeeded in doing so. He was therefore very glad to discover it in this spot.

In every temple in South India there are two images of each Deity. The name of the one is Achala-Vigraha (non moving image), which never goes out from inside the temple; the other is Sachala-vigraha (moving image), which goes out of the temple, being carried on vehicles during the times of festivals; it is also called the Utsava-vigraha. One day 'Yadavadripati appeared to Ramanuja in a dream and said, 'Ramanuja, My child, I am pleased with your service. But as I have no Utsava-vigraha here, I cannot go out of the temple to bless My devotees and free the fallen ones from sin. Therefore, hasten to bring My second image, named Sampatkumara, which is now with the Emperor[1] of Delhi.'

Being thus commanded, Ramanuja, with a few disciples, set out next morning for Delhi, which he reached after two months. The then Emperor of Delhi was much gratified to see the lustre of his body, his scholarship, and his personality and wanted to know the purpose of his visit. Ramanuja petitioned for the image of Sampatkumara and the Emperor granted his prayer. Ramanuja was taken inside the hall, where he found many of the Deities removed from the temples of India. Though Ramanuja made a thorough search, he did not find the image he wanted. Now, when the emperor showed an image which was very dear to his daughter, Ramanuja at once recognized it as Sampatkumara and with the consent

---

1. See Appendix A.

of the Emperor, took the image and started along with his disciples towards the south.[1]

They walked day and night without any rest, for Yatiraja knew for certain that, if the princess wanted the image restored to her, the loving father might again take it back from him.

Now when the princess came to know that some Brahmanas had gone away with the object of her greatest love, her grief knew no bounds. She was overwhelmed with sorrow and could not be consoled by her father. Day by day she grew sick with longing. Frightened at this, the Emperor ordered a regiment of soldiers, 'Go immediately, and bring back the image forcibly from the Brahmana.' Then the princess said, 'Father, with your permission, I too shall accompany them.' The fond father acceded to her importunities. The princess, who was followed by a large retinue of maid-servants and men-servants, rode in a nicely decorated palanquin and had the command of the troop of soldiers. Meantime, Kubera, a prince in love with the emperor's daughter, had been trying for long to win the favour of the princess and hoping to be betrothed to her. When he found the princess Bibi Lachimar going after the image like an insane woman, he too followed her.

Ramanuja and his disciples, walking day and night, had crossed the boundary of the emperor's territories. Bibi Lachimar who was pursuing them was still far behind them. Ramanuja arrived at Melkote with the image of Sampatkumara and installed the Utsava-vigraha in a secret spot inside the temple. On his way, he was immensely helped by the Chandalas. Had they not carried the image all the way, Ramanuja might have fallen into the hands of the emperor's

1. It is said that when Sri Ramanuja saw Ramapriya, he called Him by His name, and lo! the image jumped down from the couch on which the princess had placed him, and walked towards Ramanuja who embraced the moving Deity with all the fondness of a parent finding his long-lost son. In commemoration of this event, Ramapriya was given the name 'selva-p-pillai' (Sampatkumara)—which means 'Darling'— by Ramanuja; even today the image of Ramapriya is called by that name.—Ed.

soldiery. Hence the Chandalas were given the right to enter the temple of Yadavadripati for three days every year.[1]

Like the unlimited, non-dual and formless aspect of God, His concrete forms are also real. God sometimes descends on the earth in the form of an image, accepts the worship of devotees up to the end of a cycle of creation and fulfils the desires of their hearts. These holy images are called the Archavataras of Sri Hari. Like those of Amarnath, Kedarnath, Badrinarayana, Chandranath, Jagannath, Dvarakanath, Srinath, Omkarnath, Pasupatinath, Tarakanath, Srihinglajesvari, Kalikamata, Sri Ramanath, so too Yadavadrinath is an Archavatara.

Ramanuja was pursued by the emperor's daughter while he was coming away with Sampatkumara, the Sachala or Utsavavigraha of Yadavadripati. To gross eyes, this image may not appear different from the other images; but Yatiraja, with his subtle vision, knew that it was Sri Vishnu Himself who incarnated in the form of the image and fell into the hands of the Emperor so as to be taken to the palace to be united with Bibi Lachimar, the supremely devoted princess, and make her blessed. By the divine power of her devotion, acquired through many births, Bibi Lachimar could recognise Sampatkumara as her Chosen Deity and by accepting Him, got immersed in the ocean of beatitude. It was nothing strange that, unable to bear the pangs of separation, she should be ready to sacrifice her life in the quest of her Chosen Deity.

Without food or sleep or rest and with the vast regiment of soldiers following her, the Princess proceeded southward in pursuit of her dearest One. But when she crossed the bounds of her father's empire and still could not recover Him, she

---

1. More than eight centuries ago when Sri Ramanuja granted this right to the 'untouchables', it was indeed a bold pioneering act of magnanimity. At present with the abolition of 'untouchability 'under Article 17 of the Constitution of India all Hindus irrespective of caste have equal rights to enter any public place of worship belonging to their religion. And according to The Untouchability (Offences) Act, 1955 (Act No. 22 of 1955) any person preventing another to exercise the above right is liable to punishment.—*Tr.*

resolved to give up her life. The pangs of separation tormented her heart and tears flowed from her eyes. The words of hope uttered by Kubera did not enter her ears. She only exclaimed, 'My Lord! Ah, my Lord! 'and thus gave vent to the agony of her heart. One night, without the knowledge of the soldiery, she entered the dense forest southward. Only Kubera followed her. All the while meditating only on her Chosen One, she proceeded further south. Kubera sometimes brought her wild flowers and fruits. She took a little to appease her hunger and thirst. When night fell, unable to discern the way, she would be forced to take rest. After thus travelling many days, she at last reached Melkote. As one with eyes does not require the help of any one else to see the sun, so the Princess, who was all devotion to Sri Hari, and whose vision had been cleasend by the collyrium, of knowledge, did not require the help of others to be united with Sampatkumara, who was dearer to her than her own life.

Thus was brought about their longed-for union. The river came to be merged in the ocean. She was satisfied like a hungry man with a pot filled with nectar.

Yatiraja and his disciples were amazed to see her intense devotion. Though born of a Muslim family, she was allowed to enter the temple; for, a genuine devotee has no caste whatsoever.

Now came to an end Bibi Lachimar's journey in the wilderness of this world; her desires were fulfilled. The remaining days of her life were crowned with indescribable happiness born of communion with the Lord of her heart. At last her pure frame got dissolved in the body of Sri Sampatkumara.

Prince Kubera used to serve Lachimar like his own Chosen Deity. When the empress of his heart got dissolved in the body of Sampatkumara, he was not able to stay there any longer. He gave up all his Muslim ways, went to Srirangam and took refuge at the feet of Sri Ranganathaswami. Not permitted to enter the temple, he

stayed outside and took refuge at the blessed feet of Seshasayi
Narayana with undivided devotion. If any one gave him
anything, he would take a part of it to appease his hunger
and thirst. Once, while absorbed in deep meditation, he
heard a voice saying, 'O the best among the Yavanas! I am
here to grant liberation to Vaishnavas who take refuge in
Me; and Lord Jagannatha is there to grant liberation unto
the fallen ones.'[1]

Being thus ordered, this Muslim devotee started the
next morning for Sri Jagannathakshetra. After a few months
he arrived at Sri Puridhama where he was blessed with the
divine vision of Sri Purushottama, the Redeemer of the
fallen.

It is said that Mahatma Kubera was one day baking
his bread on the oven when a dog came and suddenly ran
away with the bread. At this, he ran after the dog with the
pot of ghee in his hand, shouting, 'O Narayana! wait a little,
let me smear ghee on the bread; otherwise You won't relish
it.' Kubera, with the capacity to see the same reality everywhere, realized the same Brahman in a cow, an elephant,
a dog, and a Chandala alike.

When one has shed body-consciousness, one is free
from the pride of caste. In the body alone are found name,
caste and Ashrama. It is the body to which one applies the
terms Brahmana, Kshatriya, Vaisya, Sudra, Mussalman,
Christian, English, French, Hindu and so on. Through the
grace of God, Bibi Lachimar and Kubera had ceased to
identify the self with the body and so they had no fetters
of caste. And Ramanuja himself regarded them as great
devotees. To this day the sacred image of that daughter of
the emperor is being worshipped in some Vaishnava temples
in South India. Such is the universality of Hinduism.

---

1. प्रपन्नमोक्षदानेऽहं दीक्षितो यवनेश्वर ।
    पतितानां मोक्षदाने जगन्नाथ: प्रदीक्षित: ॥

    Prapannamritam, XLVIII, 29 (second half), 30 (first half).

29

More about Kuresa

After Kubera, the illustrious devotee, had left for Srikshetra, Kuresa—who had lost his physical eyes but had his inner vision intact, who was a perfect image of devotion to the Guru,—came along with his wife and son to a place called Krishnachala to perform the worship of Bhagavan Sundarabhuja and resided there for some time. While residing there, he thought himself blessed in composing the hymns to Sri, to Sundarabhuja, to Atimanusha and to Sri Vaikuntha. Desirous of touching the lotus feet of Yatiraja, his own Guru, he went from there to Yadavadri and appeared before him and fell at his feet. Sri Ramanuja raised him affectionately from the ground and embraced him warmly and said, 'Today I have been purified and blessed by the touch of a great devotee. Ah! What an auspicious day it is for me!'

Kuresa shed tears of joy. He could not utter a single word. His wife and his son Parasara, too, experienced unbounded joy in the gracious presence of Sri Ramanuja.

After a few days, Ramanuja said to Kuresa, 'My child, go to Kanchipuram and pray for your eyes to Lord Varadaraja who will surely remove your blindness. Krimikantha is dead. There is no more reason for fear. Do not delay.'

'Be it so,' said Kuresa at the command of his Guru and straight went to Kanchipuram. Arriving there, he went to Sri Varadaraja and surrendering body, mind and speech to Him, began to hymn the Lord. Pleased with his devotion, Varadaraja asked: 'Kuresa, My child, what do you pray for? Tell Me your wish, and I shall fulfil it right now.'

'Lord, by Thy grace, may Chaturgrama[1] obtain the supreme object,' said Kuresa, the large-minded, with folded hands.

'Be it so,' said Sri Varadaraja.

Kuresa again fell to hymning the Lord.

'Kuresa, what is your wish now? Tell Me; I shall fulfil that,' Sri Varadaraja said again.

'Lord, may those who are the masters of Chaturgrama attain the supreme object,' submitted Kuresa.

'Be it so,' said Varadaraja.

Kuresa experienced unbounded joy on hearing this. Thinking himself blessed and quite forgetful of his own blindness, Kuresa went to his own place from the temple.

The master of Chaturgrama was that stone-hearted man who caused the plucking out of the eyeballs of Kuresa. Yet, Kuresa was happy and thought himself blessed by securing supreme bliss for his enemy. Is not such a one God Himself in the image of a Bhakta? This was why Sri Ramakrishna used to say: Bhagavan, Bhakta and Bhagavata—there is no difference between these three.

When Ramanuja at Yadavadri came to know from reports that Kuresa had deemed himself blessed on securing the supreme welfare of his arch-enemies and that he took no care to get back his own eyes, Ramanuja sent a disciple of his with the message: 'My child Kuresa, I am pleased to

1. Chaturgrama' literally means 'four villages'; here it refers to a man who was probably the owner of a group of four villages well-known in those days, or to a descendant of that family. This man—called Naluran in Tamil—a disciple of Kuresa, was the minister of the Chola king, who gave the suggestion to the king that there was no use in getting signatures from all Vaishnavas indiscriminately in support of the king's declaration about the pre-eminence of Siva, and that the signatures of the two veteran Vaishnavas, Kuresa and Ramanuja, alone would best serve the purpose. It was at his instance that the king sent for Ramanuja and Kuresa to get their assent to his proposition. Later Kuresa in the guise of Ramanuja met the king and refuted his statement, for which he had to lose his eyes. Kuresa knew that it was his disciple who was responsible for his being brought before the king and yet he prayed to the Lord of Kanchi for the forgiveness of his disciple and his salvation. Thus Kuresa evinced nothing but love for even his greatest enemy.—Ed.

hear that you are experiencing transcendental joy. But, in this, you have shown selfishness by keeping the joy to yourself. In order to make me supremely happy, you should now beg for your eyes at the feet of Sri Varadaraja. Don't you know that you, your body and mind, are all mine and not yours?'

Hearing this message of supreme grace from his master delivered by his brother-disciple, Kuresa danced in joy and said, 'Blessed am I today! Making this worldly-minded man an excuse, Yatiraja has to-day revealed the largeness of his heart. Instantly shall I go and do my master's bidding.'

He hastened to the temple and standing before the blessed image of Sri Varadaraja, the fulfiller of all desires, began to hymn the Deity. Being pleased with Kuresa, Sri Hari said, 'My child, Kuresa, with what prayer have you come again? There is nothing I shall withhold from you. Tell Me, and right now I shall fulfil your prayer.' Kuresa answered, 'My Lord, some time ago, I had, through some Wrong turn of my fate, lost two things dear to my master. May I, through Thy grace, get them back today?'

'My child,' said Sri Varadaraja, 'may two divine eyes adorn your pure body and bring unlimited joy to your master. I am here only to see and serve devotees like you. As they solicit My vision and service, likewise, I too find joy in seeing and serving them. They are to me as the rays are to the sun.'

On hearing these words of Sri Hari, Kuresa experienced unspeakable joy, and lost consciousness of the outer world. After some time, he came to know of the regaining of his eyes. Glad beyond measure, shedding tears of joy, and looking with folded hands at the image in front of him, he said, 'Lord, it is You who gave it ; it is You who took it; and now it is You who have given it back. O Playful One, how can an insignificant Jiva like me comprehend the mystery of Your sport? In the beginning, in the end and in the middle You are pure bliss. You create in joy; You sustain in joy; and that slumber of Yours, which brings about dissolution, that too is full of joy. Only those like me, who are blinded by ignorance, imagine this creation of Yours to be of the nature of misery, and Yourself, the very essence of bliss, as the cause of that misery. Through Your grace, my ignorance has been dispelled today. How great is my good fortune! And how great Your grace!'

Mad with joy, Kuresa began to dance. All were surprised and blessed to see him regain his eyes and there was the awakening of deep devotion in every heart towards the Lord and His devotee.

News of this spread in all directions and all knew that Ramanuja and his disciples were endowed with superhuman powers. All the people of South India believed them to be the God-ordained reformers of religion. When Ramanuja heard about the supreme mercy of Kuresa towards his terrible enemies, he danced with upraised arms before all, and said, 'My attaining the supreme goal is now assured. For, when Kuresa has been able to secure Moksha for his enemies, then, it is certain that I too shall find liberation through his goodness.'

It is natural for the great and godlike to exalt the glory of their devotees.

30

Divine Qualities of
the Disciples of Sri Ramanuja

Vatiraja left Yadavadri along with his disciples, en route to Srirangam, stopping on the way at Vrishabhachala (Tirumalirumcholai) in order to worship Lord Sundarabahu there. This place is situated near Madurai. Previously Andal had prayed in her hymn to Sundarabahu:

> O Hari, if You would graciously accept my hand, I shall offer You a hundred jars full of sweet rice prepared with milk and other delicious things, and a hundred jars full of butter along with that.[1]

The Lord fulfilled this prayer of Andal. But that immaculate woman, who was all love for the Lord, could not keep her word, for soon after attaining Sri Hari, she got dissolved into Him. So, in order to fulfil her pledge, Ramanuja offered to Sri Sundarabahu a hundred jars full of sweet rice and a hundred jars of butter. For having done this act befitting a brother, Ramanuja came to be renowned as Godagraja, or the elder brother of Andal.

From there Ramanuja went to Srivilliputtur to see the birth-place of Andal. After having the Darsan of the Seshasayi Narayana of that place, he entered the temple dedicated to Andal and considered himself blessed by worshipping and hymning her with devotion. There he stayed for some time and then moved to Sri Kurukanagara (Alvar Tirunagari). Thence he went to other holy places. At long

---

1. कुरुषे यदि देव पाणिग्रहणमङ्गलम् ।
     क्षीराद्यनेकसंयुक्तगुडान्नस्य घटीशतम् ।
     समर्पये हरे तुभ्यं नवनीतघटीशतम् ॥

     Prapannamritam, LIII, 3, 4 (first half).

last he came to Srirangam along with his disciples and
had the Darsan of Seshasayi Narayana. And then he
entered his own monastery. The news of Yatiraja's return
brought back life as it were into men and women of the
place.

On hearing of the return of his Guru, Mahatma Kuresa
hastened to fall at his blessed feet. And so did his wife and
his son Parasara. No matter in what state they were, when
people heard of the return of Ramanuja, they ran at once
to see him. The monastery of Yatiraja assumed a festive
appearance. When Kuresa and Yatiraja met, they experienced indescribable joy.

Two years passed. Disabled in body now, Kuresa
became confined to bed. Then one day, in the presence
of Yatiraja, surrounded by devotees, while hearing the loud
chanting of the Lord's name, shedding tears of joy and
holding to his heart the lotus-feet of his Guru, Kuresa passed
away. All were immersed in grief. Tears rolled down from
the eyes of Yatiraja. Controlling himself and consoling others with words of wisdom, he said: 'Devotees of the
Lord! Parasara, the son of Kuresa, is in fact the son of Sri
Ranganathaswami Himself. From today accept him as your
king. He will keep under his control the vast Vaishnava
empire of the future. His devotion equals his father's and
the depth of his natural wisdom is incomparable.'

So saying, Yatiraja himself seated Parasara on the throne,
placed on his head a crown of flowers, decorated him
with garlands and asked all the devotees to utter words
of blessings. Then he himself embraced him and transmitted
the Vaishnavi-sakti in full to Parasara and thus made him
blessed.

Kuresa's sacred body was cremated on the banks of the
Kaveri and the day passed in congregational singing of the
Lord's name. Thanks to the influence of Yatiraja,
there remained no trace of grief in any one's heart. And then
followed month-long celebrations to which came from all
directions hundreds of Vaishnavas, as also poor, blind and

lame people, who happily took the Prasada of Sri Ranganathaswami and deemed themselves fortunate.

Thereafter, Yatiraja never left Srirangam. Many men and women came from far and near to see him. He was now sixty years of age. After this, he lived there for another sixty years in supreme bliss at the feet of Sri Ranganathaswami, surrounded by disciples and doing good to people. Andhra-purna was ever busy in his service. To him, Ramanuja was all in all, his only God.

Once Sri Ranganathaswami, with His retinue, came out of the temple to make His devotees blessed by granting them Darsan. Eager to see the Lord, all came out into the streets, laying aside the work on hand, and began to worship the Consort of Lakshmi, the Lord of the three worlds, who was beautifully decorated with flowers and garlands, and carried by bearers on their shoulders. With his disciples Ramanuja too came out from the monastery, saw the Lord, and offered worship and felt blessed. At that time, Andhrapurna was boiling milk for Yatiraja. He could have easily taken it down from the oven and gone to offer worship to Sri Ranganatha-swami. But he did nothing of the sort. Service to the Guru was for him the highest duty. When Yatiraja asked him, 'We all went out to see the Lord, and what were you doing alone inside the monastery all the time?' Andhrapurna replied, 'O refuge of the lowly! if I went to see the Lord outside, the service to the Lord inside would suffer. How then could I go out and have Darsan of Sri Ranganathaswami? At that time I was engaged in cooking.'

All the disciples of Yatiraja were endowed with sterling qualities. The disciple named Anantacharya who had, by the command of his Guru, gone to live at Srisaila along with his wife, kept himself constantly busy in the worship of the Lord; for he knew that to be the only stay of the Jiva. While staying at Srisaila, he saw that the people of the place experienced great difficulty due to scarcity of water. So he resolved to dig there a lake with his own hands. He began the work of digging. His wife used to carry the earth in a basket and throw it far away. For many years, they kept themselves engaged in this work. Once, while his wife— then in the family way—was carrying the excavated earth with slow steps and throwing it at a distance, she felt tired. After carrying a few more basket-loads, she was utterly exhausted and sat under a tree. Soon she fell into a deep slumber. Tradition has it that, seeing this, Sri Hari, the Redeemer of the sufferings of all, assumed her form and began to clear out the earth in an earthen pot. He did this work so speedily that Anantacharya, who was busy digging the earth, got suspicious and looking up at Her, asked, 'With your big body, you were at first carrying the earth with slow steps, and now when you should feel tired, you are doing the work far more quickly. How is it?'

Thus questioned, God in the form of his wife looked in his face without giving any reply, smiling all the while. At this, Anantacharya, who grew more suspicious by this time, came out of the pit, leaving his work aside, and found that his wife was fast asleep under a tree on the bank of a tank. Then, with glowering eyes and spade lifted in chastisement, as it were, he looked at the smiling dame and said, 'You are the great conjurer. You are not satisfied even with deluding the entire universe with Your Maya? And You have today taken on this woman's form to deprive this poor Brahmana couple of the merit of service. We are Your devotees. What power has Maya to do harm to Your slaves? Though You Yourself are all good, yet a harm caused to Your devotee is Yours as well. Now, what have You not suffered for Your slaves? It is well known that You had to get fried in burning oil and fall under the feet of elephants[1]; become a messenger and a charioteer of the Kshatriyas[2]; go in exile

---

1. The reference here is to Prahlada who was tortured by his father Hiranyakasipu, the king of the Asuras, in order to punish him for his devotion to Vishnu, whom he considered to be his enemy.
                                    Vide *Srimad Bhagavatam*, VII.
    2. The allusion is to Sri Krishna who acted first as a messenger of the Pandavas to the court of Dhritarashtra in order to explore the possibility of an amicable settlement of the disputes between the

to the forest[1]; and become bound with a rope by the Gopi[2] Why, Lord, are You causing harm to us by disturbing our service and thus doing harm to Yourself?'

While uttering these words, Anantacharya, the great devotee, began to shed tears of joy at the vision of God. The spade fell on the ground from his hands. That smiling form of a woman assumed the all-perfect and supremely captivating form of Sri Krishna. Overwhelmed by joy at this vision, Anantacharya, who had been hymning the Lord, fell on the ground unconscious. Meanwhile, his wife got up from sleep by the grace of the Lord and had the vision of that world-bewitching son of Yasoda whom her husband used to worship. She too lost herself in joy and found her place by the side of her husband. Now the Lord too after revealing His profound grace to His devotees, became invisible behind the veil of Maya.[3]

Even today that lake at Srisaila dug by Anantacharya and known as Anantasarovara proclaims the fame of the great soul.

Pandavas and the Kauravas; and then as the charioteer of Arjuna in the great war of Kurukshetra.

Vide *Mahabharata:* Udyoga and Bhishma-parvans.

1. It was the Incarnation of Sri Rama who went in exile to the forest for fourteen years in order to fulfil his father Dasaratha's promise to Kaikeyi. Vide *Valmiki Ramayana: Ayodhya-kanda.*

2. Here it is again Sri Krishna who was tied by Yasoda for his childish mischief of breaking the churning pot and giving away the butter to a cat. Vide *Srimad Bhagavatam,* X, ix, 14-16.

3. An interesting variation of this episode which explains a very important custom prevailing in the temple of Tirupati up to this day is as follows: As the wife of Anantacharya was carrying the basketloads of earth and emptying them elsewhere, her returns were slow at first but later rapid. When she was questioned about it, she explained that a Brahmachari boy was helping her in carrying the load. Anantacharya, enraged at the boy's meddling with his service uninvited, ran after the boy and gave him a poke under the chin with his crowbar, and the boy ran away as if in fright. But the temple authorities found, and Anantacharya too found later, that the Lord of Tirupati in the shrine was profusely bleeding in the chin. This they stopped by stuffing camphor into the wound. This is done even to this day and the camphor is distributed to devotees as Prasada.—*Ed.*

What profound devotion Ramanuja used to cherish towards those who were broad-minded and pure-hearted is shown by the following incident:

Once a simple-hearted Brahmana of a devotional temperament came to Yatiraja and said: 'I wish to purify my soul through service to you. You are the great Guru, the purifier of all. By serving you, I shall no more fall into the clutches of the three kinds of miseries and shall thus be saved from untold afflictions.'

'O Brahmana,' said Ramanuja, 'you are right. There is no other way but service for the liberation of the Jivas. If you like to please me through service, let me tell you what you have to do while living with me.'

'Revered Sir,' said the eager Brahmana, 'kindly tell me. I am ready to do it.'

'O Revered Brahmana,' said Ramanuja, seeing the intensity of his earnestness, 'I have resolved that I shall make myself pure by taking the water touched by a Brahmana's feet and then sit for my daily worship. Fortunately, by the grace of Sri Hari, I have received a pure-natured Brahmana like you. Stay here and make me blessed by giving me every day the pure water touched by your feet. Only if you do so, you shall have done real service to me.' The large-hearted, simple Brahmana agreed to this.

Every day he would wait for Yatiraja at the monastery. Every noon after finishing his ablutions in the sacred water of the Kaveri, Ramanuja would take the blessed water with which the feet of the Brahmana were washed, and then take his seat to worship his Chosen Deity. One day, importuned by one of his disciples, after finishing his ablutions in the Kaveri, Ramanuja went straight to the disciple's home to take alms. There, after finishing the worship of Sri Narayana, partaking the consecrated food, and taking a little rest, he entered into spiritual talks with the devotees assembled. It was late in the night when he returned to the monastery. But Yatiraja found the noble-hearted Brahmana waiting at his fixed place. Astonished, Yatiraja asked him: 'Great one, are you still waiting for me? I suppose you have had your meal?'

'How can I partake of the Prasada before I have finished my service unto you?' the Brahmana replied smiling.

Supremely pleased with the words of the Brahmana, Yatiraja said, 'You are indeed blessed. You have attained the zenith of Dasya-bhakti. Through devotion you have for all times made God a captive of your heart.'

So saying, Yatiraja drank again and again the water used for washing his feet and gave it to his disciples also. Through the influence of Yatiraja, the Brahmana also became supremely blessed.

31

Installation of His Image and the Passing Away

When Ramanuja was about to leave for Srirangam the devotees in Yadavadri were sorely afflicted by the thought of the separation which was to follow. At this, Ramanuja got a stone image of himself made, and after transmitting his own powers into it, handed it over to the devotees of the place and said, 'My dearest ones, know this image of mine to be my very self. When you feel the desire to see me, you will get peace of mind by looking at this image.'

With these words he took leave of his devotees.

A short time after this, the devotees of Sriperumbudur, his own birth-place, made an image of Yatiraja and invoking life in it according to the Vedic rites, installed it inside a huge temple. It is said that at that time Ramanuja was seated in his monastery at Srirangam expounding the Sastras to his disciples. All on a sudden, he became silent and indrawn, his entire body was still, like an inert thing. And two drops of blood trickled down the corners of his eyes. After a time when he regained his consciousness, being questioned by the astonished disciples, Ramanuja said: 'Today the people of Sriperumpudur have made me a captive of their love. After infusing life into the stone image, they have now finished the rite of opening the eyes of the image.'

Hearing this, the disciples, who had their beloved Guru in person with them, deemed themselves more fortunate than others.

Undoubtedly the devotees who were the residents of Srirangam were the most fortunate; for during the last sixty years of his life, Yatiraja did not once leave the blessed feet of Sri Ranganathaswami. Thousands of men and women

238

from all quarters would assemble there to see him and to hear his nectar-like words of wisdom and devotion. Purified inwardly by seeing and hearing him, the assembled devotees would experience joy beyond expression and return home blessed. Within a short time, through the power of his teachings which could remove all miseries and afflictions, all South India appeared to be like Ramarajya, being drawn near to the feet of Sriman Narayana. Thus after living on the earth 'for the good of the many, for the happiness of the many' for twice sixty years, making the world an abode of happiness like Vaikuntha and bringing up his chosen disciples to the level of his own merits, this large-hearted incarnation of Lakshmana, Bhagavan Srimat Ramanujacharya, the Ubhayavi-bhutipati, grew indrawn and silent in preparation to enter the Supreme Realm. When all the disciples came to know the cause of this indrawn mood of their Acharya, like helpless, hapless orphans, they began to shed tears. Some began to wail aloud. At this, the mind of Yatiraja who was so gracious to the devotees, grew unsettled and his meditation broke. Seeing the distress of his attendants, Yatiraja said: 'My dear children, why on earth are you thus confounded, like ignorant ones? I do reside in your hearts for ever. It is not possible for me to be even for a single moment without you. Why are you under the sway of delusion and why do you behave like mere boys?'

In one voice spoke forth all the disciples, 'O Lord, what you say is true; but it is unbearable for us to suffer the disappearance of your divine frame, which is the supreme purifier, the abode of all that is good, the destroyer of all afflictions, and the fountain of ineffable joy. Out of pity for your children, do preserve your body for some time more.'

According to the prayers of the devotees, the great Acharya, acquiesced in the continuance of his life on earth with them for three more days. He then had all his devotees summoned near him and gave them seventy-four gems of instructions.[1] They are infinitely more valuable than worldly treasures. The fortunate man who has made his own even a single one of these gems of instructions enjoys happiness and peace not only in this life but also in lives to come.

Enriching his disciples with this real wealth, Yatiraja thus addressed them: 'My children, all your ignorance now stands dispelled. You have fully realised that Bhagavata, Bhakta and Bhagavan are but one. How can then a real devotee remain separated from God? I am within you; you are within me, for ever. Grieve not over the disappearance of this perishable body.'

At this, Dasarathi, Govinda, Andhrapurna and a few other disciples said: 'Those two feet at the touch of which ignorant men like us have been freed from nescience, the mother of death; that noble heart which is the abode of Sri, which is full of the milk of compassion for Jivas; that lotus face marked with the insignia of the feet of Sri Vishnu, from which has flowed the purifying Ganga of words, making all Bharata Vaikuntha-like—can this all-powerful body of yours be considered perishable even after it has established the imperishableness of the Jivas who are imbued with the idea of perishableness? Our creature-bodies are perishable, your divine body is eternal. Therefore, deign graciously to ordain that we be not deprived of the sight of your blessed form.'

Being thus importuned by the devotees, that setting sun of knowledge, that delight of the devotees' hearts, took pity on them and said, 'Bring some skilled sculptors and order them to make a stone image of mine.'

In three days, the stone image of Yatiraja was completed. Then having had the image properly bathed in the-holy water of the Kaveri and installed on a pedestal, Yatiraja transmitted his own powers to that by breathing into the crown of the head.[2] And then addressing his

---

1. For a gist of this last message of Sri Ramanuja see Appendix C-III.

2. ब्रह्मरन्ध्रं समाघ्राय स्वशक्तिं तत्र दत्तवान् । *Prapannamritam*, LXVI, 16.

disciples said: 'My children, this is my second self. There is no difference whatsoever between this and myself. Casting this worn-out body aside, here I go to reside in this new body.'

So saying. Ramanuja, the large-hearted one, kept his head on the lap of Govinda and his two lotus feet on that of Andhrapurna, and looking at the two wooden sandals of his own Guru placed before him, entered into the supreme realm of the feet of Lord Vishnu. It was noon on a Saturday, the tenth day of the bright half of the month of Magha of 1059 Saka era (1137 A.D.).

After a few days of the passing away of Sri Ramanuja, Govinda, the playmate of his childhood, followed him into the supreme realm. His other disciples, under the leadership of Srimat Parasara Bhatta, remained engaged in the work of preserving Dharma, living in the shade of Yatiraja's life-like image. They did not suffer from the pangs of separation, for through the power of devotion they could always feel the presence of their Guru in their own hearts.

THE END

यो नित्यमच्युतपदाम्बुजयुग्मरुक्म-

व्यामोहतस्तदितराणि तृणाय मेने।

अस्मद्गुरोर्भगवतोऽस्य दयैकसिन्धो:

रामानुजस्य चरणौ शरणं प्रपद्ये॥

वैकुण्ठस्तव:

—कूरेश:

*I take refuge at the feet of Sri Ramanuja, our vene-
rable teacher, the unparalleled ocean of compassion,
who, prompted by an impassioned desire for the precious
wealth of the lotus feet of the Lord, viewed every other
things as mere straw.*

VAIKUNTHA STAVA
—KURESA

Appendix - A

P. 12.

The traditional dates of the births of Alvars as given in Sanskrit couplets are to all intents and purposes indefinite, incomplete and unreliable; and neither scholars nor historians have satisfactorily ascertained those dates beyond all dispute. Under the circumstances Pandit M. Raghava Iyengar after careful research and scrutiny of available material has fixed in his book *Alvarkal Kala-Nilai* the dates in the case of seven Alvars with considerable perspicacity. Hence his considered opinion is given below. The opinion of Sri Manavala Mamuni, as given in his verse, represents the traditionally accepted view regarding the chronological order which coincides more or less with the historical view and appears to be highly probable. There is no mention of Andal and Madhura Kavi Alvar in the recorded list, since it is well known that Andal was the foster-daughter of Perialvar and Madhura Kavi Alvar took refuge in Nammalvar as his Guru.

Acharya Nathamuni: A.D. 825 to 918.

So all the Alvars belong to an earlier period, before 825 A.D.

The first three Alvars—Poigai, Bhuta and Pey—between the 5th and 6th century A.D.

Tirumazhisai Alvar—beginning of the 7th century A.D. Perialvar—the first half of the 8th century A.D.

Andal—born 716 A.D.; sang Tiruppavai 731 A.D.; lived for a few years more.

Tirumangai Alvar (the latest)—8th century A.D.

The chronological order of the appearance of the Alvars according to Sri Manavala Mamuni, a great Acharya of the Srivaishnavas, is as follows: Poigai, Bhuta, Pey, Tirumazhisai, Nammalvar, Kulasekhara, Perialvar, Tondaradippodi Alvar, Tiruppanalvar and Tirumangai Alvar.

—*(Upadesaratnamalai-4).*

P. 49.

According to the tradition of Srivaishnavism, the image of Sri Ranganatha—the family deity of the Ikshvaku line of kings who ruled over Ayodhya—was given to Vibhishana by Sri Ramachandra. Vibhishana wished to install Sri Ranganatha in his own country, Ceylon, but on the way the Lord expressed His desire to make the island of Srirangam His permanent abode, and hence a temple was built there for Him. So Vibhishana had to content himself with a visit to Srirangam for worship once in twelve years—thus says the tradition.

P. 78.

One day when the divine sage Narada had come on a visit to poet Valmiki's hermitage, the host asked him whether there was any person on earth who was strong, handsome, learned, truthful, compassionate, righteous and pious,—in other words, worthy to be an ideal for all mankind. In reply Narada said he knew only one such person and that was Sri Ramachandra of Ayodhya. As Valmiki was eager to know all about Sri Rama, Narada related the incidents of his life and took leave of his host.

Still ruminating in his mind over all that he had heard, Valmiki went to the banks of the Tamasa for his bath. There he found sitting on a tree two beautiful birds, a pair of Kraunchas, chirping and making love. When the poet was enjoying the beauty of the scene and the song of the birds, a sudden shaft from a fowler's bow instantly brought down to earth the cock-krauncha. Seeing her mate lying on the ground in a pool of blood, the hen-krauncha cried in agony. At this piteous sight, the poet was overwhelmed with grief and anger and cursed the man for his cruel deed. But to his surprise he noticed that he was giving expression to his emotion in regular metrical form. When Valmiki returned to his hermitage after bath, he began to brood over the slaughter of the bird by the hunter and the curse that came out of his lips. Presently Brahma, the Creator, arrived there and said consoling him that the metrical form' in which the curse was uttered was to be employed to write out the story of Sri Rama, which he had heard from Narada. The poet obeyed and the *Ramayana* was the result. Vide *Valmiki Ramayana:* Balakanda. 1st and 2nd Sargas.

P. 106.

1. After dethroning Indra, the king of Devas. Bali, the grandson of Prahlada and king of Asuras, had become the ruler of the three worlds. Aditi, the mother of Devas, observed penances for the victory of her sons over Bali. In response to her prayers Vishnu was born to Kasyapa and Aditi as their son. This son, a dwarf, became known as Vamana. After the investiture with sacred thread Vamana went to Bali who was performing an Asvamedha sacrifice and making presents. With due courtesy Bali offered to present him anything he wanted. Vamana complimented Bali and asked only for three steps of ground and nothing more. When the gift was made. Vamana assumed the cosmic form and covered the earth with one foot. With the second step he covered the rest of the universe leaving no space for the third step. Heroic Bali offered his head for the Lord's third step. The Lord graciously sent him to the nether world constructed by Viswakarma. Vide *Srimad Bhagavatam,* VIII. xvii-xxiii,

2. It so happened in the sixth cycle of Manu—that the gods were severely worsted in battles by the Asuras and by the curse of Durvasa, Indra and the three worlds lost their fortune; the sacrificial and other righteous observances came to be neglected. After an inconclusive conference among themselves, Indra, Varuna and other gods went to Brahma and sought his advice as to the means of regaining their pre-eminence. Brahma led the gods to the abode of Narayana beyond the region of darkness, offered prayers and hymned the Lord. Revealing Himself to the

gods, Narayana advised them to make alliance with the Daityas and Danavas till the tide of fortune flowed to them. He further advised them to churn the milk ocean and therefrom procure nectar, by drinking which creatures in the jaws of death could become immortal. Thus advised, Brahma and Indra went to their respective places and the gods went to Bali, the king of the Asuras, and made a truce with him. Out of the churning of the milk-ocean, in which Devas and Daityas joined and the Supreme Lord Himself also gave a helping hand, first issued a dreadful poison called Halahala. When this deadly poison spread menacingly in every direction, all the frightened creatures sought refuge in Siva, who in his supreme compassion and magnanimity drank off the poison for the safety of the creatures. The poison being drunk by Siva, the gods and demons resumed the churning with renewed vigour. Gradually there arose from the churned milk-ocean Surabhi (the 'cow of plenty' which fulfils all desires), the brilliant horse Uchchaisravas, the amazing elephant Airavata, Kaustubha the precious jewel, the wish-fulfilling Parijata tree, and the celestial nymphs. Then arose the most glorious goddess Rama, the very Lakshmi, illumining all directions with her splendour. Looking for a permanent flawless resort for herself, she chose Mukunda, the supreme Lord Vishnu, as her consort. The Father of the three worlds assigned His bosom as the permanent abode of Sri (Lakshmi), the Mother of the three worlds and the source of all fortunes. Vide *Srimad Bhagavatam*. VIII. v to viii.

3. Reference here is to the story of the Ramayana. Just on the, eve of his coronation, Sri Rama, the eldest son and heir to the throne of Ayodhya, went on exile for fourteen years in order to help fulfil a boon which his old father King Dasaratha had promised his step-mother Kaikeyi, one of the three Queens. Sita, his peerless wife, and Lakshmana, his incomparable brother—born of another Queen, Sumitra—followed him to the forest. After staying in various other places and passing through many adventures and travails, in the thirteenth year of their exile they came to settle temporarily in Panchavati in the Dandaka forest. From here one day, when Rama and Lakshmana were away from the cottage, Sita was kidnapped by Ravana, the mighty king of the Rakshasas, and taken away to far off Lanka, separated from India by sea. With the help of Sugriva, the king of Kishkindha, his monkey retinue and other friends, prominent among whom was Vibhishana, Ravana's own brother, Rama and Lakshmana causewayed the sea and invaded Lanka. After a grim battle of many days, heroic Ravana along with his valorous army was completely annihilated and Sita rescued.

According to Hindu tradition Sri Rama, though appearing as the son of Dasaratha, was none other than an incarnation of Sri Vishnu, the supreme Godhead and Sita, Sridevi Herself. Vide *Valmiki Ramayana* from Ayodhyakanda to Yuddhakanda.

P. 109.

1. In the course of their wanderings in Chitrakuta during their exile, Rama and Sita were once resting in a forest by the side of which flowed the river Mandakini. A ravenous crow—who was in fact a prodigal son of Indra in disguise—desirous to eat flesh, suddenly swooped upon Sita and tore her breast with its sharp beak. Rama woke up and was much exercised by, the situation. Seeing the crow with bloody claws, he released a blade of grass which flew after the fast flying crow, following it wherever it went over the three worlds. Unable to escape the missile, the crow at last returned and took shelter at Rama's feet. Out of his infinite compassion Sri Rama forgave the crow and saved its life, though it deserved to be killed.

Vide *Valmiki Ramayana*, Sundara Kanda, XXXVIII.

2. The reference here is to the story of king of Chedi, Sisupala, son of Krishna's father's sister and Damagosha. Sisupala was sinful from the very moment he began to lisp and became a determined enemy of Krishna. But Krishna had promised his aunt that he would pardon a, hundred offences of Sisupala. When his offences exceeded that number, challenged by Sisupala himself, Krishna killed him in the assembly where Yudhishthira was performing the Rajasuya sacrifice. The wonderful part of the story however was that as soon as Sisupala was beheaded, a fierce energy issued forth from his body and adored Krishna and then got merged in his body and thus attained union with the Lord. Vide *Mahabharata:* Sabhaparvan, XXXVII-XLV.

As to Sisupala's previous birth, the story runs as follows:

On one occasion Sanandana and other sons of Chaturmukha, who all being 'sky-clad' looked like mere children of five or six, went by chance to the regions of Vishnu during their wanderings in the three worlds, Jaya and Vijaya, who were keeping the gate, taking them to be mere children, prohibited them from entering Vishnu's abode. Angry at this, they cursed them with the words: 'You do not deserve ever to be here at the feet of Hari where Rajas and Tamas have no place. *Do* you, both being childish soon go hence and be born of the sinful Asura race.'

In their first birth they were born as Hiranyakasipu and Hiranyaksha and slain by Hari in the forms of a Man-lien and a Boar respectively In their second birth they were born as Ravana and Kumbhakarna and slain by Sri Rama. In their third, they were born as Sisupala and Dantavaktra and slain by Sri Krishna. Through their very attitude of enmity they attained the grace of the Lord, who killed and liberated them from the curse.

Vide *Srimad Bhagavatam*, VII. 1. 33-47.

P. 143.

There was a man who worshipped Siva but hated all the other deities. One day Siva appeared to him and said, 'I shall never be pleased with you so long as you hate other gods.' But the man was inexorable. After a few days Siva again appeared to him. This time He appeared as Hari-Hara—a form, of which one half was Siva and the other Vishnu. At this the man was half-pleased and half-displeased. He laid his offerings on the side representing Siva, but nothing on that representing Vishnu. When he offered the burning incense to Siva, his beloved form of the Deity, he was audacious enough to press the nostril of Vishnu lest he should inhale the fragrance. Then Siva said: 'Your bigotry is ineradicable. By assuming this dual aspect I tried to convince you that all gods and goddesses are but the various aspects of the One Being. You have not taken the lesson in good part, and you will have to suffer for your bigotry. Long must you suffer for this.' The man went away and retired to a village. He soon developed into a great hater of Vishnu, On coming to know this peculiarity of his, the children of the village began to tease him by uttering the name of Vishnu within his hearing. Vexed by this, the man hung two bells on his ears, and when the boys cried out, 'Vishnu, Vishnu', he would ring the bells violently and make those names inaudible to his ears. And thus he came *to* be known by the name of Ghantakarna or the Bell-eared. [The story given above is Sri Ramakrishna's adaptation of the classical story of Ghantakarna found in the 78th to 83rd chapters of the Bhavishya parvan (2nd part) of the *Harivamsa*. It is more likely that the author referred to the adapation and not to the original.]

P. 163.

The reference here is to the fearful she-demon Putana who was sent by Kamsa in order to kill children from among whom his destroyer was to arise according to the voice of Goddess Maya. Putana assumed the form of a charming woman and entered the house of Nanda in Gokula, where Krishna was happily asleep. With murderous intent she took the baby upon her lap and began to suckle him at her breast charged with most fatal poison. Sri Krishna suckled her breast in such a fashion that Putana gave out world-shaking screams and then fell dead covering a space of twelve miles. When her body was burnt in pieces, there arose in the sky smoke smelling like agaru.

Though she was a demoness feeding on blood, she became sinless by suckling the God-incarnate at her breast. Even that terrible creature attained liberation worthy of Yasoda, because Krishna drank her milk.

Vide *Srimad Bhagavatam*, X. vi.

P. 173.

Nala, the valorous and righteous king of Nishadhas, lost his kingdom in a fatal game of dice. He was thereupon forced to go into exile with only a single cloth on. He pleaded with Damayanti, his faithful wife of peerless beauty, to go and live with her parents, the king and queen of Vidarbha. Out of constancy and attachment to her husband, Damayanti preferred being by the side of Nala in his distress to living in comfort with her royal parents. This was, however, too much for Nala, who could not bear seeing her in that plight. So when one night she was fast asleep by his side in a wayside inn on a trade-route leading to her father's kingdom, Nala took the extreme step of leaving her there in the full faith that her chastity would protect her and the hands of destiny would eventually bring her to her father's protection, while he could be free to battle along with his evil fate until better days smiled on him.

When Damayanti woke up, she took quite some time to realise that her well-beloved husband had left her to her fate. She ran into the forest in search of Nala and during her ramblings stumbled against a hungry python looking for prey.

As the great serpent coiled itself around her body, Damayanti cried out the name of Nala. Her cries attracted a savage hunter who instantly killed the python and saved her life. But now Damayanti had to face the savage in the huntsman, who took no time to address improper words to her. Damayanti blazed up in anger and cursed the man saying: 'If it is true that I have never thought of any other man but Nala, let this man fall down dead.' And instantaneously the hunter fell dead on the ground like a tree struck by lightning.

After many more trials and travails Damayanti was reunited with Nala who regained his kingdom, and the two lived happily.

Vide *Mahabharata:* Vana-parvan, LII to LXXIX.

P. 218.

In about 1098 A.D., when Sri Ramanuja might have gone to the North to secure the image of Sampatkumara, there was possibly no 'Muhammadan Emperor' in Delhi, which was being ruled by the chief of the Tomara clan. That chief was a descendant of Anangapala, who a century earlier, had built the Red Fort, where the Kutub mosque now stands, and thus given permanence to the city which had been founded in 993-4 A.D. So the tradition of Sri Ramanuja's bringing the image of Sampatkumara from the Muhammadan Emperor of Delhi may be interpreted as only referring to a Muslim chieftain, general or viceroy, ruling somewhere in the North, 'Delhi' being used in deep south somewhat loosely to denote Northern cities or states. It is not, however, easy to identify historically the Muslim ruler. Neither is it easier to identify the adventurer who had taken away the image from Melkote. Was he one of the followers of Muhammad of Gazni whose invasions took place in India between 1000-1026 A.D.? The probability cannot be absolutely ruled out. May it not be that even before Malik Kafur's invasion of the South in 1306-10 A.D. in which Srirangam and Madurai were plundered, there was also another Muslim invasion of the South, though not in the same menacing proportions as that of Malik Kafur? In a footnote on this issue A. Govindacharya, author of *The Life of Ramanujacharya* (1906) hazards such a view saying: '.....an account given by Buchanan (p. 3151, vol. I) confirms what otherwise would be mere conjecture. He says, "Near the place (Tondanur) there is a monument dedicated to one of the fanatical followers of Muhammad of Gazni who had penetrated this length and had suffered martyrdom." '

Tradition has it that during the time of his passing away, all who were present there heard a celestial voice say, 'Dharmo nashtah', which means 'Dharma which had embodied itself is now removed from the sight of man.'

In accordance with the rule 'ankasya vama gatih' as explained in p. 73, the words 'dharmo nashtah' indicate the figures 1, 0, 5 and 9. By this the scholars have decided 1059 Saka era as the year in which Sri Ramanuja passed away.

Appendix B

1. श्रीः

स्तोत्ररत्नम्

नमोऽचिन्तयाद्भुताक्लिष्टज्ञानवैराग्यराशये ।
नाथाय मुनयेऽगाधभगवद्भक्तिसिन्धवे ॥ १ ॥

तस्मै नमो मधुजिदंघ्रिसरोजतत्त्वज्ञानानुरागमहिमातिशयान्तसीम्ने ।
नाथाय नाथमुनयेऽत्र परत्र चापि नित्यं यदीयचरणौ शरणं मदीयम् ॥

भूयो नमोऽपरिमिताच्युतभक्तितत्त्वज्ञानामृताब्धिपरिवाहशुभैर्वचोभिः ।
लोकेऽवतीर्णपरमार्थसमग्रभक्तियोगाय नाथमुनये यमिनां वराय ॥३॥

तत्त्वेन यश्चिदचिदीश्वरतत्त्वभावभोगापवर्गतदुपायगतीरुदारः ।
सन्दर्शयन्निरमिमीतपुराणरत्नं तस्मै नमो मुनिवराय पराशराय ॥ ४ ॥

माता पिता युवतयस्तनया विभूतिस्सर्वं यदेव नियमेन मदन्वयानाम् ।
आद्यस्यः नः कुलपतेर्बकुलाभिरामं श्रीमत्तदंघ्रियुगलं

प्रणमामिमूर्ध्ना ॥

यन्मूर्धिन मे श्रुतिशिरस्सु च भाति यस्मिन्नस्मन्मनोरथपथस्स

कलस्समेति ।

स्तोष्यामि नः कुलधनं कुलदैवतं तत्पादारविन्दमरविन्दविलोचनस्य ॥

तत्त्वेन यस्य महिमार्णवशीकराणुश्शक्यो न मातुमपि सर्वपितामहाद्यैः ।
कर्तुं तदीयमहिमस्तुतिमुद्यताय महां नमोऽस्तु कवये निरपत्रपाय ॥७॥

यद्वा श्रमावधि यथामति वाप्यशक्तस्तौम्येवमेव खलु तेऽपि सदा

स्तुवन्तः।

वेदाश्चतुर्मुखमुखाश्च महार्णवान्तः को मज्जतोरणुकुलाचलयोर्विशेषः॥

किं चैष शक्त्यतिशयेन न तेऽनुकम्प्यस्स्तोतापितु स्तुतिकृतेन परिश्रमेण।

तत्र श्रमस्तु सुलभो मम मन्दबुद्धेरित्युद्यमोऽयमुचितो मम चाब्जनेत्र॥

नावेक्षसे यदि ततो भुवनान्यमूनि नालं प्रभो भवितुमेव कुतः प्रवृत्तिः।

एवं निसर्गसुहृदि त्वयि सर्वजन्तोस्स्वामिन्न चित्रमिदमाश्रित-

वत्सलत्वम्॥

स्वाभाविकानवधिकातिशयेशितृत्वं नारायण त्वयि न मृष्यति

वैदिकः कः।

ब्रह्मा शिवश्शतमखः परमस्वराादित्येतेऽपि यस्य महिमार्णवविप्रुषस्ते॥

कश्श्रीः श्रियः परमसत्त्वसमाश्रयः कः कः पुण्डरीकनयनः

पुरुषोत्तमः कः।

कस्यायुतायुतशतैककलांशकांशे विश्वं विचित्रचिदचित्रवि भागवृत्तम्॥

वेदापहारगुरुपातकदैत्यपीडाद्याापद्विमोचनमहिष्फलप्रदानैः।

कोऽन्यः प्रजापशुपती परिपाति कस्य पादोदकेन स शिवस्स्व

शिरोधृतेन॥

कस्योदरे हरविरिश्चिमुखः प्रपञ्चः को रक्षतीममजनिष्ट च कस्य नाभेः।

क्रान्त्वा निगीर्य पुनरुद्गिरति त्वदन्यः कः केन वैष परवानिति

शक्यशङ्कः॥ १४॥

त्वां शीलरूपचरितैः परमप्रकृष्टसत्त्वेन सात्त्विकतया प्रबलैश्च शास्त्रैः।

प्रख्यातदैवपरमार्थविदां मतैश्च नैवासुरप्रकृतयः प्रभवन्ति बोद्धुम्॥ २५॥

उल्लङ्घितत्रिविधसीमसमातिशायिसम्भावनं तव परिब्रढिमस्वभावम्।

मायाबलेन भवतापि निगूहामानं पश्यन्ति केचिदनिशं त्वदनन्यभावाः॥

यदण्डमण्डान्तरगोचरं च यत् दशोत्तराण्यावरणानि यानि च ।
गुणाः प्रधानं पुरुषः परं पदं परात्परं ब्रह्म च ते विभूतयः ॥ १७॥

वशी वदान्यो गुणवानृजुश्शुचिर्मृदुर्दयालुर्मधुरः स्थिरस्समः ।
कृती कृतज्ञस्त्वमसि स्वभावतस्समस्तकल्याणगुणामृतोदधिः ॥ १८॥

उपर्युपर्ब्जभुवोऽपि पूरुषान् प्रकल्प्य ते ये शतमित्यनुक्रमात् ।
गिरस्त्वदेकैकगुणावधीप्सया सदा स्थिता नोद्यमतोऽतिशेरते ॥ १९॥

त्वदाश्रितानां जगदुद्भवस्थितिप्रणाशसंसारविमोचनादयः ।
भवन्ति लीला विधयश्च वैदिकास्त्वदीयगम्भीरमनोनुसारिणः ॥ २०॥

नमो नमो वाङ्मनसातिभूमये नमो नमो वाङ्मनसैकभूमये ।
नमो नमोऽनन्तमहाविभूतये नमो नमोऽनन्तदयैकसिन्धवे ॥ २१॥

न धर्मनिष्ठोऽस्मि न चात्मवेदी न भक्तिमांस्त्वच्चरणारविन्दे ।
अकिञ्चनोऽनन्यगतिश्शरण्य त्वत्पादमूलं शरणं प्रपद्ये ॥ २२॥

न निन्दितं कर्म तदस्ति लोके सहस्रशो यन्न मया व्यधायि ।
सोऽहं विपाकावसरे मुकुन्द क्रन्दामि सम्प्रत्यगतिस्तवाग्रे ॥ २३॥

निमज्जतोऽनन्त भवार्णवान्तश्चिराय मे कूलमिवासि लब्धः ।
त्वयापि लब्धं भगवन्निदानीमनुत्तमं पात्रमिदं दयायाः ॥ २४॥

अभूतपूर्वं मम भावि किं वा सर्वं सहे मे सहजं हि दुःखम् ।
किन्तु त्वदग्रे शरणागतानां पराभवो नाथ न तेऽनुरूपः ॥ २५॥

निरासकस्यापि न तावदुत्सहे महेश हातुं तव पादपङ्कजम् ।
रुषा निरस्तोऽपि शिशुस्स्तनन्धयो न जातु मातुश्चरणौ जिहासति ॥ २६॥

तवामृतस्यन्दिनि पादपङ्कजे निवेशितात्मा कथमन्यदिच्छति ।
स्थितेऽरविन्दे मकरन्दनिर्भरे मधुव्रतो नेक्षुरकं हि वीक्षते ॥ १७॥

त्वदङ्घ्रिमुद्दिश्य कदापि केनचिद्यथा तथा वापि सकृत्कृतोऽञ्जलिः ।
तदेव मुष्णात्यशुभान्यशेषतश्शुभानि पुष्णाति न जातु हीयते ॥ २८॥

उदीर्णसंसारदवाशुशुक्षणिं क्षणेन निर्वाप्य परां च निर्वृतिम्।
प्रयच्छति त्वच्चरणारुणाम्बुजद्वयानुरागामृतसिन्धुशीकरः॥ २९॥

विलासविक्रान्तपरावरालयं नमस्यदार्तिक्षपणे कृतक्षणम्।
धनं मदीयं तव पादपङ्कजं कदा नु साक्षात्करवाणि चक्षुषा॥ ३०॥

कदा पुनश्शङ्करथाङ्गकल्पकध्वजारविन्दाङ्कुशवज्रलाञ्छनम्।
त्रिविक्रम त्वच्चरणाम्बुजद्वयं मदीयमूर्धानमलङ्करिष्यति॥ ३१॥

विराजमानोज्ज्वलपीतवाससं स्मितातसीसूनसमामलच्छविम्।
निमग्ननाभिं तनुमध्यमुन्नतं विशालवक्षस्थलशोभिलक्षणम्॥ ३२॥

चकासतं ज्याकिणकर्कशैश्शुभैश्चतुर्भिराजानुविलम्बिभिर्भुजैः।
प्रियावतंसोत्पलकर्णभूषणश्लथालकाबन्धविमर्दशंसिभिः॥ ३३॥

उदग्रपीनांसविलम्बिकुण्डलालकावलीबन्धुरकम्बुकन्धरम्।
मुखश्रिया न्यक्कृतपूर्णनिर्मलामृतांशुबिम्बाम्बुरुहोज्वलश्रियम्॥ ३४॥

प्रबुद्धमुग्धाम्बुजचारुलोचनं सविभ्रमभ्रूलतमुज्ज्वलाधरम्।
शुचिस्मितं कोमलगण्डमुन्नसं ललाटपर्यन्तविलम्बितालकम्॥ ३५॥

स्फुरत्किरीटाङ्गदहारकण्ठिकामणीन्द्रकाश्रीगुणनु पुरादिभिः।
रथाङ्गशङ्खासिगदाधनुर्वरैर्लसत्तुलस्या वनमालयोज्ज्वलम्॥ ३६॥

चकर्थ यस्या भवनं भुजान्तरं तव प्रियं धाम यदीयजन्मभूः।
जगत्समस्तं यदपाङ्गसंश्रयं यदर्थमम्भोधिरमन्थ्यबन्धि च॥ ३७॥

स्ववैश्वरूप्येण सदानुभूतयाप्यपूर्ववद्विस्मयमादधानया।
गुणेन रूपेण विलासचेष्टितैस्सदा तवैवोचितया तव श्रिया॥ ३८॥

तया सहासीनमनन्तभोगिनि प्रकृष्टविज्ञानबलैकधामनि।
फणामणिव्रातमयूखमण्डलप्रकाशमानोदरदिव्यधामनि॥ ३९॥

निवासशय्यासनपादुकांशुकोपधानवर्षातपवारणादिभिः।
शरीरभेदैस्तव शेषतां गतैर्यथोचितं शेष इतीर्यते जनैः॥ ४०॥

दासस्सखा वाहनमासनं ध्वजो यस्ते वितानं व्यजनं त्रयीमयः।
उपस्थितं तेन पुरो गरुत्मता त्वदङ्घ्रिसम्मर्दनकिणाङ्कशोभिना॥ ४१॥

त्वदीयमुक्तोज्झितशेषभोजिना त्वया विसृष्टात्मभरेण यद्यथा।
प्रियेण सेनापतिना न्यवेदि तत्तथाऽनुजानन्तमुदारवीक्षणैः॥ ४२॥

हताखिलक्लेशमलैः स्वभावतस्त्वदानुकूल्यैकरसैस्तवोचितैः।
गृहीततत्तत्परिचारसाधनैर्निषेव्यमाणं सचिवैर्यथोचितम्॥ ४३॥

उपूर्वनानारसभावनिर्भरप्रबद्धया मुग्धविदग्धलीलया।
क्षणाणुवत्क्षिप्तपरादिकालया प्रहर्षयन्तं महिषीं महाभुजम्॥ ४४॥

अचिन्त्यदिव्याद्भुतनित्ययौवनस्वभावलावण्यमयामृतोदधिम्।
श्रियः श्रियं भक्तजनैकजीवितं समर्थमापत्सखमर्थिकल्पकम्॥ ४५॥

भवन्तमेवानुचरन्निरन्तरं प्रशान्तनिश्शेषमनोरथान्तरः।
कदाहमैकान्तिकनित्यकिङ्करः प्रहर्षयिष्यामि सनाथजीवितः॥ ४६॥

धिगशुचिमविनीतं निर्भयं मामलज्जं परमपुरूष योऽहं
योगिवर्याग्रगण्यैः।
विधिशिवसनकाद्यैर्ध्यातुमत्यन्तदूरं तव परिजनभावं कामये
कामवृत्तः॥ ४७॥

अपराधसहस्रभाजनं पतितं भीमभवार्णवोदरे।
अगतिं शरणागतं हरे कृपया केवलमात्मसात्कुरु॥ ४८॥

अविवेकघनान्धदिङ्मुखे बहुधा सन्ततदुःखवर्षिणि।
भगवन् भवदुर्दिने पथः स्खलितं मामवलोकयाच्युत॥ ४९॥

न मृषा परमार्थमेव मे श्रृणु विज्ञापनमेकमग्रतः।
यदि मे न दयिष्यसे ततो दयनीयस्तव नाथ दुर्लभः॥ ५०॥

तदहं त्वदृते न नाथवान् मदृते त्वं दयनीयवान्न च।
विधिनिर्मितमेतमन्वयं भगवन् पालय मा स्म जीहपः॥ ५१॥

वपुरादिषु योऽपि कोऽपि वा गुणतोऽसानि यथातथाविधः।
तदयं तव पादपद्मयोरहमद्यैव मया समर्पितः॥ ५२॥

मम नाथ यदस्ति योऽस्म्यहं सकलं तद्धि तवैव माधव।
नियतस्वमिति प्रबुद्धधीरथवा किं नु समर्पयामि ते॥ ५३॥

अवबोधितवानिमां यथा मयि नित्यां भवदीयतां स्वयम्।
कृपयैवमनन्यभोग्यतां भगवन् भक्तिमपि प्रयच्छ मे॥ ५४॥

तव दास्यसुखैकसङ्गिनां भवनेष्वस्त्वपि कीटजन्म मे।
इतरावसथेषु मा स्म भूदपि मे जन्म चतुर्मुखात्मना॥ ५५॥

सकृत्त्वदाकारविलोकनाशया तृणीकृतानुत्तमभुक्तिमुक्तिभिः।
महात्मभिर्मामवलोक्यतां नय क्षणोऽपि ते यद्विरहोऽतिदुस्सहः॥ ५६॥

न देहं न प्राणान्न च सुखमशेषाभिलषितं
न चात्मानं नान्यत्किमपि तव शेषत्वविभवात्।
बहिर्भूतं नाथ क्षणमपि सहे यातु शतधा
विनाशं तत्सत्यं मधुमथन विज्ञापनमिदम्॥ ५७॥

दुरन्तस्यानादेरपरिहरणीयस्य महतो
निहीनाचारोऽहं नृपशुरशुभस्यास्पदमपि।
दयासिन्धो बन्धो निरवधिकवात्सल्यजलधे
तव स्मारं स्मारं गुणगणमितीच्छामि गतभीः॥ ५८॥

अनिच्छन्नप्येवं यदि पुनरितीच्छन्निव रज-
स्तमश्छन्नच्छद्मस्तुतिवचनभङ्गीमरचयम्।
तथापीत्थं रूपं वचनमवलम्ब्यापि कृपया
त्वमेवैवम्भूतं धरणिधर मे शिक्षय मनः॥ ५९॥

पिता त्वं माता त्वं दयिततनयस्त्वं प्रियसुह
त्वमेव त्वं मित्रं गुरुरसि गतिश्चासि जगताम्।

त्वदीयस्त्वद्भृत्यस्तव परिजनस्त्वद्व्रतिरहं
प्रपन्नश्चैवं सत्यहमपि तवैवास्मि हि भरः ॥ ६० ॥

जनित्वाहं वंशे महति जगति ख्यातयशसां
शुचीनां युक्तानां गुणपुरुषतत्त्वस्थितिविदाम् ।
निसर्गादेव त्वच्चरणकमलैकान्तमनसा
मधोऽधः पापात्मा शरणद निमज्जामि तमसि ॥ ६१ ॥

अमर्यादः क्षुद्रश्चलमतिरसूयाप्रसवभूः
कृतघ्नो दुर्मानी स्मरपरवशो वञ्चनपरः ।
नृशंसः पापिष्ठः कथमहमितो दुःखजलधे-
रपारादुत्तीर्णस्तव परिचरेयं चरणयोः ॥ ६२ ॥

रघुवर यदभूस्त्वं तादृशो वायसस्य
प्रणत इति दयालुर्यश्च चैद्यस्य कृष्ण ।
प्रतिभवमपराद्धुर्मुग्ध सायुज्यदोऽभू-
र्वद किमपदमागस्तस्य तेऽस्ति क्षमायाः ॥ ६३ ॥

ननु प्रपन्नस्सकृदेव नाथ तवाहमस्मीति च याचमानः ।
तवानुकम्प्यस्स्मरतः प्रतिज्ञां मदेकवर्जं किमिदं व्रतं ते ॥ ६४ ॥

अकृत्रिमत्वच्चरणारविन्दप्रेमप्रकर्षावधिमात्मवन्तम् ।
पितामहं नाथमुनिं विलोक्य प्रसीद मद्वृत्तमचिन्तयित्वा ॥ ६५ ॥

Appendix C-I

A COMPLETE LIST OF SRI RAMANUJA'S WORKS

1. *Vedantha-Sangraha*—a treatise setting forth the principles of Visishtadvaita, reconciling the different conflicting Srutis.
2. *Sribhashya*—a detailed commentary on Badarayana's *Brahmasutras*.
3. *Gita-bhashya*—a detailed commentary on the *Bhagavad-Gita*.
4. *Vedanta-dipa*—a brief commentary on the *Brahma-sutras*.
5. *Vedanta-sara*—a brief commentary on the *Brahma-sutras* and intended for beginners.
6. *Saranagati-gadya* and 7. *Sriranga-gadya*—tell about Saranagati or self-surrender.
7. *Sri Vaikuntha-gadya*—describes Sri Vaikuntha and the state of the liberated.
8. *Nitya-grantha*— a short manual, intended to guide the devotees, to perform their daily round of duties, particularly in the worship of the Lord.

****

C-II

VISISHTADVAITA

THE PHILOSOPHY OF SRI RAMANUJA

The system of philosophy associated with the name of Ramanuja is known as Visishtadvaita. The chief contribution of Ramanuja, apart from his effort to systematize the philosophy of the Upanishads, is his attempt to develop a complete system which synthesizes the concept of God with the philosophy of the impersonal Absolute. We should not think that Ramanuja developed any new philosophy, and he makes no claim of originality. He was the culmination of the movement that started from the Vedas and was nourished by the Alvars, Nathamuni and Yamunacharya. Ramanuja's genius and supreme efforts resulted in the systematic presentation of Visishtadvaita, which emphasizes the spiritual experience of God without ignoring the critical methods of philosophy. Visishtadvaita owes not a little of its influence on the subsequent development of the philosophy of religion to his clear and rational interpretation of it. In his exposition of the Vedanta, he claims merely to follow the doctrines of Bodhayana, Tanka, Dramida, Guhadeva, Kapardin and Bharuci, many of whom preceded Sankara, and the *prima facie* views mentioned in Sankara's writings show that Ramanuja's assertion as following an ancient tradition is not unfounded. His works, nine in all, give an idea of masterly exposition and consistency of philosophy. Prof. Berriedale Keith says that 'the *Sribhashya*, his commentary on the *Brahma-sutras*, conveys an impression of no mean philosophical insight, and it is fair to assume that his work in substantial merit and completeness far outdid any previous effort to find in the *Brahma-sutras* a basis for monotheism.'[1]

Ramanuja accepts as ultimate three kinds of entities, matter (acit), soul (cit) and God (Isvara). Though equally real, matter and soul depend on God and constitute His body or attributes, the relation being conceived as that between body and soul. Individual souls and matter form the body of God and He is the Soul of souls and matter. God is the central Reality of soul and matter, and neither can exist without Him. They exist in Him and are absolutely inseparable. Thus the three realities are all ultimate and eternal, each having its own distinctiveness.

It is rather difficult to find an English equivalent for the Sanskrit term Visishtadvaita. It is sometimes erroneously rendered as 'qualified non-dualism '. This conception may be illustrated by taking a common example like a 'mango'. Here the colour, the taste, the smell, the flesh, the shell and the fibre which constitute the whole fruit can be distinguished as being different from one another. Though each element in the fruit has its own distinctive attributes, the synthetic whole is regarded as a mango. What is common to all the different parts of the fruit is their inseparable existence. Of the various parts which form the mango, we can regard any particular one as the substantive (Viseshya) and the rest of attributes (Viseshanas). Likewise if God, the chief factor, comprehends in Himself matter and the souls, the Reality may be regarded as Advaita, one without a second. God, the substantive factor, directs and predominates over the attributive factors. Though the world of matter and souls have real existence of their own, they are entirely subject *to* the control of God in all their conditions. Here the 'qualified non-dualism' is not a synthesis of the distinctions between the attributive factors and the substantive factor, but that God, who is the Soul of souls and matter, is one. It is the non-dualism of the qualified whole. By this definition, the identity and difference of matter and souls with God are maintained. By their very nature, the souls and matter are neither identical with God nor with one another. Perhaps it may not be incorrect if we interpret the term 'Visishtadvaita' as signifying that whatever exists is contained within God, and so the system admits no second independent factor. According to Sankara, Bhaskara and Yadavaprakasa, identity is primary and difference secondary, but for Ramanuja difference is primary and identity secondary.[2]

Ramanuja accepts only two categories: substance (Dravya) and non-substance or attribute (Adravya). The non-substance is tenfold: five qualities of the Panchabhutas, Sattva, Rajas and Tamas, potency (Sakti) and conjunction (Samyoga). Substance is that which has modes or which undergoes change. It must be noted here that the substantive factor (Viseshya) in itself is changeless, and attributive factors (Viseshanas) alone undergo change, for which reason the synthetic whole (Visishta) is imagined to undergo change. God and souls, viewed as the substantive factor, are immutable. The Dravyas, which are divided into two classes as Jada (matter) and Ajada (immaterial), are six: The Jada comprehends

---

1. *Encyclopaedia of Religion and Ethics,* Vol. X, p. 572.
2. See *Darsanodaya,* p. 194.

nature (Prakriti) and time (Kala), and the Ajada includes attributive consciousness (Dharmabhutajnana), super-nature (Suddhasattva), soul (Jiva) and God (Isvara). Jada is that which is devoid of pure Sattva. Now we shall say a few words regarding Prakriti, Jiva and Isvara who form the most important Dravyas:

Prakriti: This is the substratum of the three Gunas, Sattva, Rajas, and Tamas, and not the complex of the Gunas as in Sankhya. Prakriti is not independent of God, but constitutes His body as His mode. The entire universe evolves out of Prakriti under the will of God and is entirely under His control. Prakriti is the seat of soul and, indirectly through it, of God. The relation between them, viz., matter and soul or Prakriti and its evolutes is Aprithak-siddhi (inseparable relation). The evolutes of Prakriti provide appropriate bodies to souls according to their past Karma.

Jiva: Like Prakriti soul also is a mode of God. It is entirely dependent upon Him, though distinct from Him. It also constitutes His body, since He is the Soul of soul and inner controller. It is of the essence of consciousness and bliss. It is not a fabricated complex, but an eternal reality, a Karta (doer) and a Bhokta (experiencer). The souls are many and there is no difference among them as far as their essential nature is concerned. The soul is monadic in nature. In its natural state, its attributive consciousness expands and is able to apprehend everything. But in Samsara, as a result of its past Karma, its consciousness contracts, though never absent. The contraction of consciousness and bliss is itself Samsara, and expansion of the same through constant communion with God is itself Moksha. The souls are of three kinds: those that are ever-free and never experience bondage (Nitya), those that have attained release from transmigration (Mukta), and those that are still in Samsara.

Isvara: God is the absolute Reality, endowed with all auspicious and excellent attributes which are unsurpassable. He too is of the nature of consciousness and bliss, all-powerful, all-pervading and all-compassionate. He is the inner ruler of matter as well as souls. As already pointed out, God with souls and matter as His body constitutes an organic unity, sustaining and controlling them for His purpose. Since God cannot be separated from His modes or attributes, He is determinate and not indeterminate. God possesses two states as cause and effect. In the state 'of cosmic dissolution (Pralaya), which occurs at the end of a Kalpa, matter and souls exist in a subtle state possessing none of the qualities which make them objects of experience or cognizing subjects. Brahman in this subtle body is said to be in a causal state. From this subtle state, creation evolves by the will of God. Subtle matter develops into gross form, souls expand their consciousness, entering into connection with the bodies appropriate to their past Karma. In this gross condition Brahman is said to be in the state of effect. Thus God is the material cause as well as the efficient cause of the universe. This change of body from subtle to gross state does not affect the nature of God, because it is His body that undergoes modification, while as the soul of the cosmic body, He remains unchanged. Thus the self-determining Isvara is the Absolute of Ramanuja.

In the theology of Ramanuja, which is an inheritance from the ancient Bhagavata school, God manifests Himself in five forms. The first is the highest (Para), in which as Parabrahman or Narayana, He dwells in the domain of Nitya-vibhuti. The second form of manifestation is known as Vyuha which is fourfold: Vasudeva, Sankarshana, Pradyumna and Aniruddha, these being forms assumed for purpose of worship by the devotees, instruction, creation, etc. The third is Vibhava in which the Supreme manifests Himself as Avataras. The fourth manifestation is Antaryamin, in which he dwells in the heart of all embodied beings as their friend. The last is called Area in which the Deity dwells in consecrated images. In all these manifestations, the chief purpose is to help the erring souls, by His unsurpassable love and compassion.

Before proceeding further, it is necessary to deal briefly with Ramanuja's theory of knowledge. Attributive consciousness (Dharmabhutajnana), according to Ramanuja, can manifest itself and other objects. Since soul also is of the nature of consciousness, this has been described as *attributive* consciousness to distinguish it from self-consciousness or Svarupa-bhuta-jnana. The manifestation of attributive consciousness is never for itself, but for the individual soul, of which it is the attribute. Unlike soul 'it can only show but cannot know'. Jnana which is a modification of attributive consciousness functions through the mind (Manas) with or without the help of some sense-organ through which it reaches its objects, which exist already independent of the mind. This is called Satkhyati, since Sat (what exists) alone is cognized. When it comes in contact with an object, it reveals it to the soul in question. It may be noted that all mental states like desire, hate, etc. are the modifications of attributive consciousness.

There can never be a knowledge of an unqualified bare object, and it necessarily points to an object as characterized in some way or other. Hence according to Ramanuja, there is nothing like a pure indeterminate (Nirvikalpa) stage; for even there something is cognized, though the features of the object may not be clear. It follows from this that Ramanuja never admits an attributeless or non-differenced Brahman. Even the negative statements of the Upanishads 'not this, not this' (Neti, Neti) negate only certain attributes.

Another important point to be noticed is that all knowledge is of the real, since it never reveals any object that is not presented. Valid knowledge not only agrees with outside reality, but also facilitates its own adaptation to life. There is no error in the logical sense, as even error is incomplete knowledge. If all knowledge is true, how is the distinction between truth and error to be explained? The distinction between truth and error is made from the practical or empirical standpoint. When a firebrand is swung round rapidly, it touches all the points of the circle described without our being able to apprehend the intervals. As a result we see a fiery wheel. Here the cognition is no illusion in the logical sense. What has happened is that the perceiver has failed to apprehend the intervals due to the rapidity of the movement. In the cases of other errors like nacre-silver, yellow conch, etc., the distinction between truth and error is explained on a practical basis. In Samsara, all knowledge in a way reveals partial truth, and in its perfect expanded state reveals reality without any blemish. Ramanuja clinches the subject by concluding that Brahman—while creating the entire world for the souls according to their good and ill deserts—creates certain things which become common objects of consciousness, pleasant or unpleasant, to all souls, while certain other things are created for individual experience for a limited time only. And it is this distinction which makes the difference between 'the sublating' (Badhaka) and 'the sublated' (Badhya). Ramanuja accepts only three valid means of knowing: perception (Pratyaksha), inference (Anumana) and verbal testimony (Sabda).

Spiritual discipline begins with Karmayoga as expounded in the Bhagavadgita, which bids an aspirant perform acts without desire of reward; it includes worship, penance, charity, pilgrimage, etc. It purifies the heart and makes an aspirant fit for Jnanayoga, in which he realizes the true nature of his self as distinct from matter and as a mode of Brahman. Self-realization serves as a preparation for God-realization. This again leads to Bhakti or Prapatti, both of which are the direct means for attaining the vision of God.

Bhakti, according to Ramanuja, is not a mere devout meditation but a loving contemplation of God. It is a continuous process of meditation till the final goal is achieved. This ever-growing continuous meditation is promoted by subsidiary means, including discrimination (Viveka), mental detachment (Vimoka), practice of meditation (Abhyasa), performance of the five great sacrifices (Kriya), practice of such virtues as truth, non-violence, etc. (Kalyana), cheerfulness (Anavasada) and non-exultation (Anuddharsha). Thus promoted, the meditation becomes so perfect as to result in a vivid perception of the Supreme. The final intuition of the Supreme is not at all a means, but an end itself. The final liberation, which results only after physical dissolution, is constant communion with God which is the consummation of Karma, Jnana and Bhakti.

Prapatti, on the other hand, is absolute self-surrender to the Supreme, involving complete conformity, avoidance of opposition, the confidence of protection, the choosing of the Divine as the saviour, and surrender of one's self to God in all meekness. This implies complete surrender of 'I' and 'mine' to God. This sincere and complete transfer of spiritual responsibility to the Supreme liberates an aspirant at once from human efforts and foibles and creates the condition for the flow of the divine grace. When one sacrifices his ego at the altar of the Supreme, the Lord himself steps forward to receive him. Prapatti is usually prescribed as the direct means for those who feel incompetent in the classical pathway of meditative Bhakti and too impatient to wait for the perfection of Bhakti. It may be noted here that Bhakti and Prapatti are not antagonistic to each other as some people think. In Bhakti there is always an element of surrender and surrender involves an aspect of Bhakti. The predominence of one or the other element in spiritual practice determines whether the path is Bhakti or Prapatti.

*****

C-III

THE LAST MESSAGE OF SRI RAMANUJA

Sri Ramanuja after having lived on earth for a period of 120 years, out of which 60 years were spent in the holy island of Srirangam, one day approached the Lord Ranganatha and sought permission of Him to lay down the burden of the mortal body that he was bearing even beyond the allotted full span of human life. The Lord was at first silent but when Sri Ramanuja persisted in his request in an appealing manner, He granted his wish. Sri Ramanuja then went to his Math and assembling all his disciples, announced his intention to depart from the world, and exhorted them not to deviate from the path leading to salvation. The disciples gave vent to their feelings of unbearable sorrow, but the Guru consoled them and commanded them to gather together after taking their night meal. When they did so, Sri Ramanuja gave them the quintessence of his teachings thus:

'Worship Sri Vaishnavas exactly as you would do in the case of your spiritual preceptor. Have sincere faith in the teachings of the great Acharyas of yore. Never be slaves to your senses. Be not satisfied with the acquisition of worldly knowledge. Go on reading repeatedly the books dealing with the greatness of God and the wonders of His creation. If perchance you are favoured with scintillating wisdom by Guru's grace, then the attraction of the senses will cease for you. Learn to treat all your feelings with indifference. Enjoy the utterance of the names and glories of God's devotees with as much relish as the utterance of God's name and glories. Bear in mind that he who renders service, to God's devotees attains God speedily; therefore unless you dedicate yourself to the service of God and His devotees, you will not be saved, however wise you may be. Do not consider the life of a Vaishnava as a means for acquiring any selfish advantage. You must endeavour to realise the ideal.

'Devote a portion of the day, at least one hour, to the contemplation of the greatness of your spiritual preceptor and some time every day to the reading of the sacred writing of the Alvars or the Acharyas. Always seek the company of those that pursue the path of self-surrender to God and avoid the company of those that say, 'There are other paths leading to salvation.' Do not associate with people who are always in quest of filthy lucre and sense-enjoyment, but mingle with the devotees of God to the extent possible. Whoever looks upon the sacred images of God as mere stones, his own spiritual teacher as an ordinary human being, eminent devotees as high or low according to the caste of their birth, the holy water that has touched the feet of God and as a consequence has the power to purify and purge one of all sins as mere water, the sacred Mantras as a collection of sounds, and the Supreme Lord of all the worlds as one not higher than the Devas,—let him be considered as one fit to dwell in the infernal regions.'

When Ramanuja finished this discourse, the disciples requested him to exhort them as to how they should live in the world till life departed from the body. Thereupon the Acharya commanded them to abide by the following instructions:.

'He who has truly surrendered himself at the feet of God should not bestow any thought on his future, which is entirely at His disposal; for the least anxiety felt in that connection betrays the hypocrisy in his self-surrender. His present life is entirely determined by his past Karmas; so

Appendix 263

it is not proper to grieve over it. Let not the performance of your duties be regarded as a means for achieving worldly ends, but consider it as service rendered to the Supreme Being.

'Study the Sribhashya and teach it to others—this is a service most pleasing to God. If this be not possible, study the holy writings of Saint Satakopa and other great souls and teach them to qualified disciples. Failing this, spend your lives in service done to the Lord in the sacred places on earth. Else construct a hut at Yadavadri and live there in perfect peace. Or remain where you are, throwing all your burdens on God or your own Guru and ever immersed in the contemplation of the Dvaya Mantra. If none of the above is possible, seek a Vaishnava who is full of wisdom, devotion and desirelessness, and move with him in such a way that he may be kind towards you; uprooting all your egoism, abide by the Vaishnava's words—this itself is a means for your salvation.

'In this life on earth, find out by careful discrimination your friends, enemies and the indifferent. Sri Vaishnavas are your friends; those who hate God are your enemies; the worldly are the indifferent ones. Let your heart rejoice at the sight of friends as though you have come across fine betel, flowers and scents. At the sight of your enemies let your heart tremble as though you have faced a snake, a tiger, fire and so forth. At the sight of the indifferent, do not mind them any more than when meeting stocks and stones before you. Such should be the conduct of those who have taken refuge in God. Association with your friends, the Vaishnavas, will confer spiritual illumination on you. Shun the company of your enemies, and regarding the indifferent too, do not talk to them, and never show respect to them in consideration of the worldly benefits thereby accruing to you; for such benefits are sure to make you soon an enemy of God. Remembering that the All-merciful Being is ready to supply you all that you pray for, never beg of your enemies.'

Glossary[1]

Acala-vigraha— Non-moving image of the deity which is daily worshipped in a temple as distinguished from the image which is taken out during festivals.

Ācārya—Spiritual guide or preceptor. One who propounds a particular philosophy.

Acyuta—*Lit.*, not fallen; also meaning imperishable, permanent. A name of Vishnu, the almighty Being, the second of the Hindu Trinity.

Adharma—Unrighteourness. opposite of dhartna.

Āḷvār—In Tamil language the word refers to the supreme devotees of Lord Vishnu whose number is once for all fixed to be twelve.

Aṁśa—A part, share, portion.

Aṁśin—One who has amsa or part.

Ananta—Endless, infinite, a name of Sesha (the divine serpent forming the bed of Vishnu); also a name of Vishnu.

Aṅkaṇa—The act of marking religious insignia.

Antaryāmin—One who regulates the soul or internal feelings; the Supreme Spirit as guiding and regulating mankind.

Arcāvatāra, Arca—Manifestation of Vishnu as images or other sacred symbols which are worshipped in temples and houses.

Arjuna—Name of the third Pandava who was a son of Kunti by Indra.

Āryāvarta—Abode of the noble or excellent ones, the sacred land of the Aryans. Name of northern and central India extending from the eastern to the western sea and bounded on north and south by the Himalayas and Vindhya mountains. Entire India is also signified by the word.

Āśrama—A hermitage, dwelling or abode of ascetics. A stage or order or period of the religious life. These are four: brahmacharya, the life of the students; garhasthya, the life of the householder; vanaprastha, the life of an anchorite or hermit; sannyasa, the life of one who has renounced the world for realization of God.

Āśramīn—One living in a particular stage of life.

Aṣṭāvakra—Name of a celebrated sage (figuring in *Mahabharata:* Vanaparvan CXXXII—VI), son of the great sage Kohoda, the student and later son-in-law of the preceptor Uddalaka. Ashtavakra was born with a crooked body because of the curse of his father. When he was a mere boy

---

1. The scheme of transliteration adopted in these pages to indicate the pronunciation of most of the non-English words occurring in the book is the one that is widely in vogue. There is only one change to which we may draw the reader's attention: the letter '1' with two dots below (1) represents the Tamil letter (ழ This may be pronounced holding the tip of the tongue turned up and curled backwards without touching the palate.

he defeated Vandi, the foremost controversialist of Janaka's court and rescued his father who had-been drowned in the sea after being defeated at Vandi's hand. Thus rescued, Kohoda blessed his son as a result of which the crookedness of Ashtavakra's body disappeared.

Bandi (also spelt as Vandi)—Name of the foremost controversialist in Janaka's court, who was defeated by Ashtavakra.

Bhagavān—Revered, venerable, divine. An appellation applied to Gods, Incarnations of God and holy persons.

Bhagavad Gītā—The well-known Hindu scripture comprising eighteen chapters from the 25th to the 42nd of the Bhishma Parvan of the *Mahabharata*.

Bhāgavata—A devotee of Vishnu or Sri Krishna. *See also Srimad Bhagavatam.*

Bhāgīrathī—The sacred river Ganga, called so after the name of Bhagiratha. This ancient king of solar dynasty, the great grandson of Sagara, brought down, by practising the most austere penances, the celestial river Ganga from heaven to the earth and from the earth to the lower regions to purify the ashes of his 60,000 ancestors, the sons of Sagara.

Bhakta—Devotee of God.

Bhārata—Another name of India.

Bhāva—Being, existence; spiritual mood.

Bhūdevī—One of the three forms of the consort of Vishnu. Also, Goddess of Earth.

Bodhāyana—Name of an ancient teacher and author of the Brahma-sutra-vritti (also said to have commented on *Bhagavad-Gita* and the ten Upanishads). Sri Ramanuja studied his vritti before writing the *Sribhashya*.

Brahmā—The Creator God; the first of the Hindu Trinity, the other two being Vishnu and Siva.

Brahmaloka—The plane of Brahma, where purified pious souls repair after death and enjoy spiritual communion with Personal God.

Brahman—The Absolute, the Supreme Reality of Vedanta.

Brāhmaṇa—One of the four varnas or castes of the Hindu social system.

Brahmarākṣasa—The ghost of a Brahmana, who died with his sins unexpiated.

Brahma-sūtras—An authoritative treatise of aphorisms on Vedanta philosophy by Badarayana, who is again identified with Vyasa. The work is also known as Vedanta-sutras, Vyasa-sutras and Sariraka-sutras.

Brahmeśvara—The Creator God.

Cāṇḍāla—A general name for the lowest and the once most despised of the mixed castes of the Hindu society.

Cārvāka—Founder of the atheistic or materialistic school of Hindu philosophy. His doctrines are embodied in the *Barhaspatya-sutras*. The follower of Charvaka also goes by the same name.

Damayanti—An illustrious character in the *Mahabharata* exemplifying the wife's fidelity to the husband. See Appendix A.

Dāna—Giving away in charity, munificence.

Darśan(a)—Seeing; paying a visit to a deity or a holy man; a system of philosophy.

Dāsya-bhāva—The attitude of a willing servant; one of the five attitudes assumed by spiritual aspirants of the path of devotion towards their chosen ideals.

Dāsya-nāma—Name given to a devotee at the time of his religious initiation by his guru.

Dharma—Righteousness, duty. The inner constitution of a thing, which governs its growth.

Dhyāna—Meditation, contemplation.

Dvāpara—The third of the four *Yugas* or world cycles. *See Yuga.*

Gaṇapati (also Ganesha or Gananatha)—Name of the God of wisdom and obstacles (in the Hindu pantheon). Though Ganapati causes obstacles, he also removes them. Hence his favour is invoked at the commencement of all undertakings.

Garumat (also Garuda)—Name of a mythical bird akin to the eagle (the chief of the feathered race and the enemy of the serpent race), vehicle of Vishnu.

Gaurāṅgadeva—A saint from Bengal (A.D. 1485 to 1533) who preached ecstatic love for God. Also known as Sri Krishna Chaitanya, he is widely revered as an incarnation of God.

Gāyatrī—The most sacred vedic prayer—described as the 'Mother of the Vedas',—occurring in the Rig-Veda and named after its metre, which literally means, 'the saviour of the singer'. When this is orally communicated to one by the spiritual preceptor, one becomes spiritually reborn, as it were. By devoutly reciting this prayer during the three junctures of the day (sandhya), morning, noon and evening, such twice borns make spiritual progress.

Gopā (or Yaśodharā)—Wife of Prince Siddhartha before he renounced the world. After illumination when the Buddha revisited his home town Kapilavastu, Gopa applied for ordination. After some hesitation, she and Mahaprajapati were accepted as the first nuns of the Buddhist Order.

Gopīs—The milkmaids of Vrindavan, companions and devotees of Sri Krishna.

Govinda—A name of Sri Vishnu.

Guṇa—According to Sankhya philosophy, Prakriti (nature), in contrast with Purusha (soul), consists of three gunas (qualities or strands) known as sattva, rajas and tamas. Sattva stands for balance or wisdom, rajas for activity or restlessness and tamas for inertia or dullness.

Guru—One's spiritual teacher.

Hari—A name of Vishnu, since He removes the sins of His votaries.

Hayagrīva—Name of an incarnation of Vishnu in which He had a horse's head.

Hṛṣīkeśa—Lord of the senses, meaning Sri Krishna; also the name of a holy place in North India.

Indra—The King of the gods; the god of rain.

Iśvara—The Personal God; the Supreme Being.

Jagannātha—The Lord of the universe, Vishnu; name of the deity worshipped in the famous shrine of Puri.

Janaka—*Lit.,* a father, progenitor. Name of a famous King of Videha or Mithila, the foster-father of Siṭa. He was remarkable for his philosophical knowledge, good works and holiness.

Jaṭāyu—A son of Syeni and Aruna, a semi-divine bird. He was a great friend of Dasaratha, whose life he once saved while the latter had come under the ire of Saturn. When Ravana was carrying away Sita, he fought hard with the demon king to rescue the helpless princess. But he was mortally wounded and remained in that state till Rama and Lakshmana came to the place in their search after Sita. Jatayu told Rama about Sita having been carried away by Ravana and then breathed his last. His funeral rites were dutifully performed by Rama and Lakshmana.

Jīva—Living being, the individual soul.

Jñāna—Knowledge of Reality; also means learning and knowledge of any subject in ordinary parlance.

Jñāna-kāṇda—The part of the Vedas that teaches philosophical wisdom, viz., the Upanishads.

Jñāna-miśra-bhakti—Bhakti or devotion mixed with knowledge.

Jñātā—The knower, the cognizer.

Jñātṛtva—The consciousness that one knows.

Kaliyan—Another name of Tirumangai Alvar. *See p. 32 et seq.*

Kaliyuga—Name of the last and the worst of the four yugas or ages. *See* Yuga.

Kamaṇdalu—The waterpot of a monk.

Karma—Action in general; duty; ritualistic worship.

Karma-kāṇḍa—The part of the Vedas that deals with rituals and sacrifices.

Kārtikeya—The name of a son of Siva and Parvati. He is popularly regarded as the General of the gods, because he leads the Devas against the demons. He is also called Kumara, Skanda and Subrahmanya.

Kaumodaki—Name of the mace of Vishnu given to Him by Varuna.

Kaustubha—Name of a celebrated jewel obtained with thirteen other precious things at the churning of the ocean, and suspended on the breast of Vishnu.

Kṛṣṇa, Śrī—*Lit.,* black, dark-blue. Name of the most celebrated Avatar or' incarnation of Lord Vishnu. The life of this great hero and teacher is delineated in the *Mahabharata, Harivamsa* and *Srimad Bhagavatam.*

Kṣatriya—A member of the warrior-caste in Hindu society.

Kubera (or Kuvera)—The god of riches and treasures; also the regent of the northern quarters.

Kurukṣetra—Name of the extensive plain near Delhi, the scene of the great war between the Kauravas and Pandavas.

Kurus—Name of a race of ancient India and of their country near about the regions of Delhi. Kuru is the ancestor of both Pandu and Dhritarashtra, though the patronymic derived from his name is usually applied onty to the sons of the latter, the sons and descendants of the former being called Pandavas.

Lakṣmaṇa—Name of a son of Dasaratha by his wife Sumitra. He was the younger brother of Rama and accompanied him to the forest during his exile.

Lakṣmī—Name of the Goddess of fortune and beauty, the consort of Vishnu. Also known as Sri Devi.

Mādhava—A name of Sri Krishna.

Mahāprasāda—The very holy consecrated food after it is offered to a deity devoutly worshipped.

Mahāpuruṣa—A great saint, sage or ascetic.

Maharṣi—A great seer.

Mahātma(n)—A great soul.

Mahāvākyas—Lit., great sayings. Name of the four most sacred and philosophically most significant utterances of the Upanishads.

Mantra—Lit., 'instrument of thought', sacred text or speech, a prayer or a song of praise. A vedic hymn or sacrificial formula; that portion of the Veda which contains the texts called Rik or Yajus or Sama. A sacred formula addressed to any individual deity. A mystical verse or magical formula or incantation.

Mantra-śāstra—Science of sound symbols.

Maṭh—A Hindu monastery.

Māyāvāda—The doctrine of Vedanta philosophy denoting ignorance obscuring the vision of Reality; the cosmic illusion on account of which the one appears as the many, the Absolute as the relative; mysterious power of God.

Māyāvādin—One who accepts and upholds mayavada.

Nandaka—Name of the sword of Vishnu.

Nārāyaṇa, Śrīman—Name of Lord Vishnu, the Preserver God of the Hindu Trinity. The word 'Sriman' means along with Sri or Lakshmi, the consort of Narayana.

Nīḷādevi—One of the three manifestations of the consort of Vishnu.

Nirvāṇa—Extinction of the flame of life, dissolution, death or final emancipation from matter and re-union with the supreme spirit. According to Buddhists and Jains absolute extinction or annihilation of individual existence; perfect calm or repose or happiness; highest bliss or beatitude.

Nitya—Eternal.

Padmanābha—Name of Vishnu from whose navel sprang the lotus which contained Brahma, the future Creator.

Pāñcajanya—Name of Vishnu's conch, made from the bones of the demon Panchajana.

Pañcama—*Lit.,* the fifth. The Hindu population outside the four original castes.

Pāñcarātra āgama—Name of sacred books accepted by Sri-Vaishnavas as revealed by Sriman Narayana.

Pīṭhādhipatī—The pontiff of a seat of religious institution.

Prabandha—Any literary production. The sacred compositions of Alvars.

Prakṛti—The Primordial Nature; the material substratum of creation, consisting of sattva, rajas and tamas.

Prasāda—Food offered to a deity or the remnants of food taken by a holy man.

Puruṣa—A term of Sankhya Philosophy denoting the conscious principle. The universe evolves from the union of Prakriti and Purusha. In Vedanta the word also denotes the soul and the Absolute.

Puruṣottama—*Lit.,* the best of men, an excellent or superior man. The highest being, Supreme Spirit; a name of Vishnu or Krishna.

Rāgānuga-bhakti—Supreme devotion.

Rājarṣi—A king who leads a saintly life.

Rajas—The quality of activity or restlessness. *See* Guna.

Rājasika—Pertaining to or possessed of rajas.

Rāmacandra, Śrī—The hero of the famous Hindu epic *Ramayana.*

Rāmarājya—*Lit.,* the kingdom of Rama. The concept of an ideally governed state in which none practises violence on another, justice is denied to none and everyone is so placed in material welfare and ethical situation as to be able to live a spiritually progressive life. In such a state the king is only a regent of Dharma which is the sovereign ruler.

Rāmāyaṇa—The famous Hindu epic written by sage Valmiki.

Ranganatha—Name of the image of Sri Vishnu as worshipped in the famous shrine at Srirangam.

Raṅganāyakī—The consort of Sri Ranganatha.

Sacala-vigraha—The moving image of a deity which is carried in procession etc. during festivals as distinguished from the non-moving image which is worshipped in a temple. Also called utsava-vigraha.

Sādhaka—The striving spiritual aspirant.

Sādhanā—Practice of spiritual discipline.

Sādhu—A holy man.

Saguṇa Brahman—Brahman with attributes; the Absolute conceived as the Creator, Preserver and Destroyer of the universe; also the personal god according to Vedanta.

Sahadharmiṇī—A lawful wife, who participates in the righteous living of the husband.

Saṁsāra—The course or circuit of worldly life, mundane existence; metempsychosis; worldly illusion.

Saṃskāra—Making perfect, refining, polishing; consecration, sanctification; the self-reproductive quality, faculty of impression; a purificatory or sacred rite or ceremony.

Sanaka—One of the first four offspring of Brahma, the Creator, begotten of his mind. The names of the three others are Sanatana, Sananda and Sanatkumara. They are considered to be highly spiritual persons.

Sanātana dharma—*Lit.,* the Eternal Religion. Refers to Hinduism formulated by the rishis of the Vedas.

Saṅkarācārya—One of the greatest Saint-philosophers of India and an exponent of Advaita Vedanta (A.D. 788-820).

Sāṅkhya Kārikā—A Sanskrit treatise on Sankhya philosophy—one of the six systems of Indian philosophy—by Isvara Krishna, who wrote it before the 5th century A.D.

Sannyāsīn—A Hindu monk.

Śāradāpīṭha—One of the four pontifical seats established by Sri Sankaracharya and situated in Kashmir. The other three are at Puri, Sringeri and Dwaraka.

Śārṅga—Name of the bow of Vishnu.

Śāstra—Scriptures, religious treatises; code of law.

Sattva—The quality of balance and wisdom. *See* Guna.

Sāttvika—Possessed of or pertaining to the quality of sattva.

Sāvitrī—Name of the wife of Satyavat, King of Salva. One of the most exalted characters of the *Mahabharata (vide* Vanaparvan CCLXII to CCLXVIII), Savitri—along with Sita, Damayanti and a few others—is considered to be the highest pattern of conjugal fidelity and an eternal ideal of Hindu womanhood.

Śeṣa—Name of a celebrated mythological thousand-hooded serpent regarded as the emblem of eternity, whence he is also called Ananta, the infinite. He is sometimes represented as forming the couch and canopy of Vishnu whilst sleeping during the intervals of creation; sometimes as supporting the seven nether worlds with the seven regions above them and therefore the entire universe. According to some legends he became incarnate as Lakshmana and then Balarama. Sri Ramanuja also is

considered to be an incarnation of Sesha. Also means 'one who exists for
the purpose of sesin, or one who is in tune with the will of God'.

Sesatva—Conscious dependence on Vishnu, like property on its owner, for
being appropriated solely for His own purposes.

Sesin—One who utilizes the Sesha for His purpose.

Simhāsanādhipatis—The seventy-four direct disciples of Sri Ramanuja who
came to occupy pontifical seats.

Sītā—The exalted consort of Sri Rama.

Śiva—The Destroyer God. the third of the Hindu Trinity, the other two being
Brahma and Vishnu.

Smṛti—The law books, subsidiary to the Vedas, guiding the daily life and
conduct of the Hindus.

Śrāddha—A religious ceremony in which food and drink are offered to
deceased ancestors.

Śramaṇa—A Buddhist or Jain monk or mendicant.

Śrī Devī—Name of Lakshmi, the consort of Vishnu; the goddess of
prosperity and beauty.

Śrīmad Bhāgavatam—Same as Bhagavata. A sacred book of the Hindus,
specially of Vaishnavas, dealing with the lives of different incarnations of
Vishnu, and elaborately of Sri Krishna.

Śrīnivāsa—Name of the presiding deity of Tirupati or Venkatagiri. Also called
Venkatanatha, Venkatesa or Balaji.

Śrī-śaila—Name of Tirupati or Venkatagiri.

Śrī-sampradāya—The class of devotees who worship Sri Vishnu or Sriman
Narayana as the Supreme Godhead according to the philosophy of Visishtadvaita as expounded by Sri Ramanuja.

Śrī-sampradāyin—One who belongs to Sri-sampradaya.

Śrī-Vaiṣṇava—See Vaishnava.

Śrī-Vaiṣṇavism—The faith of the devotees belonging to Sri-sampradaya. As
the Mother Goddess Lakshmi or Sri acts as the mediator of salvation on
behalf of the devotees of Vishnu, the faith is known by this name.

Sudarśana—Name of the discus of Sri Vishnu.

Śddha-bhakti—The pure devotion unmixed with knowledge.

Śūdra—The last of the original four castes of Hindu society.

Sumeru—The sacred Mount Meru of Hindu mythology, around which all the
planets are said to revolve.

Sumitrā—Mother of Lakshmana, the faithful and beloved younger brother of
Sri Rama.

Svarāṭ—A self-ruler.

Swāmi(n)—Lord, master, spiritual preceptor.

Tamas—The principle of inertia or dullness. See Guna.

Tapas—Spiritual austerity.

Tridaṇḍa—The triple-staff carried by the Vaishnava monk signifying the three-fold control of thought, word and act.

Trivikrama—One who traversed the three worlds in three steps; a name of Vishnu.

Tulasī—A plant sacred to Vishnu.

Umā—The daughter of King Himalaya and the consort of Siva; She is an incarnation of the Divine Mother.

Upāsanā—Worship.

Ūrdhvapuṇḍra—The religious mark worn by Sri-Vaishnavas on the forehead.

Utsava-vigraha—See Sachala-vigraha.

Vaidhi-bhakti—Devotion to God associated with rites and ceremonies prescribed in the scripture.

Vaikuṇṭha—The heaven of the Vaishnavas.

Vaiṣṇava—Lit., relating or belonging or devoted or consecrated to Vishnu. A worshipper of Vishnu. One of the main sects of Hinduism. The Vaishnavas identify Vishnu with the Supreme Being and are exclusively devoted to His worship. Followers of Ramanuja, Madhva, Vallabha, Chaitanya, Nimbarka and Ramananda, though not following an identical philosophy, are all known as Vaishnavas.

Vaiṣṇvāparādha—The offence of showing discourtesy to a worshipper of Vishnu.

Vaiṣṇavī-śakti—The energy of Vishnu.

Vaiśya—The third or the merchant caste in Hindu society.

Vākula (or Bakula)—A kind of tree bearing tiny fragrant flowers. Mimascope Elengi.

Vālmīkī—The celebrated author of the great Hindu epic Ramayana.

Varuṇa—One of the most pre-eminent of the Vedic gods, he is often regarded as the Supreme Deity, being styled, 'King of Gods' or 'King of both Gods and men' or 'King of the universe'. Later on Varuna came to be considered as the presiding deity of the ocean in the Hindu mythology.

Vibhīṣaṇa—A brother of Ravana, the monster-king of Lanka, whom he succeeded as the ruler of Lanka. Unlike his brother, Vibhishana was a devotee of Rama. It was considerably through his help that Rama vanquished Ravana and rescued Sita.

Vibhūti-bhūṣaṇa—Lit., one who is endowed with superhuman powers or one who is smeared with sacred ashes; a name of Siva.

Vidura—An exalted character of the Mahabharata. Vidura is the younger brother of Pandu. A great devotee of Sri Krishna, he was remarkable for his wisdom, righteousness and impartiality.

Viṣṇu—The Preserver-God; the second of the Hindu Trinity, the other two being Brahma and Siva. The Vaishnavas regard Vishnu as the Supreme Being and identify Him with Narayana.

Visistādvaita—*Lit.,* non-duality of the qualified Whole, also translated as qualified non-dualism. The philosophy systematized by Sri Ramanuja.

Virāt—The spirit in the form of the universe; the all-pervading spirit.

Visnupriyā—The second wife of Sri Chaitanya in his pre-monastic days.

Vivarta—(In Vedanta) An apparent or 'illusory' form, an unreal appearance which is caused by *avidya* or human ignorance and removed by *vidya* or true knowledge. This is a favourite doctrine of the non-dualistic Vedantins according to whom the whole visible world is an unreal and illusory appearance while Brahman or Supreme Spirit is the only real entity; as a serpent is a *vivarta* of a rope, so is the world a *vivarta* of the real entity Brahman. This illusion is removed by Vidya or true knowledge.

Vraja—Same as Vrindavana. A town on the bank of the Yamuna river (in the Uttar Pradesh) associated with Sri Krishna's childhood.

Vyāsa—Name of the celebrated sage, author and compiler, to whom is ascribed the compilation of the Vedas, and the authorship of *Brahma-sutras* and the eighteen puranas. He is also known as Badarayana or Krishna Dvaipayana. He was the father of Dhritarashtra, Pandu. Vidura and Suka.

Yajña—Act of worship or devotion, offering, oblation; a sacrifice.

Yama—*Lit.,* the act of checking, curbing; restraint, self-control, forbearance, any great moral rule of duty. Name of the god who presides over the Pitris and rules over the spirits of the dead.

Yaśodā—Name of the wife of cowherd Nanda; Krishna's foster-mother who nursed and brought him up.

Yuga—A cycle or world period. According to Hindu mythology the duration of the world is divided into four yugas, namely, Satya, Treta, Dvapara and Kali. In the first, also known as the Krita Yuga or Golden Age, there is a great preponderance of virtue among men, but with each succeeding yuga virtue declines and vice increases. In the Kali Yuga, there is a minimum of virtue and a great excess of vice. The world is said to be now passing through the Kali Yuga.

Tamil equivalents of the names figuring in the book

Āndhrapūrṇa	—	Vaḍuga Nambi
Bhāṣyācārya	—	Mahā-bhāṣya-bhatta
Dāśarathi	—	Mudaliyāṇḍān
Devarājamuni	—	Arulāla Perumāḷ
(also Yajñamūrti)		Emperumānār
Dhanurdāsa	—	Piḷḷai Uraṅgā Villi Dāsar
Dīptimati	—	Perīya Pirāṭṭi
Goṣṭhīpūrṇa	—	Tirukkoṭiyūr Nambi
Hemāmba	—	Ponnāciyār
Kaliyan	—	Tirumangai Āḷvār
Kāñcīpūrṇa	—	Tirukacci Nambi
Kūreśa	—	Kūrattāḷvār
Mahāpūrṇa	—	Periya Nambi
Mālādhara	—	Tirumalai Āṇḍān
Munivāhana	—	Tiruppāṇ Āḷvār
Rakṣakāmbāḷ	—	Tanjamambāḷ *
Rāmamiśra	—	Maṇakkāl Nambi
Sampatkumāra	—	Śelva Piḷḷai
Śaṭhāri	—	Nammāḷvār
Śrīnivāsa	—	Śrī Veṅkaṭeśa
Śrī Śailapūrṇa	—	Tirumalai Nambi
Uttamapūrṇa	—	Uttamanambi
Yādavādripatî	—	Tirunārāyaṇan
Varadarājā, Śrī	—	Aruḷāḷa Perumāḷ
Yāmunācarya	—	Āḷavandār

---

* In the original Bengali biography the name of Sri Ramanuja's wife (before he became a monk) is given as Jamamba, which obviously is an abbreviation of Tanjamambal, the Tamil name. In the translation we have used the Sanskritized name Rakshakambal for the sake of uniformity.—Tr.

Index